LOOKING BACK

MEMOIRS

LOU ANDREAS-SALOMÉ

EDITED BY ERNST PFEIFFER

TRANSLATED BY BREON MITCHELL

MARLOWE & COMPANY

NEW YORK

First paperback edition, 1995

Published in the United States by

Marlowe & Company
632 Broadway, Seventh Floor
New York, N.Y. 10012

This American edition is based upon Ernst Pfeiffer's latest, revised
edition of *Lebensrückblick*, published in 1973.

All notes and critical material for this edition have been
translated by Kristine Lindemann.

Book Design by Barbara M. Bachman

Library of Congress Cataloging-in-Publication Data

Andreas-Salomé, lou, 1861-1937.
[Lebensrückblick. English]
Looking back : the memoirs of Lou Andreas-Salomé / edited by
Ernst Pfeiffer ; translated by Breon Mitchell.
p. cm.
Translation of: Lebensrückblick
ISBN 1-56924-848-6
I. Andreas-Salomé, Lou, 1861-1937—Biography. 2. Authors,
German—20th century—Biography. I. Pfeiffer, Ernst. II. Title.
PT2601.N4Z513 1991
838'.809—dc20
[B] 9047431
CIP

Manufactured in the United States of America

LOOKING BACK

MEMOIRS

LOU ANDREAS-
SALOMÉ

TRANSLATOR'S NOTE

The discursive, highly personal style
of these memoirs, written while Lou
Andreas-Salomé was in her early
seventies, approaches that of spoken
language. The flow of thought is
reflected in the loosely structured,
baroque fullness of individual
sentences and paragraphs. I have tried
to remain faithful to this style, which
reveals both the person and the
personality of the author.

In translating verse, I have
concentrated on providing poetic
equivalents which convey the poem's
sense as accurately as possible.
The German
texts of all poems have been included
in the Appendix, p. 217.

Passages marked with an asterisk are enlarged upon
in the Notes, p. 153.

CONTENTS

Human life—indeed
all life—*is* poetry.
It's *we* who live it,
unconsciously, day by day,
like scenes in a play,
yet in its inviolable wholeness
it lives *us*, it composes *us*.
This is something far different
from the old cliché ''Turn
your life into a work of art'';
we are works of art—
but we are not the artist.

—Lou Andreas-Salomé

LOOKING BACK

MEMOIRS

LOU ANDREAS-SALOMÉ

THE
GOD EXPERIENCE

OUR FIRST EXPERIENCE, remarkably enough, is that of loss. A moment before, we were everything, undifferentiated, indivisibly part of some kind of being—only to be pressed into birth. Henceforth a tiny residue of the whole must strive to avoid contracting into even less and less, must stand up to a world which rises before it with ever-increasing substantiality, a world into which it has fallen, from universal fullness, as into a deprivating void.

We feel that earlier state as something at odds with the present. What we will later refer to as our first "memory"* consists simultaneously of shocked disappointment at the loss of that state of being, and a residual awareness that it should still exist.

This is the problem of earliest childhood. Likewise, in all the early stages of Man, self-awareness based on practical experience is accompanied by a continuing memory of at-oneness with the universe, like the potent legend of an immortal partnership in cosmic power. Early Man retained a confident faith in that power, and the entire world of appearances seemed subordinated to humanly controlled magic. Man never entirely discarded this disbelief in the general validity of the exterior world, which had once seemed insepar-able from himself. He constantly bridged the gap with the help of his imagination, even if the divinely corrected model he proposed had to mold itself more and more closely to his increasingly accurate perceptions of the external world. This realm above and beyond the world, this imaginary duplicate—made for hushing up the unpleasant things that had happened to Mankind—was called religion.

Thus today's child, or yesterday's, if he is immersed as a matter of course in his parents' faith, may absorb religious beliefs as automatically as sense perceptions. For it is precisely in the earliest years, when the ability to make distinctions is as yet undeveloped, that a child still believes all things are possible. That the highest powers may magically appear within the human realm is to him the most natural thing in the world—until he has rubbed himself sufficiently against the mediocrities and differentiations of the real world.

Even a child untouched by religion goes through this primal stage. Every child begins in the realm of infinite possibilities, due to his insufficient analytic powers and the overwhelming strength of his desires. As our sense of at-oneness with the universe gives way to rational judgment, a shimmer from the past settles upon those objects to which we were most attached, or surrounds the events which first moved us deeply, like a transfiguration, lifting them into a higher dimension—as in a universal embrace. Suppose today or tomorrow the trend of the times tends to insulate a child from this realm, hoping to spare him inevitable disillusionment. Suppose he is called upon to develop his critical faculties at too young an age, abnormally repressing the natural desire to exercise his imagination, which is active long before his rational faculties. Would we not have good reason to fear a reaction against rationality, a revenge of the imagination in which objective standards are abandoned?

Moreover, a normal child usually outgrows an all-too-"religious" upbringing on his own, turning his critical attention to the world about him—just as his preference for fairy tales gives way to a burning interest in reality. If this does not happen, it generally is a case of arrested development, a discrepancy between the drive toward life and a reluctance to come to terms with life's restrictions.

Since birth creates a gap between two types of existence—between two worlds—some form of mediation is desirable. In my own case various childhood conflicts caused a certain regression. Having already begun to adapt myself to rational judgment, I retreated into a stage of pure fantasy in which my parents and their viewpoints were in a sense abandoned (almost betrayed) in favor of a more all-embracing absorption. I devoted myself to a higher power and shared in its authority, even its omnipotence.

Perhaps one might picture it this way: I had moved from my parents' lap, slipping down as one must from time to time, and was now in the lap of God—a grandfather who spoiled me mightily, who approved of everything I did, who enjoyed giving me gifts so much it seemed his pockets were overflowing. I felt almost as omnipotent as he, if not as "good." He combined, in a sense, both parents' attributes: maternal warmth and the perfection of fatherly power. (To separate the two, and differentiate between them as spheres of power and of love, is already a major disruption of primal well-being.)

But what enables a person to accept a fantasy as real? Only the refusal to limit oneself to the external world, to the imposition of something which is

Outside Ourselves, the refusal to give full recognition to something does not include ourselves within it.

Surely this was the major reason why I was surprisingly undisturbed by the total invisibility of this third power, superior even to my parents, who after all received all they had from it. That's how it is with all true believers. In my case there was a second reason as well, which had to do with a strange thing about our mirrors. Whenever I looked into one, I was disturbed to see so clearly that I was no more than what I beheld: so limited, so restricted; forced simply *to stop* by everything around me, even what was nearest at hand. If I didn't look in them I could spare myself this feeling, yet somehow my own sensibility seemed to demand my presence in each and every one, as if without my image in the mirror I would be homeless. It seems quite abnormal, because I seem to recall experiencing this again from time to time on later occasions as well, at a point when the image in a mirror normally bears an innocuous and interesting relationship to one's own image. In any case such early thoughts contributed to the fact that I found nothing at all disturbing about the omnipresence or the invisibility of God.

Of course it's clear that such an image of God, patched together from so many early sensations and feelings, can hardly have lasted long; not as long as our more rational, more comprehensible constructions—just as grandfathers tend to die before our parents do.

One small memory illustrates my method of holding off doubt. My father had returned home from some festival at court with a splendid surprise, a small package which one could pop open. I got the impression it contained golden dresses. When I was warned that the clothes in it were simply made of paper trimmed in gold, I decided not to open it. Thus the clothes *remained* golden in my mind.

Nor did I need to see the gifts I received from my God-grandfather. Their value was beyond measure, they were innumerable, and I was sure to receive them. Moreover, they weren't contingent on my behavior, unlike the presents I got for being good, for example. Even the gifts which sparkled on my birthday table were only there because I was well-behaved, or because they hoped I would be. Now I was often a "naughty" child, painfully acquainted with the birch switch—something I never failed to complain vigorously about to God. It turned out he agreed with me completely, and in fact he seemed so angry at times about my parents' use of the birch switch that, if I happened to be in a noble mood (which didn't occur all that often), I would try to convince him just to drop the whole matter.

Naturally these fantasies often spilled over into my daily life, a fact which was usually passed over with a smile. Until one day I returned home from a walk with a relative, a little girl a bit older than I was. When we were asked, "Well, little misses, what did you see on your walk?" I replied with an entire unabridged drama. My little companion, who found her childish honor and truthfulness offended, stared at me at a loss and interrupted with a loud shriek: "But you're lying!"

I think my subsequent efforts to state things precisely date from that moment. This meant not adding the slightest jot to my descriptions, although I was deeply depressed by such enforced stinginess.

In the dark of night I didn't just tell God what had happened to me that day—I also told him entire stories, in a spirit of generosity, without being asked. These stories had a special point. They were born of the necessity to provide God with the entire world which paralleled our secret one, since my special relationship to him seemed to divert my attention from the real world, rather than making me feel more at home in it. So it was no accident that I chose the material for my stories from my daily encounters with people, animals, or objects. The fairy-tale side of life hardly needed to be emphasized—the fact that God was my audience provided adequately for that. My sole concern was to present a convincing picture of reality. Of course I could hardly tell God something he didn't already know, yet it was precisely this that ensured the factual nature of the story I was telling, which was why I would begin each story, with no small degree of self-satisfaction, with the phrase:

as you know

I first recalled the details of the abrupt end to this somewhat questionable imaginary relationship when I was nearing old age. I recounted it in my little story *Die Stunde ohne Gott** (The Hour Without God). In that tale, however, the child is placed in a foreign milieu, and in altered circumstances— perhaps because I still felt the need to create some external distance from such intimate details. What actually happened was as follows.

Each winter a servant brought fresh eggs to our city residence from our house in the country. One day he announced to me that he had found a "couple" standing in front of my very own miniature house in the middle of the garden. They were requesting entrance, but he had told them to go away. The next time he came, I asked about the couple immediately, no doubt because I was worried that they might have starved or frozen to death in the meantime; where could they have turned? —Yes, he said, they were still there. —Then they were still standing in front of the house? —No, not exactly: the couple had changed, gradually but thoroughly, getting thinner and thinner, smaller and smaller. They were so run down that they had finally collapsed. As he was sweeping in front of the house one morning, he had found nothing left but the black buttons from the woman's white coat; of the man only a battered hat remained. But the ground where they had stood was still covered with their frozen tears.

It was not my sorrow for the couple which bothered me most about this gruesome story, but the riddle of their transitory nature, the way in which they had simply dissolved away. It was as if something were preventing me from seeing the obvious solution because it was all too simple, while everything in me searched with increasing passion for an answer. That same night, I struggled with God over the answer. Normally he had nothing to do with such matters, he was only serving as an ear, so to speak, for what he already knew. But I wasn't asking much of him this time either. He just needed to let a few brief words pass over his invisible lips, from his speechless mouth: "Mr. and Mrs. Snowman." The fact that he didn't, however, was catastrophic. This was not simply a personal catastrophe, it opened the curtains violently to reveal something unspeakably sinister lurking behind them. For the God painted upon the curtain didn't disappear just for me, he disappeared totally—he was lost to the entire universe as well.

When something like that happens with a living person, forcing us to come to terms with our disappointment, with the feeling that they've left us, abandoned us, the possibility always exists that we may learn to see things aright at some point, that we may be able to correct the misperception we had of them. Something of the sort happens to each of us, to every child. Sooner or later a break occurs between what we expect and what we find— and experience teaches us that whether it proves to be more or less serious, more or less remediable, is simply a matter of degree. But in God's case the difference is qualitative. This can be seen for example in the fact that the disappearance of a belief in God in no way entails a loss of the God-granted power to believe in imaginary beings in general. Thus I recall a moment during our customary religious services at home in which the name of the devil or demonic powers was read aloud, and I was awakened from my lethargy: was *he* still around, then?! Was *he* the one, after all, who had allowed me to fall from the lap of God, where I had nestled so comfortably? And if he was responsible, why hadn't I fought against him? By not doing so, had I not positively assisted him?

In attempting to analyze that moment, which was so fleeting and yet so deeply engraved in my memory, I want to bring out one tone in particular: not a feeling of shared *guilt* in the loss of God, but a sense of *collusion* in that loss—a premonition of what would happen. For the astonishing insignificance of the event which caused me to put God to the test makes it highly improbable that I could not have solved the riddle myself—that I could not have discovered the couple to be Mr. and Mrs. Snowman, given the propensity of children's hands to build them.

The notion of the sinister which was awakened in me played no further major role in my childhood: it only served to increase the difficulty of making myself at home in the real world, the world without God. Strangely enough, the loss of God had one unexpected result in the moral realm. It caused me to become a good bit better as a child, more well-behaved (thus godlessness did not make me devilish). This was presumably because dejection generally puts a damper on unruly behavior. But there may have been a positive reason as well: a sort of instinctive sympathy for my parents. I didn't want to cause them trouble since, like me, they had suffered a blow—for God was lost to them as well,—*they just didn't know it*—.

Of course for a time I made attempts to turn the situation around, to imitate my religious parents, just as I had received everything from them in the past, learned everything from them, assured myself of the reality of things with their help. In the evenings I would fold my hands hesitantly, in my despair and humility, like a little stranger called from the outermost edge of an immense solitude into an unbelievably distant land. But the attempt to bring this supposedly distant land in harmony with the old, familiar divine intimacy failed. In spite of all my humility, it was still something forced, an active approach to a totally different, uninterested stranger, and this case of mistaken identity increased my solitude through the shame of having bothered someone who knew nothing about the matter.

In the meantime I continued to tell my stories before I fell asleep. As before, I took them from simple sources, encounters and events in my daily life, although they had suffered a decisive reversal as well, since the listener was gone. No matter how hard I tried to embellish them, to guide their destiny along a better path, they too disappeared among the shadows. You could see that in the act of telling they had not rested for a moment in God's gentle hands, had not been given to me as a gift from his great pockets, sanctioned and legitimized. For that matter, was I even sure that they were *true*, since I had ceased to receive them and pass them on with the confident words "as you know"? They became a cause of unconfessed anxiety for me. It was as if I were thrusting them, unprotected, into the uncertainties of the very life from which I had drawn them as impressions in the first place. I recall a nightmare—one which was often retold to me—which occurred during an attack of the measles, when I was in a high fever. In it I saw a multitude of characters from my stories whom I had abandoned without food or shelter. No one else could tell them apart, there was no way to bring them home from wherever they were in their perplexing journey, to return them to that protective custody in which I imagined them all securely resting—all of them, in their thousandfold individuality, constantly remultiplying until there was not a single speck of the world which had not found its way home to God. It was probably this notion which also caused me to relate quite different external impressions to one another.* For example, a passing schoolboy and an old man going by, or a sapling and a towering tree. To me they represented various stages in the life of the same individual. It was as if they belonged together from the first. This remained the case even when the sum total of such impressions gradually began to overload my memory, so that I began to use threads, or knots, or catchwords to orient myself within the ever more densely woven tapestry. (Perhaps something of this habit carried over into later life when I began to write short stories; they were temporary aids in getting at something which was after all a much larger coherent whole, something which could not be expressed in them, so that they remained at best makeshift.)

My concern for the characters in my stories was not a matter of motherly care, as might have been expected in a little girl. Even when we were playing with dolls, it was my brother, who was three years older, who put the dolls to bed afterward and led the animals we had required for our games back to their stalls. They had served their purpose for me as occasions for play. Strangely enough, it was my brother who by these actions seemed to me to have the stronger imagination.

I didn't usually talk about my divine "experiences" when I was with little girlfriends my own age (one of my particular friends was a distant relation, who, like us, was from a Franco-German family on her mother's side only; her sister later married my second brother). I kept things vague, as if I weren't sufficiently sure that they would recall similar experiences. But the memory of those experiences faded for me as well over the years. So I remember how struck I was much later when I came across a torn and tattered sheet of paper upon which I had once scribbled a poem. It was written in Finland, under the magical glow of the white summer nights:

Oh bright heaven overhead*
I place my trust in you:
Do not allow desire or dread
To screen you from my view!

You who stretch above us all
From end to windswept end,
Show me the road before I fall,
To find you once again.

I do not wish to flee from pain
Nor ask that love be true;
All I want is some broad plain
To kneel upon beneath you.

It was like reading an unknown poem. I even looked it over with impartial vanity for its value as verse! And yet the basic feeling behind it has colored all my subsequent actions and experiences, as if that feeling did not arise gradually from the normal series of joyful or sad events, but sprang instead from my earliest childhood, a reliving of that primal shock all men experience when they consciously awaken to existence, to be felt throughout our life.

In spite of all autobiographical sincerity, it is difficult to convey the sense of such matters. Perhaps a concrete example would be better. A little calendar of fifty-two biblical sayings had been placed above my bed, to be changed each week throughout the year. And when at one point I Thess. 4, 11, appeared in the window, I simply left it there: "Study to be quiet, and to do your own business, and to work with your own hands." I probably couldn't have said then why I did it. But it must be the continuing reverberation of that early feeling of desertion and the absolute resignation which accompanied it that explains why the little calendar with that very saying still hangs on my wall today. That Biblical passage, so unchildlike, remained throughout the years of my estrangement from God. I didn't remove it, both for the sake of my parents, and because the words had penetrated my heart. The final proof of this came while I was living abroad, when I was sent the little calendar along with several other things. Then it routed even the replacement from Goethe that Nietzsche suggested when he heard about it: "Turn away from half measures,* and be resolute in living wholly, fully, beautifully."

These handwritten words may still be found today, behind the faded lines of print.

The fact that these impressions come from very early childhood may seem surprising. They were, as I've said, tied to an infantile regression, or an arrested development at the infantile stage. My conception of God arose too soon, and stood so at odds with its own spiritualization that its collapse was much more drastic and disturbing than is normally the case. It was as if I had been thrust into the world a second time, to be confronted henceforth with a sobering reality.

When I was seventeen years old, the first direct memories of my earliest struggles with faith came to me from an external source: during confirmation instruction with Hermann Dalton* in the Reformed Evangelical church. On these occasions something in me took sides with the faded image of God from my early childhood, for *he* had required no such demonstrations and lessons. A sort of secret, pious anger arose, rejecting the rational proofs of his existence, his justice, his incomparable power and goodness. It made me feel ashamed, as if, from the depths of my childhood, he were being forced to listen to all this in astonished bewilderment; thus in a sense I spoke for him.

The actual outcome of the matter of confirmation was as follows: because my father had fallen ill, I allowed Dalton to talk me into starting a second year of instruction, to avoid any upset that might have been caused by my leaving the church at that time. But, having done this, I then officially withdrew. I did this in spite of the fact that in my own mind, rationally, I felt that I had done something far worse than if I had simply gone through the motions, which would have spared my pious family both pain and worry. It wasn't any fanatical attachment to truth which led me to this step, but an irresistible, incontrovertible compulsion.

Over the course of my life my studies and various other factors led me into areas of philosophy, and even theology, more often than into areas which I might otherwise have chosen for myself. However, this is not a reflection of my "pious" nature as a young child, nor has it anything to do with my subsequent rejection of such piety. Nothing I've studied or thought about systematically has ever stirred up the early faith I once had—almost as if that faith felt out of place in the realm of "adult thought." As a result, all those academic fields, including theology, remained of purely *intellectual* interest to me, they never touched, let alone mingled with, the areas of *feeling* I once experienced. I might almost say they soon seemed to me like—confirmation instruction. Of course I recognized, and often even admired, the way in which others created a substitute—of a quite enlightened and spiritual kind—for their original piety through such studies, and how they managed to combine the past into a coherent whole with their mature thought. It was often the best means they had to move *themselves* forward, intellectually, to learn the whole of life's lesson, much better than I, who was never able to repeat it without a good deal of stammering and stuttering. But such means remained as foreign and distant to me as if we were talking about completely different fields or subjects.

What attracted me most strongly to those individuals, living or dead, who dedicated themselves totally to such thoughts was always their quality as human beings. No matter how subtly they expressed it in their philosophy, you could always tell that in some deep sense *God* remained the first and most important experience in their lives. What else in life could compare? I never ceased to love them, with a love that seeks to penetrate the human heart, where our most intimate destiny unfolds.

Now someone may well ask, if I failed to achieve this balance in my life, between desire and truth, emotional expectations and rational knowledge, a balance which so often takes place gradually and quite normally in the course of development—in what respect did these earliest religious feelings continue to exercise their effect on me? In all honesty I can answer only by saying, in terms of God's very disappearance. For what remained at the deepest level, no matter how the surfaces of life and the world changed, was the unalterable fact of a universe abandoned by God. And perhaps it is precisely the childish nature of the previous construction of God in such cases which makes it appear impossible to replace or redress the image by later formulations.

But in addition to this negative result, the childish aspect of God's disappearance also had a positive side: it thrust me into real life with equal irrevocability. I am certain that for me—judged autobiographically to the best of my ability—any substitute concepts of God which might have merged with my feelings would only have restricted, deflected, impaired this result. I freely grant that many others make quite different use of such substitutes, a use that carries them further than I could ever go.

The primary impact of all this upon me was the most positive aspect of my life: *the profound feeling of a deeply shared destiny with all things.* This was awakening darkly in me from early childhood, with a constant and penetrating force which has never ceased. Thus "feeling" is a better word for it than "perception," which is tied to objects; a sensuous conviction that we share a destiny. And this feeling is not limited to human beings alone, but opens simultaneously even to the dust of the cosmos. As such it is unalterable by any scale of human measurements or values in the course of a life, as if there were no way to further justify, elevate, or debase anything given the simple fact of its existence—just as nothing can affect the significance of any thing, neither murder, nor destruction, unless it be to fail to show this final *reverence* to the weight of its existence, which it shares with us, for, at the same time, it *is* us.

In saying this I've let slip the word in which one may well be inclined to see the spiritual residue of my early relationship to God. For it is true that throughout my life no desire has been more instinctive in me than that of showing reverence—as if all further relationships to persons or things could come only after this initial act. So that this word seems to me but another term, a second name, for that bond of universal destiny in which the greatest is included without reference to size and even the smallest is rendered meaningful. Or to put it another way: anything that "is" bears within itself the whole weight of existence, as if it were all things. Is the ardor of such belonging conceivable *without* an indwelling reverence—be it the least visible, and least recognized substratum of our emotional life?

In what I am setting out to narrate here as well, reverence is already a part of the story. Yes, it may be reverence alone which is its subject, in spite of all the other words that must be devoted to so many matters that swirl around it, while this single, simplest word rests silently beneath.

Illogical as it may be, I must confess that any type of belief, even the most absurd, would be preferable to seeing Mankind lose its sense of reverence entirely. *

THE EXPERIENCE
OF LOVE

IN EVERY LIFE there is an attempt to begin again, to be reborn: the old saying is true—puberty is a second birth. After years in which we managed to conform to the life around us, to the rules and judgments which overpowered our young minds so easily, a sudden primal urge arises so vehemently within our maturing bodies that it is as if the world is only now to be created, that world into which we have been delivered—naive, incapable of learning in the face of all the deep desires which assail us.

Even the most sensible of us falls prey at some point to this magic spell: the feeling that a new and totally different world has arisen, and that whatever contradicts that feeling involves some incomprehensible misunderstanding. But because it is not given to us to persevere in this bold belief, and because we must, in the end, give in to the world as it really is, this "romantic" period wraps a veil of nostalgic melancholy about us in later days—like shimmering moonlight on a woodland lake, or the lure of ghostly ruins. Then we confuse that innermost pulse with the unproductive and disproportionate excesses of emotion which once were tied to some particular period in time. But in fact what we incorrectly call "romanticism" arises from the most indestructible part of our being, the most robust, the most primal, the force of life itself, which alone can balance external existence with an internal power, and thus provide a common ground for outer and inner reality.

The transitional years to physical maturity, which by their very nature result in inner struggles and agitation, are at the same time most strongly suited to come to new terms with the confusions and inhibitions of our earlier life.

That happened in my case as well, as I found the dreams and fantasies of my childhood pushed aside in the real world. A living person took their place:* he did not appear beside them, but rather incorporated them—became himself the very embodiment of reality. There is no simpler and shorter way of expressing the violent emotion he released in me than by a phrase which united my ultimate sense of the marvelous with a feeling of deep primal intimacy, something I had never considered possible, and had always been waiting for: "a real person!" As a child, I felt such intimacy only with God, *because* he was imbued with the marvelous, as opposed to everything surrounding me, and in that sense he was not actually "present." Now the same all-encompassing and all-ascendent qualities had appeared within a *human being*. Moreover, this divine mortal proved to be opposed to all fantasy. As a teacher he aimed at the unlimited development of clear and rational thought, and the more difficult I found it to convert myself to this view, the more passionately I listened to him. Still, elevated by the intoxication of love, I was able in this way to come to terms with reality. Up to that point, on my own, I had not even approached the brink of that reality he now represented.

This teacher and educator, first visited in secret, then accepted by the family, also helped prepare me for further studies in Zurich. Thus he proved to be, even in his severity, as generous as my former "God-grandfather," who always fulfilled my wishes. It was as if he were Lord and instrument in one, educing and seducing me toward my own deepest inclinations. The extent to which he thus remained for me a duplicate, a doppelgänger, a revenant of the God of my childhood, first became clear when I proved unable to bring the love affair to a real, human conclusion.

Of course there were many factors I could use as excuses, not the least of which was the disparity in our ages, equivalent, frankly, to the emotional distance between obsession and first awakening. Then there was the fact that my friend was married, and the father of two children about my own age (which didn't bother me in particular, since God too is bound to all human beings, without this preventing the closest and most personal individual relationship with him). Moreover my still childlike nature—a result of the delay in physical development common in northern climes—initially forced him to conceal from me that he had already spoken with my family about marriage. When the moment of decision unexpectedly required me to descend from the heavenly to the earthly I refused. At one blow, that which I had worshiped fled from my heart and mind into foreign lands. Something that had its *own* demands, something that not only did not fulfill my desires, but even threatened them, that wanted to bend the endeavors which he had assured me were aimed toward pleasing me alone to serve the being of another—like a bolt from the blue The Other rose before me. It was indeed *someone else* who stood before me: someone I had not recognized clearly under the veil of divinity. Nevertheless I was right to have deified him, for up to then he had been the person whose influence I needed to reach my own potential. This dual relationship, present in a sense from the very start, resulted in the curious fact that in spite of loving one another, I never once used the familiar form of address with him, although he did with me. Thus throughout my life the use of the polite form retained for me a note of intimacy, while the familiar form meant less.

My friend was attached to the Dutch embassy. There had been a strong Dutch colony in Russia since the time of Peter the Great, and a clergyman was needed to perform official duties, particularly the swearing in of sailors. Sermons were delivered in both German and Dutch at the chapel on Névsky Prospect. Since my friend spent so much of his time helping me, it was really no great matter that I also wrote a sermon for him now and then: of course in *that* case I never failed to attend church, since I was burning with curiosity to see if the audience (he was a first-rate orator) would be sufficiently enthralled. That all came to an end when, in the heat of composition, I got carried away and chose "Feeling is all! Name is but sound and smoke" from Goethe's *Faust*, as the text for the day, instead of something from the Bible. This earned him a reprimand from the ambassador, which, deeply annoyed, he passed on to me.

Since Holland is blessed by the total separation of church and state, the fact that my friend was a licensed minister proved helpful to me in another way. The Russian authorities had refused to issue me a passport prior to my trip to Zurich,* since I had left the church. He suggested that he could arrange a certificate of confirmation for me through a friend of his who served as pastor of a tiny Dutch church in a small village. We were both moved by this strange ceremony, which was conducted strictly according to my wishes. It took place on a normal Sunday in the presence of the local peasants, in the beautiful month of May. But it meant that we would have to part—and I feared this like death itself. Fortunately my mother, who had traveled with us, couldn't understand a word of the blasphemous Dutch sermon, nor the words of confirmation with which it closed—almost like a marriage vow: "Fear not, for I have chosen you, I have called you by your name: you are mine." (In fact he *had* given me my name, since he found the Russian "Lyola" [or "Lyolya"] too difficult to pronounce.)

The surprising turn which my youthful love story had taken, and which at the time I only half understood myself, was fashioned into a tale I wrote ten years later* (*Ruth*). That story was somewhat unclear, however, since it lacked one necessary narrative precondition: a knowledge of the pious background, the latent residue of an identity between my relationship to God and the love affair. It's true that the worshiped lover suddenly disappears, just as God disappeared without a trace for me. But the fact that the comparison was missing, and with it any deeper meaning, gave the basic plot of *Ruth* a "romantic" tinge rather than anchoring it in the abnormal, repressed aspects of a young girl's development. But precisely because of my immaturity, this incomplete experience of love retained an incomparable and unique charm, a rightness which never had to be tested against life itself. Therefore its sudden conclusion, in contrast to the sorrow and affliction when my childhood God disappeared, which was in other ways so similar, led in this case toward freedom and joy: and even to a continuing relationship with this first man who was so fully real, whose will and wisdom had helped to set me free, had granted me the inner freedom through which I finally learned how to live fully.

If the course of these events already reveals sufficient traces of irregularity stemming from a somewhat abnormal childhood, it was even more clearly evident in my physical development, which did not match my spiritual and mental growth. My body had to react to the erotic impulses to which it had been subjected, without those impulses having been accepted or counter-balanced by my spiritual side. Left to itself, my body even fell ill (coughing blood), and I had to leave Zurich to be taken south. * Later that seemed to me analogous to the behavior of certain animals, for example a dog which remains by its master's grave until it starves, although it has no idea *why* it's lost its appetite. We human children don't suffer the physical consequences of having a faithful heart without becoming consciously aware of it.

In my case I not only felt inexplicably happy at parting, I also regarded my physical distress as something foreign, situated outside my rising joy in life. Yes, one could almost speak of a certain arrogance, as when, amidst all the love poems which are typically produced at such times, I lent a note of willed cleverness to a song of illness entitled "Deathbed Request":

When at last I lie upon the bier*
—a spark that slowly fades,
Stroke my hair again my love,
Before I join the shades.

Before my dust returns to dust
As it must surely do,
Place one last kiss upon the mouth
That loved no one but you.

And do not think I truly rest
In a coffin made of wood,
For all my life was placed in you
And now I'm yours for good.

Such a trick, offering mortality as a symbol (indeed as a prerequisite) of an even deeper total marriage, reveals again the unconventional nature of this love. Although I must add: unconventional only in comparison to middle-class marriage and all it entails, for which I was still too immature, and unconventional as a result of my childhood experience of God. For against that background my love was aimed *from the very first* not toward a normal consummation, but toward a symbolic image of my beloved that was almost religious.

However, just as events which fail to follow the common pattern still reveal certain normal traits in an intensified form, so this relationship revealed something about love in general. For in matters of love the partner—without necessarily taking on the divine attributes we've been discussing here—is still magnified in an almost mystical manner, so that he or she becomes the symbol of everything wonderful. Love in its fullest sense presumes that we give ourselves to each other totally—from pure and irresistible ecstasy to the most manifold relationships of the passions. But we also expect that this period of "losing ourselves" will gradually be followed by a "coming of our senses," not only in order to deal with the other demands of life, but also in light of the duties and responsibilities we are assuming toward each other. Which is not to say that those who have been enmeshed in love's questionable excesses, though such passions may be criticized or smiled at in the cold light of reason, don't owe a unique debt of gratitude to that which they have experienced—precisely *because* that experience is measured so differently, *because* it allows us to break through to what seemed to us most necessary, most self-evident, prior to our acquaintance with the real world. The person who possessed the power to make us both *believe and love* remains a royal figure deep within us, even if he later appears as our opponent.

Therefore, even in quite normal cases of consummated love, both partners must be willing to excuse excesses outside the bond—in spite of the difficulty posed by the strange blurring of borders between fidelity and infidelity. While the most strongly visionary breakthrough may be accompanied by the strongest actual demands on other people, the beloved is scarcely more than that bit of reality which moves the poet toward his poem. The poem itself can make no further demands upon its object in the real world. There is more of the poet in each of us than there is a rational being; in the deepest sense, what we *are* when we are creating poetry is more than what we *were*—apart from all questions of value, far, far deeper than such questions, simply in the irrevocability with which a sentient Mankind is forced to come to terms with that by which we are merely carried, and upon which we must attempt to find our way about together.

Our love for one another is a life jacket which allows both partners to learn to swim, yet we behave as if the other person is instead the sea which carries us both. That's why the Other becomes so uniquely precious in our eyes, an ultimate homeland, yet as misleading and confusing as infinity. We, who have become sentient and therefore disparate and discrete bits of the universal cosmos, have to help each other as we are tossed to and fro in this state, so that we can bear it, and bear each other up. We must prove our basic oneness by consummating it bodily. We must embody it. But this positive, material realization of the basic fact, an apparently irrefutable proof, is still the merest claim, since it can not overcome the ultimate isolation of each individual within the self.

Therefore two souls in spiritual love may well fall prey to the curious delusion that they are floating, free of their bodies, united somewhere, somehow, above themselves. For the same reason, however, the opposite may happen: instead of such a spiritual display, our body may achieve a total consummation by possessing an object in which it has no further interest. That is why we tend to make distinctions between Eros, which attracts us, and eroticism, which seduces us; between sexuality as something quite common, and love as something which stirs us deeply, something we are inclined to think of as an almost "mystical" experience; depending in each case on whether it finds expression in our innocent physical natures, for which banality remains invisible, and satisfaction is found in a pleasure as elemental as breathing—or whether we small creatures celebrate the mystery of our primordial relationship to all things with the whole of our being.

The perfect gift of an eroticism without inner contradictions is granted only to the animals. In place of the human tension between loving and not loving, they alone know that inner regularity which expresses itself in heat and freedom in a purely natural manner. We alone can be unfaithful.

There are only two factors which reach from the world of animal instincts into our realm of human complications, beyond all individual decisions: *fertility and motherhood.* (The fact that we can say so little about love in general, except that it breaks through our notions of orderly human life, is a result of our inability to "understand" anything except in its relationship to our rational or sensual desires—but rationality and pleasure are extremely constricted conceptual vessels with which to draw much water from the well of experience.) And so we allow ourselves to become mothers. Beyond all problematics, a deep healthiness within woman affirms the continuation of life—even when the drive has not personalized itself in terms of the conscious wish to bring about a rebirth of the childhood of the desired man within herself. There can be no doubt that the failure to experience motherhood bars a person from the most valuable part of being a woman. I remember how astonished someone once was when, in a long discussion of similar matters in my later years, I confessed, "Do you know I never dared to bring a child into the world?" I'm certain that this attitude wasn't even a product of my youth, but came from a much earlier period in which such questions are not even rationally considered. I knew God better than I knew the stork. Children came from God, and if they died, they returned to God—how else were they *possible* except through Him? Now I really don't want to claim that God's momentous disappearance weakened, or even killed, the idea of motherhood within me. No, I don't mean to imply anything for my own particular case. But it can't be denied that the full meaning of "birth" is dependent to a great extent on whether a child comes from nothingness or from the whole of things. Aside from their own personal hopes and desires, most people overcome their hesitation in such matters with the aid of commonly held expectations, and no one objects if they want to indulge in the whole optimistic notion by means of which our children are supposed to finally fulfill all the hopes and dreams we never achieved for ourselves. But it is not the moral or everyday considerations which make the question of creating a new life a matter of such deep moment, it is the situation itself, which transports us from the personal realm into a state of creativity in which our personal decision is accepted and lifted from us: at this most creative moment of our lives. If it is true that all our actions are inevitably subject to a similar permutation in which we place our signatures beneath a text which was dictated to us, the two realms are manifestly united in the case of what we call acts of creation (in all areas!). For no matter how honestly and seriously the parents' responsibility for the child is divided between them: that responsibility will be overwhelmed by the force of what is to come—by the intimate nature of our own psychic and spiritual makeups *and* by distant events, beyond all influence, striding invisibly toward us. It is easy to understand, then, if among all the true believers, it is the *mother* who requires faith most intensively: God must remain steadfast at least in this one spot—above the head of the child she has borne. There is not a single Mary anywhere on the globe who is Joseph's wife and nothing more—not a one who does not undergo as well the immaculate conception of life's ultimate riddle, that she is the chosen vessel.

Activated by Eros, beyond all those things which bind two beings personally or procreatively, there is another deeper relationship which is quite rare and is not so easily described as those we immediately understand on the basis of the merest hints. Perhaps one could risk attempting to picture that relationship by means of an analogy to what we have discussed above. Imagine a couple who see their consummated love solely and exclusively as a means of bearing a child; now imagine this desire lifted above the biological plane into a higher, spiritual realm. Here too, the most tangible and personal realm is united with that which is most distant, most absent from the couple. The ecstasy which transfigures them both is not turned upon each other, but toward a third object of their mutual desire, which lifts them from the profound depths of being into their own sight, so to speak, into their own vision. Their point of reference is not the world around them, but the common ground upon which they stand: it permits them a *mutual* conception.

Such an inadequate description, with its seemingly delphic pronouncements, would hardly be necessary, were it not for the fact that the relationship would otherwise be inevitably and wrongly confused with what we generally refer to as "friendships"—insofar as these too are not based upon a physical union, but rather upon shared interests of other sorts, be they spiritual, intellectual, or practical in nature. This not only differs from what I am describing as hills do from mountain peaks, it is of another nature altogether, as if two people, instead of bearing children, decided to adopt them: no matter how right and good that might be, nor how happy it made them. It is only in early youth, perhaps, that friendship shares something of the transports of which we are speaking: in those years when the great creative talents rise to the surface and make their claims, before the maturing body draws full attention to itself and its needs. Only rarely do these early feelings persist to reach their *own* full maturity: the rarest and most glorious human relationship created by Eros. It consists in The Other remaining—like a transparent image—the means *through* which our own deepest desires are fulfilled. In this case being "friends" means an almost unprecedented resolution of the strongest contradictions of life: both of you are in the realm of what for you is the divine, sharing the mutual loneliness—*in order* to make that loneliness even more profound—so profound that within The Other you see yourself as open to everything procreatively human. The friend protects you from ever losing that sense of loneliness—you are protected even from *each other*.

The basic nature of the first great love of my early youth was no doubt related to what I've just been describing, and it is for that reason, perhaps,

2 0 • LOOKING BACK

that I have dared to make this feeble attempt to put into words just what I mean. That relationship remained incomplete and unfulfilled in life as well. Thus I must confess that in all three forms of consummated love (marriage, motherhood, and the pure bond of Eros) I cannot match the success that others may have had on occasion. But that's not what counts: just as long as what we were able to grasp was Life, and affected Life, and as long as we continued to work creatively, as living beings, from the beginning to the end of our days.

Perhaps one might put it thus: whoever reaches into a rosebush may seize a handful of flowers; but no matter how many one holds, it's only a small portion of the whole. Nevertheless, a handful is enough to experience the nature of the flowers. Only if we refuse to reach into the bush, because we can't possibly seize all the flowers at once, or if we spread out our handful of roses as if it were the *whole* of the bush itself—only then does it bloom apart from us, unknown to us, and we are left alone.

How other young women came to terms with the problems of love and life in those years I only know in scattered cases. Even then my attitude toward things was a bit different from theirs—though I could not have given an account of my position. This was probably due to the fact that the "longing and fearing in pain and suspense" [Goethe] common to those years soon lay behind me, due to my decisive meeting with the man who threw open the gateway to Life, leaving me more in a state of boyish readiness than feminine acquiescence. But that wasn't the only reason. In their youthful optimism, other girls my age still tended to view everything they longed and hoped for in the rosiest of hues. But I lacked something necessary for such optimism— or perhaps I knew too much: some sort of ancient knowledge must have impressed itself upon my basic temperament. Like an immovable stone beneath my foot, although I could walk so surely across old moss and wilted flowers. But perhaps I've expressed this too strongly, since I've always approached everything the future held with joy, and willingly, without exception.

For "Life" was something I loved, awaited, embraced with all the strength within me. Not the elements of power, control, and determination, where compliance is expected. But rather some thing or person like myself, in my situation, sharing my incomprehensible existence. When and where does Eros cease? Shouldn't that be in this chapter, "The Experience of Love," as well? The entire ardor of youth flowed toward Life beyond all questions of possible happiness or pain, hopes or desires, an undirected emotional state, which, like the state of love, expressed itself in verse. The most typical example is a poem I wrote in Zurich upon leaving my Russian homeland, with which I close this chapter. I entitled it "A Prayer to Life":

Indeed, I love you life, as friend*
Loves friend, in all your mystery—
Whether I wept or laughed again,
Whether you brought me joy or pain.

I *love* you even for the harm you do;
And if you must destroy me,
I'll tear myself away from you
As I would leave a friend.

I embrace you with all my might!
Let your flames set me on fire,
And in the glow of that last fight
I will explore your riddle's depths.

To be for centuries! to live!
Wrap your arms about me once again:
If you have no more joy to give—
At least you still grant pain.

(Once I wrote it down from memory for Nietzsche and he set it to music in more solemn, slightly longer lines.)

FAMILY LIFE

FRATERNAL SOLIDARITY was so much a part of my experience within the family, as the youngest sibling and only sister, that it continued to exercise its influence upon my relationship to men throughout my life: regardless of how early or late I came to know a man, I always felt a brother was hidden within him. But this was due as well to the nature of my five brothers themselves, three of them in particular, since the oldest and the fourth were not granted long to live. Although my childhood was often one of lonely fantasy, although the entire development of my thoughts and aspirations ran counter to family tradition and was a constant source of irritation, although I spent my later life abroad, far from my loved ones, my relationship to my brothers never changed—and with the passing years and the physical distance an increasingly mature judgment allowed me to recognize their value as human beings even more clearly. Indeed in later years, whenever I began to question or criticize my own nature, I comforted myself with the thought that I came from the same family they did. And indeed every man I ever met, insofar as he showed integrity of thought, or manliness, or warmth of heart, awakened within me the living image of my brothers.

Even when our ninety-year-old mother died,[*] they gave me a double share of the estate, although the two who were married had fifteen children to care for between them, and I had none. When I kept asking about the will, they told me that was their business: didn't I know that I would always be "their little sister"? The oldest of them—Alexandre, or "Sasha"[*]—had always been a sort of second father to us, filled with energy and goodness, and like our father active and helpful in the widest of circles. He had a wonderful sense of humor, and the most infectious laugh I ever heard. His humor arose from the combination of a very clear, rational mind with a warmth of heart which found its most natural expression in aiding others. When, as a fifteen-year-old in Berlin, I received the unexpected news of his death by telegram, my first shocked and self-centered reaction was to think: "Who will protect me now?" My second brother—Robert, or "Roba" (the most elegant dancer of the mazurka at our winter balls) had all sorts of artistic talent and a sensitive nature. He would have liked to be a military man like his father, but his father wanted him to become an engineer, which he proceeded to do. The patriarchal family order also forced my third brother—Eugene, or "Zhénya"—who was a born diplomat if there ever was one, to become a doctor against his wishes, but also a successful one. For in spite of all their basic differences, my brothers shared one extraordinary characteristic: the ability to devote themselves absolutely to the *technical* aspects of their respective professions. My third brother bore this out as a pediatrician— even as a boy he had shown an interest in little children. But he always remained in some sense a private person and "diplomatically" secretive. Another childhood memory I have of those days is his scolding me for resisting our family rules too openly. One time I got so mad I tried to throw my cup of hot milk at him, but instead I spilled it all over myself, and wound up with hot liquid down my neck and back. My brother, who was of course as impetuous as any of us, said with satisfaction, "You see, that's what happens when you try to do something wrong." Long after he had died of tuberculosis at the age of forty, I began to understand more about him. For example, why, in spite of the fact that he was tall, thin, and not at all handsome, he nevertheless awakened the strongest passions in women, although he never chose one as a mate for life. It sometimes seemed to me that his overflowing charm had something almost irresistible about it. At times it was combined with a great deal of humor, as once when he decided to take my place at one of our dances, a beautiful wig on his otherwise shaved head, his slender body in a thoroughly modern corset. He received most of the ribbons during the cotillions, from young officers who didn't know the family well, but knew vaguely that there was a young daughter in the house who was not yet grown up, and who tended to keep to herself. What I liked in particular were the flat dancing shoes. I enjoyed wearing them from the first time I took lessons, and would glide across the parquet floor of the great hall as if on ice. I was tempted into the other grand rooms as well, with their high, churchlike ceilings. My father's official residence in Morskaja was located in a wing of the general officers' building on the Moika, and the suitability of these rooms for gliding made it one of my favorite pastimes. When I think back, I always see myself *gliding* this way: it was like being alone.

My older brothers married early, having already made their choice while I was still taking dancing lessons. They were loving husbands and fathers, and lived very happy lives. Their relationship to their wives reflected to a large extent that of our father to our mother—for example, he always stood up when she entered the room, and so did we, without even thinking. That didn't exclude the possibility of occasional blow-ups, due to his stormy

temperament, which we all inherited. At the same time he was truly innocent and open to the end of his days, and we used to tell a funny story about
that. Mushka, as we called our mother, had warned him to watch out for
someone who was supposedly slandering him, and at the same time pointed
out how much another person liked him: whereupon Father immediately got
the two mixed up, and took one for the other. In his youth he enjoyed all the
pleasures of life in the splendid imperial city of Petersburg under Nicholas I
and Alexander II. He was a member of the generation which included
Pushkin and Lermontov, and as an officer he knew them both. After his
marriage, however, both he and his wife, who was nineteen years younger,
experienced a true religious conversion under the influence of a Baltic
minister named Iken, who brought a spirit of devout piety into the somewhat
moralistic and dry evangelical church in Petersburg. The *reformed* evangelical churches—French, German, and Dutch—formed, together with the
Lutheran church, a sort of coherence of faith among the non-natives, that is,
the non–Greek Orthodox, although in all other respects we were thoroughly
Russianized. Therefore my break with the church resulted in social censure
as well, which caused my mother in particular a good deal of pain. On the
other hand I was certain that my father, who passed away shortly before it
happened, would have approved of my action, even though he was deeply
troubled by my lack of faith, and was himself closely tied to the German
Reformed church, since it was through his intercession with the emperor
that the church had been given permission to establish itself there in the first
place. He tended not to talk about religious opinions, and it was only after his
death, when I was given the Bible he had reserved for his own personal use,
that I gained a picture of his true faith, on the basis of the many passages he
had neatly underlined. I was so deeply moved by the nature of his devotion,
the quiet, humble, and childlike trust of this strong and active man, used to
wielding his own authority, that I was seized with longing for everything I
had missed knowing about him as a sixteen-year-old.

As a very young child I remember that my father and I were bound by
small, secret demonstrations of tenderness, which, as I vaguely recall, we
would break off when Mushka entered the room, since she did not favor such
open expressions of feeling. After having had five sons, my father badly
wanted a little girl, while Mushka would have preferred a round half-dozen
boys. After his death, I was going through old letters from my father to my
mother written while she was traveling abroad for the holidays with the
children, and found the following postscript: "Give our little girl a kiss for
me"—and another time: "Does she think about her old papa from time to
time?" Warm memories came rushing back. When I was a few years old, and

troubled by a passing phase we referred to as "growing pains," I had some trouble walking. As a form of consolation, I was given a pair of soft, red leather shoes with gold tassels, and was carried about in my father's arms so happily that the affair took a turn for the worse: for I was slow to reveal that the pains had passed, and that same tender father, with heavy heart, but firmness of purpose, brought a small birch switch to bear upon precisely that portion of my body which had nestled upon his arm. I recalled our walks together on clear winter days. Since my mother didn't like to walk holding her husband's arm, my father had taught me that art while I was still quite young, my gliding leaps accompanying his own long, steady stride. Once, when we came across one of the numerous Russian beggars in that region, I wanted to hand him a silver ten-kopeck piece I'd been given to learn how to "handle" money. My father, however, said that was not how money should be handled: half of what one had was enough—but that must inevitably be given to one's fellow man; and it mustn't be baser that what is retained—it mustn't be a copper coin for example. And he gravely replaced my little ten-kopeck piece with with two delightfully tiny silver five-kopeck pieces.

My relationship with both parents—it now seems to me—at least in comparison to most children I knew, lacked the more impassioned feelings often present, be it in rebellion or love. Both opposition and agreement were subject to certain limits, behind which there was still room for freedom. Indeed, while I was in school, this "freedom" even went too far: when I complained that I didn't know Russian well enough after my final required courses in that language (since we were accustomed to speaking only French and German at home), my father suddenly allowed me simply to audit courses, saying with a laugh, "Education certainly needn't be compulsory in her case." I don't know where he got this tender prejudice in my favor.

I think it was freedom in my brothers' case as well which allowed them to continue a relationship of undiminished warmth and trust with our parents, even in later life. For me, the borderline which was automatically drawn meant, for example, that I was allowed in a sense to be silent, to keep to myself, in the midst of that warm sense of trust.

A minor event occurs to me as proof of this, although I've unfortunately forgotten just how old I was—I only know I was in school, which in Russia means I was at least eight. Our dog Jimka, a schnauzer, had become rabid. There were many stray dogs running loose in the street those days (both in the heat of summer and the depth of winter), and rabies was often transmitted to house pets through bites. Since it had never happened to us before, we didn't immediately realize it, and when our beloved dog suddenly bit me on the wrist as I was leaving for school, I immediately put something on it and thought nothing more. When I returned home our Jimka was nowhere to be seen: he had gone mad, and they had come to fetch him. He was taken into observation at a nearby institute and shot that same evening. In the meantime, however, he had also bitten the woman who did our laundry. The doctor declared that there was nothing to be done for her (following current belief at the time) since several hours had already passed. My shock was outweighed by the gruesome thought that my family would think that I was going mad at any moment, and that whenever I scuffled with my brothers, they would be afraid I was going to bite them. A period of secret fear followed. I learned among other things about symptoms of hydrophobia, and thereafter I would worry all night about having to brush my teeth the next morning. (Fortunately I didn't know that this symptom applied to tea and milk as well.) But another thing I learned was that rabid dogs attacked their own masters first, and I recall my terrified conviction—the most horrible thing I had to face: "I'm going to bite Papa." I think that meant I loved him most, although I had no knowledge of this preference over my mother. How small a role the conscious mind plays in such matters is proved as far as I'm concerned by a memory from my earliest childhood. In the summer, I was often allowed to go to the beach with my mother (quite gladly) in our cabriolet. I could see her splashing about in the pool through a little window in the bathhouse, and I yelled out to her, "Mushka, couldn't you please drown just once?" She yelled back laughing, "But dear, if I did, I'd be dead!" Upon which I roared back as loudly as I could the standard Russian reply "Nichevó!" ("So what?"). But in my heart I didn't distinguish between my parents. No doubt because my father always treated my mother with the utmost chivalry in front of us, I always respected her as highly as he did. And so, when I was only half-grown, it was a shock to me to learn that my respect wasn't always self-evident. It happened this way: the key to some locked door had been misplaced, and my brothers came running to help—but I had already managed to open the door without any tools. As I was in the process of recounting this triumphantly to my mother, she asked, "What did you open it with?" to which I replied "My fingers!" I watched her face turn to stone. She said only, "I would never have dared to answer *my* mother like that—I didn't think you opened it with your feet!" I stared into the unknown—so frozen myself that I was incapable of explaining to her what I meant.

My parents understood one another wordlessly, in spite of how dissimilar they were (except for their strong temperaments and their faith). They remained constantly true to one another, in mutual trust and understanding. A major factor in their relationship was that, without really thinking about it, they sensed throughout their lives how important it was to combat their own biases—not so much in a moral sense, but to avoid being trapped within their own points of view. (They both were completely lacking in arrogance, and in its complement, subservience.) Given my mother's character, that meant submerging her independent and active nature in the role of wife and mother, the value of which was ordained by God, without making too much of it. The resulting composure and self-control which she chose to display was expected of others as well. In other matters there may well have been a touch of the rebel's blood in her veins. While she was still young she had taken on the responsibility of running a large household after her grandmother died, in order not to be under the control of her stepfather's sister. And I still recall with wonder a fleeting image from our summer trips to Switzerland: I see her standing in the hall before the door to our room, looking out into the courtyard in fascination at two men who were engaged in a knife fight. Not only was she quite brave physically, but I also think if left to her own devices she might well have preferred to fight things out rather than settle them peacefully. During the revolution of 1905, when she was in her eighties, she could be restrained only with difficulty from rushing out into the crowded streets where people were being fired upon, while the two faithful servant girls shrank back, wringing their hands.

My mother, having outlived my father by almost four decades, was mercifully spared having to witness the October Revolution. The families of my two oldest brothers, however, went through many years of bitter misery and hardship during the revolution and civil wars. It was almost impossible to get letters through to Germany except at great intervals. My second brother, Robert, when he was finally able to return from the Crimea, discovered not only that his job, his apartment, and everything he owned had been taken from him, but also that he was dependent upon the generosity of his former servant, who had been given the small estate outside the capital where Robert used to spend his summers, together with the little house and its contents. The man allowed him and his family a bit of room on the top floor and some cabbage soup for lunch if he helped in the fields. During the day Robert gathered mushrooms and berries with his grandchildren to help satisfy their hunger. His wife never really got over seeing the peasant's wife wearing her clothes, nor the sight of her naive joy in doing so. But in spite of it all, it wasn't the horrors of that period which were conveyed most movingly by the brief letters which made it through now and again: it was the extent of the revolution itself, which affected the very nature of the people themselves. It wasn't as if my brother had reversed his political opinions (he had been loosely associated with the Cadet party).* But when he told how the servant and he sat together on a bench in front of the house in the evening—resting and watching the revolutionary changes in the world—it didn't seem as if master and servant had traded places, one raised on high and one cast low, but rather as if a third person were speaking for both of them, one who was also experiencing that renewal. Perhaps there was something specifically Russian in the peasant's makeup that also contributed to this. My brother wrote admiringly: "How clever and friendly this illiterate fellow is!" From what we could tell, one could hardly speak of resignation on one side, or a sudden growth of self-confidence on the other: what altered both men was having been placed on the margin of a turning point in world history—as if they had been redrawn and enlarged in a more simplified and abstract form by the force of that situation.

The most touching aspect of all, however, was that the intimacy of the family bond developed most fully at the very moment in which it seemed to be dissolving in social terms. It wasn't just that hardships forced the family to huddle together as if they were on a small island in the midst of the pounding surf, while up to that point arguments and personal differences had no doubt divided them in the normal way. No, it was the inner importance of the familial relationships, the happiness and warmth that supported and consoled them: even as it was dying away at the level of the state, the old poetry of a life beyond the merely material blossomed here with a renewed and vital power. While on the other side there was no doubt an equally powerful stirring among the youth who had now been set free—together with new possibilities for self-indulgence and brutality.

Our elderly mother* was also spared seeing the death of her oldest son, her adviser and protector, who died of a heart attack shortly after the outbreak of the war, having suffered unspeakably painful premonitions of what was to come. Living alone, yet with her beloved children and grandchildren nearby, she was happy still. Her greatest problem toward the end was that we children had saddled her with a companion in her old age, so that we would know she was well cared for—a relative she liked of course, but not quite as much as she liked being alone and free to do exactly as she wished. Although she enjoyed having her sons and grandchildren about her, she loved living on her own, and she kept busy to the last. Even her reading was seldom dependent on the recommendation of others; one of the very last books she read, with great enthusiasm, was the Iliad.

In recounting her life between the age of eighty and ninety, I cannot help recalling the great and victorious struggle she revealed to me during one of my visits: as a deeply religious person, she felt it was her duty to do away with the devil once and for all before her life came to a close. When I asked, with

true concern, whether she didn't run the risk of losing God as well, since he
was really the one to decide such matters, she tried to calm me by
explaining patiently: "You don't understand: none of this affects Him. And
I've been talking it over with Him for some years now—of course He'll still
be there, but He'll dismiss the devil." She didn't deny that the origin of this
late, energetic turn of mind lay in the fact that she had watched her children
gradually falling prey one by one to the devil and unbelief, even though my
brothers—in chivalric fashion—continued to take part in certain ceremonies for the sake of their wives, and for Mushka. Throughout this period,
she never did anything which might have resulted in an inner spiritual
conflict: one could see in each instance that she would follow her immediate impulses, which she would then think over later in detail, and justify in
terms of the circumstances. One memory which often comes to me concerning her state of inner peace is that of her at breakfast, sitting there with a
twinkle in her deep-blue eyes; when we became annoyed, thinking she must
be laughing at us, it would turn out that she was still smiling over some
wonderful dream she'd had. In the end we turned it into a joke, claiming
that whenever Mushka had to put up with a day a bit less entertaining then
most (for one couldn't really ever speak of boring days in her case), she
would make up for it with amusing dreams that night. Toward the end of
her life, when she was going deaf, she could still find pleasure in sitting with
other friends who were equally hard of hearing, with everyone talking past
each other. She laughed heartily as she recounted how each of them—
herself included—would notice that the others were not following the
conversation, but how none of them really seemed to care that their own
responses were equally off base.

Next to reading, her favorite pastime was observing nature. Summer was a
constant delight for her, and even in late autumn she would stand at her
windows in the city, conversing with the row of trees on the street as if they
were spirits, or watching the changing effects of the light upon them. Her
apartment was filled with her own large-leafed plants, although she didn't
want any animals around her. In her old age, however, she wanted to
disencumber herself of all possessions—as if to intensify her solitude. As in
all things she took good care of every item she possessed, but she was happy
whenever she could quietly give one or the other of them to us. Over time,
ironically, it became necessary to give her things in return, so that her
apartment would not be totally empty. At times she seemed like someone
who was freeing herself, or about to soar away, feathering a nest with her
various possessions for those she was leaving behind. And I felt as well that
her actions on this mundane level revealed something about her fundamental

approach to life and death: instead of being robbed by death, she felt the superfluity of wealth, since she was soon to be beyond all fear of need.

I can't speak of my mother without calling to mind how much she did for me, in spite of her disapproval of my life abroad as a young girl, and my attitudes, which were so dissimilar to hers. Having disappointed her right from the start by not being born a boy, I should at least have attempted to be an ideal daughter—and yet the very opposite occurred. But even during the period in which my mother suffered most, when I was offending social norms most grievously, Mushka quietly came to terms with the situation: she sided with me against the whole world, believing in me even in her pain, and giving the impression that she and I understood one another completely, for it was important to her to shield me from malicious and deliberate misunderstanding. While I was spending the wonderful years of my youth abroad, I never really realized this clearly: I was barely conscious of her quiet maternal support, and instead could think only of how consistently, and with what deep conviction, she challenged the way I thought and lived—but only in her exchanges with *me*. In my self-centeredness, I was neither repentant nor homesick. When she hinted in a letter that she would like to see me safely married, I replied radiantly that I felt perfectly safe with Paul Rée. Only after I was indeed married, and my mother came for a long visit, did we finally discuss all these things at length. I was deeply moved, and, looking at her white hair, I was struck by a thoroughly old-fashioned thought: "Did she turn gray because of me?" But this emotion was tinged as well with happiness, and accompanied by an upsurge of love and respect that found its natural outlet in mutual tenderness now that we were at last together again. A person who knows me well and was once listening to this story, was thoroughly incensed by it: "Instead of being eaten up by remorse and homesickness—as you should have been—you wind up being even happier and more content because of it! If that's not moral insanity. . . ."

In fact it revealed one of the strongest contrasts between my mother's basic nature and mine: *she* constantly acted in terms of duty and dedicated self-sacrifice, impelled by something almost heroic in her character; perhaps it was a manly trait, expressing itself in a refined manner, which allowed her to be so unconsciously and wholly feminine. In *my* case, struggles were never uppermost in my mind, even struggles against myself; among those things I expected or wished for, I never fought for the things that really counted: *those* found me either acquiescent or indolent—they merged so totally with both my external and inner life, with my whole existence, that it was never a question of doing battle for them (had it been, I would have preferred the guidance of this little poem: "The world won't give you anything, of that you can be sure! So if you want to have a life at all, you'd better seize it while you can"). For I always felt that whatever is most beautiful and most valuable must always come as a *gift*, not as something earned—in part because it brings with it that second gift: *the privilege of gratitude*. And *that* no doubt is the reason why, in spite of all the seeming struggle, I had to be a daughter, and not a son.

I would like to add here my thanks to my parents: it was their love and constancy—the whole atmosphere which surrounded them—which allowed this sense of trust to develop fully within me, like a *faith* in what is given. A little story from my later life illustrates how deeply such things can be rooted in a person, even in the most mature years and combined with the clearest rationality. One morning I was strolling in the woods and unexpectedly came across blue gentians, which I wanted to pick for a sick friend; but I was also in the midst of working something out in my mind, and finally decided that I shouldn't interrupt my train of thought at that moment to gather flowers. Later, as I turned toward home, I found a full bouquet of the flowers in my hand, to my utter astonishment. I can still recall how steadfastfully I had kept my eyes off the forest floor, in order *not* to pick them. It would have been easy enough to regard their unexpected appearance as a miracle. But I didn't, just as I didn't react by laughing about how "lost" in thought I'd been. Instead my first response was to find myself joyfully saying aloud: "Thank you!"

While I was abroad, I returned to visit my mother every year, or at least every year and a half. I still remember vividly the last time we said good-bye, not long before she passed away. I was traveling from Petersburg to northern Finland, and from there by ship to Stockholm. Since the train was to leave early in the morning, we said our final good-byes the night before. Toward dawn, as I was slipping through the hall as quietly as possible, my mother suddenly stood before me: barefoot, in her long nightgown, her snow-white hair loose—the locks a bit unruly and childlike—and beneath them her deep blue eyes, opened wide, those clear, penetrating eyes, of which someone once accurately observed: if you had a bad conscience, it was best not to look into them.

She looked as if called from a dream, and her appearance too was dreamlike.

She didn't say a word to me. She simply pressed herself against me. She was my height, but although she had remained slender and erect, she had grown somewhat shorter in her final years, so that I could embrace the whole of her frail body and delicate limbs.

But when had she ever done such a thing? It was as if this embrace arose from hidden depths for this one moment. Or as if she had slowly and secretly matured toward this gesture as her life was coming to its close, as a final sweetness gathers in the fruit beneath the sun before it falls.

And perhaps in the peace of this still and tender moment, we both felt the same thought, the same pain, the same heartache: "Why, why have we waited till now?" That was the final gift my mother gave me in life. Dear Mushka.

THE RUSSIAN EXPERIENCE

OUR FAMILY ON my father's side was of French, German, and Baltic origin; Huguenots from Avignon, we apparently came to the Baltic by way of Germany after the French Revolution, having first spent many years in Strassburg. A part of so-called "Little Versailles," we settled in Mitau and Windau. I often heard the family tell stories about this as a child.

My father was sent to St. Peterburg as a young boy,* during the reign of Alexander I, for a military upbringing. After the Polish Uprising of 1830, in which my father, who was then a colonel, distinguished himself, a Russian peerage was added to his French one by Nicholas I. I still remember quite clearly looking at the great book of the coat-of-arms with the emperor's declaration when I was a child: the earlier French escutcheon, golden-red with transverse bands below, and above it the Russian arms with two golden-red slanting bands beneath the helmet; and I recall equally clearly the brooch made by imperial order for my mother, an imitation of the golden sword of honor, intended to display in exact miniature all my father's medals.

My mother, who was born in St. Petersburg, came from the north German area of Hamburg, and was Danish further back on her mother's side; her German family name was Wilm, and her Danish ancestors were called Duve (Dove).

It's hard to say which was our first language in Russia: Russian, which was dominant only among the common people, would have soon given way to French or German in any case. We spoke German almost exclusively;* it remained the bond which united us with our mother's homeland, and not only insofar as we still had friends and relatives in Germany, but as a sign of a true affinity—even if in our case (as opposed to many of the German nationals we knew in Petersburg), the affinity was to those who spoke German, rather than to German politics; for we didn't think of ourselves simply as in the Russian "service"—we considered ourselves Russian. I grew up surrounded by officers' uniforms. My father was a general. Later, in the civil service, he was a state councillor, then a member of the privy council, then an undersecretary of state, but he maintained his commission and his office at staff headquarters throughout his life. And my early love, at about the age of eight, was directed toward a young (and really strikingly handsome) officer, Baron Frederiks, an adjutant of Alexander II, and later a court minister, who, having attained a ripe old age, had to live through both the fall of the emperor and the revolution. My intimacy with him was limited, however, to the following minor event: as I stepped out of the staff headquarters one icy day, and stood at the top of the broad flight of steps, I felt the presence of the man I admired behind me. I slipped and fell—whereupon, in his chivalric haste to come to my aid, he suffered the same fate; finding ourselves suddenly face to face, in close proximity, sitting opposite one another before the entrance, we stared at each other in surprise: he laughing merrily, and I in silent bliss.

Such memories of the world around us are far less specifically Russian than the impressions made by our nurse and household servants. (I was the only one with a nurse.) My nurse was deeply attached to me. She was a gentle, pretty woman who, after having made a pilgrimage to Jerusalem, even received a "minor beatification" from the church—which caused my brothers to whinny in laughter, although I was really quite proud of her. Russian nannies (*nyánki*) have a reputation for total devotion to children which no biological mother can surpass (although their reputation for educating them is less impressive). Many descendants of former serfs were to be found among these nurses, and they still retained a sense of servitude, but now transformed, as it were, into a more pleasant and less literal form of attachment. The other Russian family servants were mixed with strongly non-Russian elements: Tatars, favored as coachmen and footmen due to their well-known abstinence from alcohol, and Estonians; there was a mixture of Protestants, Greek Orthodox, and Muslims; prayers were directed both east and west; and both old-style and new-style calendars were used to mark religious holidays and paydays. All this was made still more colorful by the fact that our country home in Peterhof was run by Swabian colonists who retained both the language and dress of the homeland they had left so many years ago. I learned practically nothing about the actual interior of Russia. It wasn't until I had made a few trips to Smolensk to visit my second brother, Robert, who had traveled far to the east (Perm, Ufa) as an engineer, that I got to know ethnic Russian society. St. Petersburg, that attractive amalgam of Paris and Stockholm, in spite of its imperial splendor, its reindeer sleighs, its illuminated ice palaces on the Neva, its late springs and hot summers, seemed totally international.

My companions at school were also of a strongly international cast, both in the small English private school I attended initially, and in the larger one which was to follow, where I learned next to nothing.* Even so I was able to meet people there who allowed me to relate to the Russian nation in a new way—namely politically. For the spirit of revolution which found its first political program in the Naródniki,* the "people's party," was already bubbling and fermenting in the schools. It was hardly possible to be young and energetic without being affected by it, since in spite of our relationship to the former emperor,* our family attitude toward the ruling political system was far from uncritical, once the "Emancipator Czar" Alexander II, after having abolished serfdom, had turned so conservative. The only thing that insulated me from these powerful contemporary issues was the profound influence of my friend, my first great love. The fact that, as a Dutchman, he felt himself a total foreigner in Russia, must have made me feel somehow less Russian myself. He felt I should put aside my tendency toward fantasy and develop myself as an individual, with an emphasis on rational and emotionally balanced spiritual growth. The only sign of my political engagement thus remained hidden in my desk drawer—a picture of Vera Sassúlich,* who might be considered the first Russian terrorist. She had taken a shot at a city official named Trépov, and after having been declared not guilty of the charge of conspiracy (courts had just been established to try such cases) was carried out upon the shoulders of a jubilant mob. She fled to Geneva and may still be alive today. During my student days in Zurich, toward the beginning of which—in 1881—Russian students celebrated with torchlight parades and shouts of joy the assassination of Alexander II by nihilists, I knew almost none of the young women studying with me, most of whom planned to be medical doctors. It was my belief that most of them were simply using their studies as a political cover for their stay abroad, since Russia had long since made higher education available to women—far earlier than anywhere else—and fully staffed universities had been established for them, for example with professors from the Academy for Medical and Surgical Sciences. But I was completely wrong about this: for these young women, and older ones as well, who struggled and sacrificed in order to establish Russian institutes of their own, equivalent to those for men, and who, when they were forcibly closed at one point, opened them yet again, could conceive of nothing more important or more vital than to gain the greatest possible knowledge and ability in the shortest possible time. Not as a means of competing with men or contesting their rights, nor from an academic ambition to further their own careers, but for a single purpose: to go out among the innocent, suffering, and oppressed Russian people, who needed their help. A flood of female doctors, midwives, teachers, nurses of all sorts—like secular women priests—flowed without interruption from the lecture halls and academies into the most distant and forsaken villages: women who devoted themselves *totally* to the object of their strongest compassion, in spite of facing, throughout their lives, political imprisonment, exile, and death.

In fact both sexes among the revolutionaries tended to regard the Russian people as children regard their parents. Although they were the ones (coming primarily from the intelligentsia) who educated, enlightened, and taught the people, the peasant remained a model for them in the human sense, in spite of his superstition, alcoholism, and vulgarity: an attitude we know from Tolstoi, who first learned from peasant society what life and death, work and devotion, were all about. All traces of simple duty and kindness were effaced in such a love, while the entire force of each individual's spiritual life concentrated itself in a form of primitivism—a childlike state which, at the deepest instinctual level, no one ever completely escapes, even as an ambitious and mature adult. It seems to me that all this influenced sexual love in Russia as well, releasing to a certain extent the extremes of tension which in Western Europe had developed over almost a thousand years to such exaggerated heights of rapture. (The only place I've seen this point made about eroticism in Russia is in Prince Karl Rohan's important sketches entitled *Moscow*, 1929.) Debauchery and licentiousness of all sorts can occur in Russia, just as anywhere else, perhaps of an even coarser nature, but the spiritual life remains innocent and childlike in its simplicity when compared to more "mature" nations which focus upon personal love of a more "egoistic" kind. The Russian "collective" is marked by attachment to the people, to what is fundamental, an intimacy of the heart rather than the principle of civilized behavior, or intelligence, or rationality. All ecstasy finds its expression *there*, in no way diminished, with an emphasis upon the difference between the sexes: for passive submission and receptivity mesh with a sharp, active revolutionary quality in a state of spiritual alertness.

Much of this became clear to me only later, during my third stay in Paris, in 1910,* when the sister of a young woman terrorist arranged for me to be introduced into her circle. It was shortly after the Azéf tragedy* had become public, when this most monstrous and inexplicable of all double agents, led into a double betrayal by Búrtsev, left behind a nameless sense of despair. I felt then, with direct emotional clarity, that there was really no contradiction between that small group of revolutionary bomb-throwers who were willing to sacrifice their private lives totally for a murderous mission in which they believed, and the equally total passivity of the pious peasant, who accepts his fate as God-given. The passion of belief is the same in each case, on the one hand demanding submission, on the other crying out for action. The guiding principle which stands over both lives, and everything privately expressed within them, does not arise from the personal sphere; it defines each of them, and allows both types of martyrdom—that of the peasant and that of the terrorist—to become conscious of the consolation of patience, the power of violent action. When, after almost a century of action, the social revolutionaries were backed against the wall in their tragic efforts, confronted by something which went far beyond the dream they had shared to that point, a third type was created from that same inner passion of the people: a newly freed proletariat, called forth to join in the work and success, and therefore—in the face of a new type of compulsion, a misery renewed in a thousand ways—swept willingly into an orgy of action. Their previous passive submission seemed to all appearances to undergo an unparalleled translation into action in the common life of the people and in the land reforms, something which up to then had seemed like the early Christians expectations of the arrival of the heavenly realm on earth. The proletarian thus became a natural enemy of his brother the peasant, who for the most part experienced only the negative side of these developments: the destruction of a form of primitive village communism by abstract political measures which could no longer count upon the peasants' subservience and submission because those very measures were so clearly opposed to God and a belief in God. So the peasants, gathered about their church bells and crosses, saw themselves as representatives of God, confronting bolshevism, the work of the devil.

It is commonly said that the almost religious terms in which bolshevism wooed the Russian proletariat, superimposing the legend of Lenin, so to speak, upon that of Christ, was a devious and pragmatic exploitation of a pious population. But no matter how often that might have been the case, it no more explains what happened than the phenomenon of the religious person can be explained by the deviousness of priests and their love of power. What is involved is clearly the effect of the massive experiments which utilized overpowering terrorism to rock Russia on every side with vehement and bold undertakings. Regardless of whether they succeed or fail in the coming years, such experiments are inextricably linked to the religious fervor of the Russian people. For it is this which provides, beneath the materialism of political theories and the mechanism of a much-admired technology, a totally different, and thoroughly spiritual ground—unlike that of normal cultures which have reached maturity more slowly, those in which these very theories were developed.

One might say that something of this national characteristic could already be seen in Russia's late conversion to Christianity (around A.D. 900). The Russians were not converted by force, an otherwise common occurrence, but instead by chosen envoys whose Byzantine Christianity seemed closer to the Russian spirit than Islam or Buddhism. The adopted religion was then irresistibly "Russianized." Since Byzantine documents were gradually being subjected to a similar "Russianization" in the course of being copied, the church (Patriarch Nikon) eventually found it necessary to have them examined and corrected. But by this time the Russians felt such an attempt at religious enlightenment was going too far, it was an improper interference in something which was now deeply their own. Almost a third of them preferred to leave the church and return to the orthodox "Raskól" (Schism of 1654), in which the saying originated: "If you love and fear God too, then going to church is not for you." Thus what was taken over from Christianity corresponded to something profoundly real in the Russian spirit, where it persisted. Just as the true reverence of those who remained in the church was not focused upon a higher spirituality, or levels of church hierarchy, but instead was granted to pilgrims, hermits, anchorites, in whose footsteps anyone could follow, and the veneration of such figures included respect for something in them that each person could, so to speak, secretly believe he too possessed. Just as, conversely, each of them might find themselves in the place of a condemned man or a criminal: which is shown by the popular custom of giving something, be it an egg, a crust of bread, or a bright piece of ribbon, to convicts making the hard journey cross country to prisons in Siberia. There is tender compassion in such actions, but also an element which I heard in the words of a peasant who pointed out such a procession to me and said, "This time it hit *them*." The reluctance to pass moral judgments on others, and a disregard for the traditional standards which result in such judgments, is related to an ultimate reliance on God, who arranges everything as he wishes. This childlike trust is also evident in the traditional words of consolation offered whenever fate sends times of affliction upon this tormented people: "Everyone has forgotten us but God."

It's easy to see how such a religious tendency could further both the church and sectarianism, and that among the sects, all sorts of various and even contradictory variants could arise, from the brutal asceticism of the Skoptsý,* with their ritual castration, to the most extreme and repellent

forms of sensual ecstasy, which were included in ceremonies under the guise
of sexual mysteries; or the delightful human joy and peace of mind which so
moved Tolstoy and made him, to a certain extent, an apostle of the Russian
peasant. Just as this could have been explained initially on the basis of
Tolstoy's psychopathology, which was a part of his genius, so the display of
orgiastic and dissolute religious behavior has recently been taken too personally in Rasputin's case, as if it were his own monstrous peculiarity, instead
of understanding it in terms of the peculiar nature of such sects and their
religious doctrines.

That contradictions may be resolved peacefully within the human breast
is yet another characteristic of a primitive and undifferentiated state. But
even beyond that, the Russian soul is clearly less attuned to dualism: thus
what one dreams about and what one experiences tend to be less sharply
divided into separate and successive realms—nor is such a clear distinction
made between heaven and earth, the former less abstract, the latter less laden
with a sense of guilt. This was strikingly illustrated on various occasions by
those who were not born in Russia, yet spent many years there, and led to a
particularly strong attachment to things Russian. This was the case with our
family as well: my father in particular loved the *prostóy naród*, the "common
people," so much that when he spoke of how often or how severely he had to
reprimand them, a tone of respect, almost of reverence, always crept into his
voice, and communicated itself to us as well. On my mother's side, it must be
said, the feeling of being an immigrant from a Protestant country persisted
in the face of Greek Orthodoxy. And how did I feel? While still quite young,
I had been de-Russianized by my first great love, because my friend, as a
foreigner (condemned by the conditions in Russia to let his greatest talents lie
fallow, much to his annoyance) had focused all his interests and wishes
"beyond the border": *zagranítsu*, the Russian word for all foreign lands. But
whenever I returned home from Switzerland or Germany after my emigration, and reaching the Russian border, would transfer to the wider, heavier
railway cars and be stowed away for the night by a conductor who called me
"my little dove" or "little mother," and when the smell of shaggy sheepskins,
or the fragrance of Russian cigarettes, would envelop me—then the bell that
rang three times, the old-fashioned signal for departure, aroused in me an
unforgettable feeling of happiness at being in my homeland. It wasn't a
matter of returning to a familiar house, nor was it ever a case of being
homesick for the country in which I was born, or for my earliest childhood
memories there. Even now I can't pin it down precisely: I only know that it
remained substantially unchanged throughout the wonderful years in which

I was a young woman, when I was so preoccupied with other matters, so absorbed by quite un-Russian intellectual endeavors.

These were gradually converted into the pursuits and studies I was engaged in when Rainer Maria Rilke met me in 1897. The two trips* we took together to Russia awakened in both of us a steadily increasing longing to be there. It was an extraordinary experience for both of us: in his case it offered a breakthrough in his creative life, for which Russia offered the appropriate images at a time when he was still studying the country and its language. For me it was simply the intoxication of being in Russia again, enveloped by the total Russian experience: this land of the people spread about me in all its vastness, its human suffering, its resigned and patient longing. It surrounded me with such a powerful sense of reality that I never again felt impressions so strongly, with the exception of the most individual of personal experiences. The most extraordinary thing about this double adventure, however, was that identical moments in time, and identical objects, gave each of us what we needed—Rainer finding creative inspiration, while I was put in touch with my most profound needs and memories, by living through them.

But what made this possible for both us, and answered a deep-felt need, was a strange fact: throughout the vast stretches of this land—and not just those in which we traveled—along its rivers, between the White and Black seas, from the transuralic to the European borders, it seemed as if we were constantly meeting one and the same man, as if he came from the nearest village—regardless of whether he had a standard Russian nose or that of a Tatar. This unity in diversity did not arise from difficulties in differentiating among little-known groups, it came from an openness and spirituality in the Russian face, as if the basic humanity we all share found eloquent expression there. It was like learning something new and moving about yourself from the person you met—and loving him. That inevitably had a decisive effect upon Rainer, given his constant search for the most profound wellsprings of the human condition, providing for him the images with which he eventually became God's hymnist.

Much of this became clear to me only later: he was impelled toward this experience, as if to heal a secret fissure in his internal being. In a similar manner he was driven toward the East by his European over-refinement, his all-too-Western nature: as if he sensed that there, as well as in the Asiatic cultures, the fundamental basis of original man, with all the attendant advantages and disadvantages, still determined the direction of things.

While traveling, we often asked ourselves if a trip deeper into Asia would disclose the Russian culture to us in a "purer" form. But we felt that, on the contrary, we would have encountered something different, something foreign, that would not reveal itself more openly but instead close itself defensively against us. For whenever one approaches the true Orient, it is as if a section of the Great Wall of China arises; the best way to approach it is with the aid of scientific knowledge, with the tools of the academic. It is ringed by age-old cultures—complete with wonderful works, but reserved toward strangers, with the inaccessible and seemingly marvelous wisdom of its ancient traditions, into which everyone there is born, no matter who he is. It closes its face to us. Seen from the standpoint of our separation into discrete individuals, the Orient seems so totally different that it would perish if it adopted our face, while at the same time it is more advanced than our own, and superior to us in having preserved its basic unity, its own special blend of culture and nature, of form and being.

The Russian land, however, presents another aspect—even in deepest Siberia, it is turned somehow westward, as if it can't stop anywhere, as if it must go on, surrounded by invasions and influences from every side throughout history, as if that were its destiny: to confirm its vastness by a receptivity for even the most foreign elements, preparing itself by the passage between right and left for a final synthesis. As if, as a result, its own immeasurable depths, its inner universality, did not become a form of defense, a finished product, but instead the slower, heavily laden tread of the "long-term nomad" who has covered great distances: continually wandering from East to West and back again in order not to lose, by settling down too soon, any part of the precious burden he bears—to hold in readiness for *that* his dancing feet, his singer's joy in even the most melancholy of his songs, which sound a note anticipating the (possible) decline of the Western world.

Today this type of man seems forcibly drawn into an ecstasy of progress, pushed violently toward artificial goals of Western origin. While these goals have failed to be fully developed in the West, because they are felt to be a product of the previous century, something with which we have to come to terms in light of the longings of our own century, in backward Russia they have called forth the massive power of clashing extremes. There it was not a case of altering an existing cultural structure; rather, it was a question of creating a cultural form for the whole of the country for the very first time. Hence, for better or for worse, it was possible to create something new by force, both through the sudden availability of technological means, and by the Asiatic dimensions of their use. Thus in Russian bolshevism we see blood and passion flow into the dry, cold theories inherited from the West, until it no longer seems something taken from the Western world, but appears instead as the precondition for a new dawn, to which Russia invites the universe in terms beyond nation and rationality.

The most important thing for us, however, was to be in old Russia, prior to its experience of the decisive risk of revolution, in which the model was put to a test. It was important because one can understand what lies ahead only from the point of view of old Russia; only thus can one avoid the misunderstanding of the many travelers who pass through Russia today and are so surprised to find the Russians, who up to then had been regarded as simpletons, now transformed into a type of exalted machine, simply because a hypermodern knout swings over their heads in place of the old-fashioned *nagáyka*.

As we stood on the shores of the Volga, in the pain of parting, we devised a form of consolation, so that we *could* part. We thought that if or when we ever returned, be it soon (!) or in the distant future, or if it was some generation yet to come: no matter what violent or turbulent times lay ahead, what we looked upon with tear-filled eyes would still be there. We little knew how soon that picture would be altered: how the Volga would join the other rivers, channeled into one huge reservoir, from which, forced by human hand, they would roar through the Russian countryside like a single gigantic flood until they reached the quiet ocean.

But we knew and had learned: even what came could not change that part of our experience which had been most magnificent and most intimately part of our interior world.

We had received more in Russia than Russia itself, and we were able to leave.

Old Russia*

You're like a youngster still at home,
Of all your suffering unaware,
So childish all your actions seem
Compared to those who've grown.

Your houses still are colored bright,
As if you're playing as you starve:
You love the colors on the gold,
Red, green, blue, and white.

And yet, if one observes with care,
Scorn gives way to reverence mild:
Russia was built at God's own feet
By that very child.

Volga

No matter how far away you are, I see you still,
No matter how far away you are, you still remain—
Like a presence that will never fade,
Like the landscape of my life.

If I had never rested on your banks:
It seems I'd know your breadth and length,
As if the flood of each sweet dream
Would strand me on your loneliness.

THE EXPERIENCE
OF FRIENDSHIP
(PAUL RÉE)

ON A MARCH EVENING in Rome,* in the year 1882, while a few friends were gathered at Malwida von Meysenbug's,* the doorbell rang and Malwida's faithful servant Trina came rushing in and whispered to her agitatedly—upon which Malwida hurried to her desk, scraped some money together, and left the room. Although she was laughing when she returned, the fine black silk scarf about her head was still trembling a bit from the excitement. The young Paul Rée* entered with her: a friend of some years whom she loved like a son, who—having come helter-skelter from Monte Carlo—was in a rush to send the waiter the money he had borrowed from him for the journey, since he had lost everything, literally every last penny, gambling.

Surprisingly enough, this funny and somewhat sensational debut scarcely disturbed me: we made friends immediately—indeed, the fact that Paul Rée stood out because of it, as if he were on a dunce's stool, sharply separated from the others, may have played a role. At any rate I quickly warmed to his clearly defined profile and shrewd eyes when I saw the expression on his face at that moment, a mixture of humorous contrition and superior kindness.

That same evening, and every day thereafter, we continued talking excitedly while wending our way from Malwida's house in the Via della Polveriera to the pensione where my mother and I were staying. These walks through the streets of Rome beneath the moon and stars soon brought us so close to one another that I began to devise a wonderful plan by means of which we could continue in this way, even after my mother, who had brought me south from Zurich for my health, returned home. It's true that Paul Rée at first took a completely false tack, to my sorrow and rage, suggesting a totally different plan to my mother—that we get married—which made her agreement to my own plan that much more difficult. First of all I had to make him envision and understand what the "self-contained" love life I had settled upon as a permanent condition meant in combination with my impulse toward a totally unconstrained freedom.

I will confess honestly that a simple dream first convinced me of the feasibility of my plan, which flew directly in the face of all social conventions. In it I saw a pleasant study filled with books and flowers, flanked by two bedrooms, and us walking back and forth between them, colleagues, working together in a joyful and earnest bond. But there's no denying that the five years we spent together resembled this dream to an amazing degree. Paul Rée once said that the only difference was that I was slow to learn how to distinguish between books and flowers, since at first I tended to think that venerable tomes from the university were mats for flower vases, and on occasion I would deal with people in an equally confused way.

Finally, while I was still struggling with poor Mama, who would happily have called her sons to help her drag me home dead or alive, I discovered to my astonishment that Malwida was almost more prejudiced than my mother, who was backed by the still unshaken, sanctified tradition of both the world and her faith. Of course I was later to learn that Paul Rée was partially to blame, since he had originally run to Malwida in high excitement, to confess to her that we would have to "flee" from one another, since he was determined not to compromise Malwida's principles—although as far as Malwida was concerned, they had already been compromised by the way in which we "wended" our way home together (something my mother knew about). I thus discovered, to my surprise, the extent to which idealism in such matters can interfere with the urge toward personal freedom, since the idealist is anxious to avoid any possible misunderstanding, or the slightest "false impression," for the sake of his tenets, and thus is overly sensitive to the judgment of others. From Rome, I wrote a letter filled with anger and disappointment to my mentor, who didn't seem to want to help me either, in answer to one he had sent me earlier—here's the letter, addressed to him in St. Petersburg:

Rome, 26/13 March 1882

I've read your letter at least five times,* but I still don't get it. What in the devil's name have I done wrong? I thought you'd be singing my praises. After all, I'm just showing you how well I learned my lessons. First of all because I'm not simply caught up in some mere fantasy, but turning it into reality, and secondly because that reality involves individuals you might have selected yourself, filled almost to bursting with spirituality and keenness of mind. But instead you claim the whole idea is just as fantastic as any I had back then, and are only more annoyed to see it actually carried out in real life, and suggest that I can't really judge men like Rée, Nietzsche, and others, who are so much older and wiser. But you're mistaken. One either recognizes what is essential about someone immediately, or not at all—and only Rée is essential to me in human terms. He hasn't been completely won over yet. He's still somewhat perplexed by it all, but I'm coming closer to convincing him, during our nightly walks beneath the Roman moon, between 12 and 2, after we leave the gatherings at Malwida von Meysenbug's. Malwida opposes our plan as well, and I'm sorry about that, because I like her enormously. But I realized a long time ago that we two are constantly talking about different things, even when we agree. She keeps saying "we" mustn't do this or that, "we" should try this—and I really don't have any idea who this "we" is—some ideal or philosophical entity no doubt—but the only thing I know about is "I." I can't live according to some model, and I could never be a model for anyone else; but I intend to shape my life for myself, no matter how it turns out. This is not a matter of some principle I'm following, but something much more wonderful— something that exists inside me, glowing with life itself, something that wants to burst forth with a shout of joy.

And now you write that you always considered total dedication to purely spiritual goals a mere "transition" for me. Well, what do you mean by "transition"? If there are some further final goals behind these, ones for which one would have to give up the most magnificent and hard-won thing on earth, namely freedom, then I hope I always remain in transition, because I won't give up freedom for anything. No one can be happier than I am now. I have no fear of the bright, pious, and joyful battle for that freedom which is now beginning; on the contrary, let it begin! Let's see whether the so-called "insurmountable barriers" life puts in most people's way don't in fact turn out to be harmless chalk lines! But I would indeed be shocked if you didn't give me your spiritual support. You write with some annoyance that your advice probably won't do much good. "Advice!"— No! What I need from you is much more than advice: I need your *trust*. Not in the normal sense one understands it, of course—no, what I need is your trust that no matter what I do or don't do, it will remain within the circle of what we share (you see, that's a "we" I know and recognize!). Of what belongs to me and is a part of me, like head, hands, or feet—from the day I became what I am, through you:

Your little girl

Next something happened in Rome that gave us the upper hand: the arrival of Friedrich Nietzsche.* His friends Paul Rée and Malwida had informed him by letter about the situation and he had arrived unexpectedly from Messina to join us. Then something even more unexpected occurred: as soon as he learned about the plan Paul Rée and I had, Nietzsche made himself a third member of our alliance.* Even the location of our future triune existence was soon decided: it was to be Paris (after we had thought originally of Vienna), where Nietzsche wanted to attend certain lectures, and where Paul Rée had connections with Ivan Turgenev* from earlier times, as I did from my St. Petersburg years. Even Malwida was somewhat comforted, since she thought we would come under the protection of her foster daughter Olga Monod and Natalie Herzen,* who even had a small literary circle in which young women read belles lettres together. But Malwida would have really liked to see Frau Rée accompany her son, and Fräulein Neitzsche her brother.

Our pleasantries were lighthearted and innocent, for we all loved Malwida, and Nietzsche was often in such an exhilarated mood that he would abandon his normally somewhat reserved, almost solemn, demeanor.* I recall this solemnity on the very first occasion we met, when he had been directed to St. Peter's, where Paul Rée was eagerly and piously working away on his notes, sitting at a confessional box where the light was particularly good. Nietzsche's first words to me were, "From what star have we fallen together here?" What had begun so well, however, took a turn which caused Paul Rée and me renewed concern about *our* plan, since it was complicated in ways we hadn't foreseen by the addition of a third person. Nietzsche, to be sure, intended in fact to simplify the situation: he asked Rée to intercede for him and ask for my hand in marriage. We anxiously tried to figure out how we could handle the matter without damaging our Trinity. We decided to make clear to Nietzsche that I was opposed to the general notion of marriage but also to point out that I had to live on my mother's military pension, and that if I were to marry I would lose the small portion of that pension I received as the only daughter of a Russian nobleman.

When we left Rome,* that all seemed settled. Toward the last, Nietzsche had also suffered from a frequent series of "attacks"—the illness which had formerly caused him to resign his professorship at Basel, the onset of which was marked by terrible migraine headaches. Paul Rée stayed behind with him, while my mother—as I recall—thought it would be better if she went on ahead with me, so that we only met up again on the way. We made various stops together, for example in Orta among the lakes of northern Italy, where we seem to have been fascinated by nearby Sacro Monte.* At any rate

Nietzsche and I unintentionally annoyed my mother by staying on the mountain far too long and failing to meet her on time. Paul Rée, who had to keep her entertained in the meantime, was also quite vexed with us. After leaving Italy, Nietzsche took a side trip to Basel to visit the Overbecks,* but soon rejoined us in Lucerne, since he had decided that Paul Rée's intercession for him in Rome hadn't really been sufficient, and he wanted to speak with me personally about it, which he proceeded to do, in the Lucerne Lion Park. At the same time he arranged a photograph of the three of us,* in spite of strong objections on the part of Paul Rée, who suffered throughout his life from a pathological aversion to the reproduction of his features. Nietzsche, who was in a playful mood, not only insisted on the photo, but took a personal hand in the details—for example the little (far too little!) cart, and even the touch of kitsch with the sprig of lilacs on the whip, etc.

Nietzsche then returned to Basel, Paul Rée continued with us to Zurich, where he turned toward his family's West Prussian estate, Stibbe bei Tütz, while my mother and I stayed on awhile in Zurich* at the charming country place of the friends I'd been living with until my trip south. Then we went to Berlin by way of Hamburg, by that time in the company of Eugene, the brother nearest to me in age, who had been sent by my oldest brother, the father figure, to help my mother. Now the final flames of battle flared up: but I received aid on my side from the trust that Paul Rée constantly inspired in me, which gradually affected my mother as well, so that the affair ended with my brother accompanying me to the Rées'. Paul Rée came out to Schneidemühl in West Prussia to meet us, and the brigand and the protector shook hands for the first time.

I stayed in Stibbe, as planned, into late summer—a few months it must have been—until, at the opening of the Bayreuth festival,* we joined Malwida at the Wagners'. Thus I met Richard Wagner in the last year of his life, and was able to attend *Parsifal* with Paul Rée's ticket. During the Wahnfried evenings, which always took place between two *Parsifal* performances, I saw a good deal of their family life, in spite of the flood of guests around them from all over the world. Things were always brightest and gayest around the centerpoint of Richard Wagner—who was often overshadowed because of his small stature, but would spring into sight from time to time like a bubbling fountain; whereas Cosima, due to her height, stood out from everyone past whom her infinitely long train glided—both encircling her and creating a certain distance. At any rate, as a kindly gesture toward Malwida, this marvelously attractive and elegant woman came to see me personally, and thus granted me the pleasure of an extended and wide-ranging conversation. That following winter, thirteen-year-old Siegfried's young tutor, Heinrich von Stein, whom I'd met in Bayreuth, became one of the earliest and most faithful members of our Berlin circle. Among those closest to Wagner, I became particular friends with the Russian painter Joukowsky,* whose little signature shield, a scarab beetle, was to be found in the corner of the huge oil painting which immediately caught one's eye in Wahnfried: the holy family, with Siegfried as the savior, Daniela as the mother of God, and the three other beautiful daughters as angels.

I don't dare say a syllable about the the overwhelming events of the Bayreuth festival itself, since I hardly deserved to be there, being tone-deaf* myself, and lacking all understanding or merit in such matters. If I resembled anyone in this respect, it would be Malwida's faithful servant Trina, who found herself covered with dishonor and shame: it seems that Richard Wagner had prophesied that a person like her, totally ignorant about music, would have "her ears opened" here, that a true revelation would occur, and so they planned to send her to the performance several times. But in spite of the fact that she was sincerely grateful and pleased, the experiment proved a failure, since Trina could not conceal her disappointment and dismay when she discovered that she was seeing *Parsifal* for a second time, instead of "a new play."

After Bayreuth, Nietzsche and I planned* to spend several weeks in Thüringen—in Tautenberg bei Dornburg—where I landed by chance in a house whose landlord, the local pastor, turned out to be a former student of my professor in Zurich, Alois Biedermann.* It seems that Nietzsche and I argued a bit at first* over all sorts of nonsense that I still can't understand, since it had no basis in fact. But we soon put that behind us, and our subsequent experience was a rich one,* undisturbed by any third person. I was able to penetrate much more deeply into Nietzsche's thought at this period than I had in Rome or while traveling. I didn't know any of his works yet except *The Gay Science*, which he was just completing, and from which he read aloud to us in Rome. On such occasions Nietzsche and Rée would take the words right out of each other's mouths. They had both been heading in the same direction, intellectually and spiritually, for some time, or at any rate since Nietzsche had fallen out with Wagner. The preference for an aphoristic style*—forced upon Nietzsche by his illness and the way he lived—had always come naturally to Paul Rée. He constantly carried La Rochefoucauld or La Bruyère in his pocket, just as his intellectual position remained unchanged, beginning with his first small monograph, *On Vanity*. But in Nietzsche's case one could already feel what would lead him beyond his collections of aphorisms toward *Zarathustra*: the deep impulse of Nietzsche the God-seeker, who came from religion and was moving toward religious prophesy.

In one of my letters* to Paul Rée from Tautenburg, on August 18, I had already noted: "Soon after I met Nietzsche I wrote to Malwida that his was a *religious* nature, which she was very reluctant to accept. Today I would underline that twice. . . . We will live to see him as the prophet of a new religion, one which recruits heroes as disciples. How similarly we think and feel about all this, literally taking the words from each other's mouths. We've talked ourselves to death these past three weeks, and strangely enough he's now able to talk almost ten hours a day. . . . It's strange, but our conversations have led us automatically toward those chasms, those dizzying places, where one once climbed alone to gaze into the abyss. We've constantly chosen to be mountain goats, and if anyone had heard us, he would have thought two devils were conversing."

It was inevitable that I would be fascinated by something in Nietzsche's words and nature that didn't find full expression when he talked with Paul Rée. For me there were memories or half-conscious feelings of the most childlike sort involved, arising from the most personal and indestructible part of my childhood. But it was just *that* which would have prevented me from ever becoming one of his disciples or one of his followers: I was always hesitant to move in *that* direction, since I had to escape all that in order to find clarity. The fascination and, at the same time, an inner aversion, went hand in hand.

After I had returned to Stibbe for the fall, we got together with Nietzsche again* for three weeks (?) in October in Leipzig. Neither of us suspected that it would be for the last time. Nevertheless, things had changed, even though all three of us still hoped to spend the future together. If I ask myself what it was that began to affect my inner feelings toward Nietzsche, it was his increasing tendency to imply things with the intention of making me think less of Paul Rée, and also my astonishment that he could think such a method might work. Only after our departure for Leipzig did hostility toward me emerge as well, hateful reproaches, which I know only from one subsequent letter.* What happened later seems so at odds with Nietzsche's very nature and dignity that it can only be ascribed to an outside influence, as when he raised suspicions about Rée and me which he knew better than anyone else were empty. But I was protected from much of the ugliness of this period by Paul Rée, who simply covered it up—something I understood only when I was several years older. It even appears that some of Nietzsche's letters never reached me, ones that defamed me in ways which seem to me inexplicable. And not only that: Paul Rée also concealed the extent to which the current stir had incited his family against me, to the point where they hated me, which of course was particularly evident on the part of his mother, who was pathologically jealous and wanted to keep her son all to herself.

Much later Nietzsche seems to have been unhappy himself with the rumors he had started, for we learned from Heinrich von Stein,* who was a close friend, about the following episode in Sils Maria, where he once visited Nietzsche (not without having first obtained our consent). He tried to talk Nietzsche into a reconciliation among the three of us, setting aside our misunderstandings; but shaking his head, Nietzsche replied, "What I've done can't be forgiven."

Since then I've followed Paul Rée's policy: I've kept away from it all,* refusing to read any more about it, ignoring the attacks of the Nietzsche family, and indeed the whole of the Nietzsche literature since his death. I wrote my book *Friedrich Nietzsche in His Works** with complete impartiality, moved only by the fact that after he became famous, so many young writers took up his ideas without understanding them; even I fully understood Nietzsche only *after* I had known him personally, when I had examined his ideas through his works. I only wanted to understand the figure of Nietzsche on the basis of these objective impressions. And so let the image I had of him then—in purely personal celebration—remain before my eyes.

Meanwhile Paul Rée and I had settled in Berlin. Our original plan to move to Paris was at first postponed, and then abandoned when Turgenev fell ill and died. Now the communal life we'd dreamed of was fully realized, including a circle of young academics, several of them university lecturers. The circle grew quickly with the passing years, often changing its membership. Paul Rée was known in this circle as my "maid of honor" and I was called "her Excellency," as indicated in my passport, having inherited the title according to Russian custom as the only daughter of a nobleman. A few of our friends even accompanied us occasionally during university vacations when we left Berlin for the summer. I recall with particular pleasure one summer* in Celerina in Upper Engadine when we lived with mill workers. It wasn't until the first deep snow of late fall that Paul Rée and I traveled south. There was as yet no railroad through Landquart, and so we were taken on as the only passengers in a postal carriage, which replaced the omnibus in the winter. We proceeded slowly and peacefully (thus anticipating present-day travel by private auto) toward Meran-Botzen, stopping whenever we wished beneath the sun or moon.

Although we traveled a good deal, our money proved more than adequate.

I had 250 marks a month from my mother's pension, and touchingly there was an equal amount from Paul Rée, for he put that much into our common purse. When things got tight, we learned to save and economize—which was fun, and earned me enthusiastic letters from Paul's brother Georg, who was the administrator of his trust fund, and who was more than pleased at how modest Paul had become, and that he no longer was constantly pestering him for money.

We tried spending a part of winter in Vienna* once, where my brother Eugene was doing postgraduate work for a few semesters with Nothnagel; but that didn't work out so well for reasons we found humorous: in place of the somewhat stiff mistrust we ran into with landlords in Berlin when renting our three rooms, the Viennese renters received us with such transparent approval of what they assumed was our love affair that Malwida's fear of "false appearances" was transformed all too wittily into a fear of "true" ones. Following Paul Rée's good advice (and a man is a better maid of honor in such cases than any woman) we moved only in our own circle in Berlin, and others closely allied to it, and not in family homes or the bohemian society of those days—and rightly so, for the ignorant were apt to consider my interest in "belles lettres" as a mere cover.

Nevertheless it was at this period, in Gries-Maran, that I wrote my first* book. I did so because my family was trying to get me to return home, and our circle of friends discovered that you could get permission to stay in a foreign country if you had written a book; and in fact it accomplished this purpose, although under the condition that my family name could not be brought into it; so I chose as a pseudonym the given name of my Dutch friend and the one he had chosen for me (in place of the Russian one he had difficulty pronouncing). Amusingly enough, this book—*Struggling for God* by "Henri Lou"—received the best press of anything I ever wrote, among others from the brothers Heinrich and Julius Hart, whom I later came to know quite well, so that I could tease them about it; for I knew better than anyone else for what purely practical reasons that opus had been pieced together from my Petersburg sketches, and when they didn't prove to be enough, from a miscreant novel in verse, which I simply converted into prose.

Our circle included representatives of various disciplines—natural scientists, orientalists, historians, and not a few philosophers. It had originally formed around Ludwig Haller,* who after a long period of silence and hard work in the Black Forest descended with a manuscript under his arm and allowed us to share his metaphysical triumphs and sorrows in a series of very private lectures. After his work was published (*All in All: Metalogic, Meta-*

physics, Metapsychics), he committed suicide by leaping into the sea on his way to Scandinavia, an act which was clearly grounded in his mysticism.

But the fact that philosophy had an unsettling and provocative effect upon the mind was also a function of the times. The great post-Kantian systems, up to and including the left- and right-wing Hegelians, lost steam as they came into clear conflict with the opposing spirit of the so-called Age of Darwin in the nineteenth century. In the midst of clear-headed rationality and objective thought, feelings of pessimism were clearing space for themselves, whether they were hidden in the subconscious or openly admitted and even emphasized. This represented what was still a quite idealistic reaction to all sorts of practical attempts to "do away with the gods": all sorts of honorable sacrifices were made for the sake of "truth." One might almost speak of a heroic age of philosophy at that time, when (precisely because of an increasingly sharp and clear distinction between what was "true" in scientific terms, and the subjective admixture of poetry and truth) the service of truth found itself restricted to increasingly modest areas, which could easily do without the all-too-grand words. The human temperament itself became an object of investigation, and was exposed to scientific research, both with regard to the means by which it exercised an undue influence on exact knowledge and in its undeniable claims as a living supplement and fulfillment of what can be taught by science. The will of the times transformed the exactitude of logic into a psychology with its own exactitude. After bowing before "truth," a whole age of submission through self-confession arrived: an age marked by the special arrogance of an independent confirmation of human dependency.

Even in our circle—as it would diminish and swell, enlarge and change—not everyone knew much about the man whose collection of aphorisms would make this psychologizing tendency world-famous: Friedrich Nietzsche. Nevertheless he stood, like a hidden shadow, an invisible figure, in our midst. For did he not touch upon precisely the agitation of souls who *lived through*, within themselves, what the rational mind gave or took from them, and who had their pains or joys in the midst of the most objective intellectual experience? And wasn't Nietzsche's greatest genius his *power of expression* in such matters? Did not poetic *and* rational power combine in him so fruitfully because spiritual struggles and distress forced him to achieve at his highest level?

This characterizes something else as well—apart from the major resonance of Nietzsche in the human spirit of his age and the next—namely, the contrast he offered to our other friends at that time. For no matter how differently they felt about the questions that were important to them—they all agreed upon one thing: the value of objectivity—they all made an effort to draw a sharp line between emotional involvement and the will to knowledge, to separate that involvement, as far as humanly possible, from what they were trying to do as scientists or academics, to put it aside as a strictly private matter.

For Nietzsche, on the other hand, his personal situation, the depths of his misery, became the glowing furnace in which his will to knowledge was forged. The creation of form in this incandescence constitutes "the complete works of Nietzsche." The poetry in his works has more substance than the truths—which he was always changing and then adapting his theories to, with an almost feminine submission, as already indicating a certain direction. Until his prophecy: the teachings of Zarathustra, the Übermensch, and the Eternal Return, where he splits himself into the all-suffering and the all-ruling—turning himself into God. To the point at which one could say it was both "truth and poetry." Then the explorer in him reached its limits, he drew back, lowered the curtain before himself:* the curtain of his suffering and longing, so grandly and instinctively painted that it was never to rise again to free his vision.

And for me, among the others, * this contrast with Nietzsche was the most comforting thing about our circle. Here was the healthy, clear climate I was longing for, in which Paul Rée remained my spiritual comrade, even when he was wrestling with his somewhat narrow-minded and utilitarian treatment of the *Origin of Conscience* and I felt closer intellectually to a few of the others than I did to him (for example Ferdinand Tönnies and Hermann Ebbinghaus). *

Of course Paul Rée and I had been brought together for more than just a temporary alliance—it was meant to last forever. The fact that we believed this possible, and had no fear of insoluble difficulties arising, was related to his basic nature, which made him, among many thousands, a uniquely precious companion. There were many extraordinary things about him which, in my youthful inexperience, seemed to me quite natural and self-evident: above all how invariably good-hearted he was, which I had no way at first of knowing was a result of a secret self-hate, so that his total devotion to a person so different from himself, this "selfless" act, was experienced as a happy deliverance. And in fact the melancholy and pessimistic Paul Rée, who had toyed with the idea of suicide even as an adolescent, and not simply in play, changed into a self-confident and cheerful young man. His humor surfaced, and what remained of his pessimism was evident only in his charming tendency to find something amusing in everyday mishaps and disappointments of the type that annoyed or confused others, precisely because he was pleasantly surprised that they weren't as bad as he had expected. Thus I remained largely unaware of his underlying neurosis, in spite of the openness with which he admitted all his faults. Only now and then—after I had seen him fall prey again to his addiction to gambling*— did I begin to make connections between the gambler I had met that first evening in Rome and the man I knew, as I now see and understand him. And even today I'm still torn by grief to think how he might have been helped if only Freud's depth psychology had been given to the world a few decades earlier and applied in his case. For not only would it have restored him to himself, but he would have been called as few others to serve this great advance of the new century: in fact it would have allowed him, given his deep understanding of human nature, to develop his intellect fully.

When I became engaged, it was not supposed to result in any change in our relationship. My husband had declared that he understood and accepted this as an irrevocable fact. Paul Rée also acted as if he believed us when we said that the engagement would stand or fall on this. But deep down he didn't believe that anyone could truly love him, and he could only force himself to forget that he had been rejected in Rome as long as reality continued to offer evidence to the contrary. So, in spite of the honest and open discussions we had (he had insisted during the transition that I neither see nor talk to my husband, at least for a time) a fundamental misunderstanding persisted.* Paul Rée had started studying medicine at that time, and lived by himself because his anatomy class was so early in the morning. (We had even discussed whether I ought to study with him, but we laughed and said that was hardly necessary for two people who were going to spend the rest of their lives together.) The memory of the evening he left me remained a smoldering fire that never quite died out. He left late in the night, but came back up after a few minutes because it was raining so hard it was senseless to go out. Then after a while he left again, only to return for a book. By the time he finally left it was almost morning. I looked out, and was startled to see fading stars in the cloudless heavens, above perfectly dry streets. Turning from the window, I saw in the glow of the table lamp a small photo of myself as a child, which had belonged to Rée. There was a piece of paper wrapped around it, bearing these words: "Have mercy—don't look for me."

*　　*　　*

It turned out, naturally enough, that Paul Rée's disappearance pleased my husband, although he took care not to say anything about it. And it was equally inevitable that over the years I remained weighed down by sorrow over something I knew should never have happened. If I woke up in the morning feeling depressed, I knew a dream had been at work, trying to undo what had happened. One of the strangest of them was the following: I was at a party with friends, who called out to me gaily that Paul Rée was with them. I looked for him, and when I couldn't find him, I turned to the cloakroom where they had left their coats. My gaze fell upon a stranger with a potbelly, who was sitting quietly behind the coats with his hands folded in his lap. His face was so swollen with fat it was almost unrecognizable, the eyes practically squeezed shut, as if a fleshy death mask were superimposed upon his features. "No one will ever find me like *this*," he said contentedly, "will they?"

Paul Rée completed his medical studies. Later he moved to Celerina in Upper Engadine, where he served as a doctor among the poor.

There, in the surrounding mountains, he accidently fell to his death. *

WITH OTHER PEOPLE

IN ORDER TO gather my impressions of what Russia meant to me, both in my early life and later on, I've passed over several intervening years which brought me in contact with other countries and other people, in part because the multiplicity of my personal activities and my various impressions of individuals makes telling the story more difficult. One is constantly confronted by the choice of either going into things so deeply that matters would be touched upon which would be out of place—or falling prey to the danger that in treating things more superficially, one winds up with the normal sort of chatty account in which hasty formulations and accidental emphases encourage easy judgments. In the case of those with whom one became truly close, natural limits are set to such commentary. For what does it mean to get close to a person? A coming together that takes us somewhere we didn't expect to go: one of those precious relationships that falls outside the realm of what can be precisely analyzed. That part which *can* be communicated may best be conveyed indirectly, through poetic effects: for what was experienced bore in its very nature the intensity of poetry.

Therefore I won't have much to say about the first dozen or so years after my marriage, although they brought me into lively contact with others. As the times would have it, I met many people, and came to understand much about them and their actions, while my natural reticence led me from individual to individual, from one private conversation to another as it were. After an initial period at my husband's bachelor apartment in Tempelhof-Berlin, we moved into a house surrounded by elms in the middle of a park. The owners had intended to decorate it beautifully inside, but had run into difficulties and hadn't been able to finish it, so that we were able to rent it quite cheaply. We lived almost entirely in the upper level on the ground floor, where the rooms were so large that they reminded me of home and my dancing lessons: a huge library, and two rooms with wainscoting, leading out onto a broad terrace. They included deep, built-in wall cupboards, so that we only had to add a few pieces to our small store of furniture. So we made our home at the southern edge of the city, where the only way to get into

Berlin was by charabanc—equipped with runners in the winter—at the cost of one groschen. But most of those we got to know* that winter lived at the "edge" of the city as well: among the first, Gerhart Hauptmann in Erkner, with his wife Marie and three sons, Ivo, Ecke, and Klaus; also Arne Garborg and the charming wheat-blonde Hulda Garborg. Bruno Wille, Wilhelm Bölsche and the two Hart brothers were in Freidrichshagen, and soon drew a whole train of others behind them—Ola Hansson-Marholm, August Strindberg, and others with whom we met from time to time in the Schwarzes Ferkel (The Black Pig) in Berlin. I remember the first gathering at our place, on the terrace surrounded by flowers, and in the adjacent dining room. I can still see Max Halbe, young and slender, with his little bride, whose hair was done up like Psyche; Arno Holz; Walter Leistikov; John Henry Mackay; Richard Dehmel, who still disliked his own name; and others. *Vor Sonnenaufgang* (Before Sunrise) had served as a spiritual rallying point. Gerhart Hauptmann's first play, in the midst of all the controversy attending the irresistible rise of naturalism, brought something to the stage which was to aid in the triumph of that new direction in art and literature: a restrained touch of lyricism, in spite of the didactic nature of the play, and its grosser aspects, which so provoked the good burghers.

Paul Rée had intentionally avoided bohemian literary circles in the days before my marriage, and we had socialized almost exclusively with academics, but this now changed. I had never been particularly interested in literature as such (Russians had interested me in other ways), I was "uneducated" when it came to literature, and knew nothing of the earlier period of easy optimism against which this new war was now being waged. But what moved me most about it was the human element: the gay buoyancy, the lively youth, and the self-confidence with which the new spirit was being preached, even when dealing with the gloomiest and most depressing of themes. Even the older generation was carried away, as we know in the case of Fontane. Another who capitulated was Fritz Mauthner, with whom I often spoke after we had moved from Tempelhof to Schmargendorf, where it was only a short walk through the woods to his house in Grunewald. Henrik Ibsen's fame in Germany was an important factor. My husband introduced me to his works by reading them aloud to me from the Norwegian editions, translating them into German as he went. Two "Freie Bühnen" (Independent Theaters) arose, and one of them lasted. Brahm took the lead in the increasingly successful struggle, along with Ibsen and Hauptmann. My friendship with Maximilian Harden—the cofounder of the Freie Bühne—which lasted many years (into the world war), dated from that time as well. Besides Gerhart, Dr. Carl Hauptmann, who until then had been seeking a position in philosophy, developed an enthusiasm for drama as well. Otto Hartleben joined in actively, together with his good-hearted Moppchen. Young people abandoned their academic ambitions in favor of literary and political goals. I recall many evenings spent in debate or agreement with Eugen Kühnemann, who didn't seem ready at that time to devote his life to a university career. Among those to whom I was closest, Georg Ledebour was most important to me in human terms: let these lines serve as a greeting to him.*

We were already in our second apartment in Schmargendorf by then, right at the edge of the forest. It was such a comically small place that for a long time we didn't need anyone to take care of it. Then I went to Paris*—in 1894—where similar changes were taking place on the literary scene. It was around the time of Carnot's assassination, people on all sides were becoming politically involved, and I was able to listen to Millerand and Jaurès personally in the Chamber. Antoine's "Théâtre libre," corresponding to the Freie Bühne, was founded, and Lugné-Poe's *Oeuvre* appeared. Hauptmann's *Hannele*, whose heroine had been portrayed in Berlin by Paula Conrad, who was later to become Schlenther's wife, was staged by Antoine with a poor, pale little girl from the streets in the title role. She brought the house down (although the French language interfered at times with Hauptmann's poetry, for example when Hannele had to replace the single word "Fliederduft" (the fragrance of lilacs) with "je sens le parfum de lilas"). The most moving *Hannele* I ever saw was later in Russia: moving because of the restrained and naive Byzantine stylization of both Heaven and Our Savior.

In Paris I found the same lively interaction of literary circles, the same interests, opposed only by the old generation who were waiting for it all to pass. In the newly founded publishing house set up by Albert Langen and the Dane, Willy Gretor, I met Knut Hamsun, who looked like a Greek god in those days. The Scandinavian colony was heavily represented, long before Albert Langen himself joined it by marrying into the Björnson family. At first I lived with a young Danish woman I knew named Therese Krüger. I remember Herman Bang, who lived on Saint-Germain, quite vividly. He fairly bubbled with energy, although he was often ill. I can recall one conversation with him almost word for word, in which he portrayed with a shiver how frightened he became whenever he set out on a new poetic project: how he would keep running to the window in hopes he would see something he could use as an excuse not to start. You could almost see the inexorable effect of the artistic process as it visibly transformed material from the deepest layers of his repressed consciousness, and the fear that overcame him during that transition. Although I knew about Herman Bang's chronic back problems, I could never see him after that without the involuntary thought that he was transforming his fears into a more active form on the physical level as well. Anyone who realizes how closely Bang's novels are based on his personal memories (such as *Das weiße Haus* [The White House] and *Das graue Haus* [The Gray House]) will also sense the terrors which accompanied their composition.

A tiny companion accompanied me everywhere: a little pitch-black poodle—an even more childlike "Toutou"—I've forgotten where he came from. When I would return home late at night, he would sit up straight in the little basket he slept in and look at me with penetrating and suspicious eyes, wondering what I'd been up to without him. During the day he caused me problems with his fondness for those "apples which never fall far from the horse." My little poodle, Toutou, would dart into the streets, which were filled in those days with brightly shining carriages instead of autos, and then run from me—a far-too-large apple in his widely opened, much-too-small mouth—scampering like a black flea across the immense squares and avenues, until he found some protected corner where he could devour it; and I would dash after him. But not alone, for often there were passersby who would call out quite freely: "Ô là là, le joli Toutou" and try to grab him and, he no doubt feared, his prize as well.

I spent more time in Paris with Frank Wedekind* than almost anyone else. But that was later on. Because at first, after meeting him at the home of the Hungarian countess Nemethy and accompanying him and the others to an onion soup restaurant in Les Halles, where we continued our lively conversation into the early hours of the morning, a misunderstanding arose on his part, as he later recounted quite openly and without any attempt to exonerate himself. (I later used this as a scene in a short story.) He could usually be found sitting at one of those sticky marble tables in front of some café in the Latin Quarter, scribbling poems—forerunners of the later *Galgenlieder* (Gallows Songs)—for example the elegy "Indeed it's true I killed my aunt, but she was old and gray—and it's my youth, bloodthirsty judge, you take from me today." Wedekind had a butcher's hands, but they were balanced by tender, even softhearted, qualities. Without any real means of support or permanent abode, he would sit among the grisettes (the term was already out of use), hoping that one of them—once the café had closed and she had filled her purse sufficiently—would be kind enough to take him home, give him shelter, breakfast, and a little loving care. But Frank Wedekind could be found in other places as well. For example, he took me, with no little pride, and to my great pleasure, to one of the poorest rooms in the poorest part of Paris, where he spent entire evenings: it was the apartment of the sixty-year-old widow of Georg Herwegh,* who suffered from dropsy, to whom he brought a carefully chosen meal.

If one chose to visit the nightclubs of the Latin Quarter or Montmartre, usually in the company of one or two journalist friends, it was because the prostitutes were always interesting, for two reasons. One was their openness and frankness, which was not only a characteristic of their profession, but served as a bond with all humanity, eliminating self-contempt, shame, and furtive secrecy; secondly the majority of them demonstrated—in their tact and manners—the traditional culture of their nation as a whole, which permeates society from top to bottom. This made conversations with those one accidently met from the "lower levels" of society a valuable experience. The same is true for the "higher" levels of society: nowhere can a woman be more certain of polite treatment, even if she finds herself in an inopportune situation on the way home at night, meeting some man on the street; for any Parisian would be ashamed to fail to live up to a situation in a gentlemanly fashion, or to misunderstand it. But along with this impression, one has the equally strong sense that it's best to leave things at that. There is little temptation to get to know someone better; traditional and ingrained cultural gestures have turned too much of the inner person outward for much to remain preserved within. This was the exact opposite of the impression I received in Russia. Paris was the first major foreign capital, after Berlin, in which I lived for an extended time, and every experience I had there was sharply distinguished from what I'd known up to then: the inexpressible charm of its seasoned maturity seemed to me that of a lovely woman who is constantly putting on new jewelry, who, when youth's splendor has fled, is still adorned with precious objects immune to rust or moths.

During my visits to the Louvre, I met someone on the street I'd like to tell a story about. She was an elderly woman from Alsace by the name of Madame Zwilling,* who supported her consumptive son by selling flowers. One evening I dropped by their small apartment to see them both and discovered that she had been carried in unconscious from the street. Her large baskets of fresh flowers from Les Halles were beside her, and I quickly decided to sell them in her place. Baroness Sophie von Bulöw was with me, and readily agreed to my plan: we borrowed Madame Zwilling's Alsatian dresses, and by two-thirty early the next morning we had sold every last flower, at a good profit, to the men at the cafés of the Latin Quarter, which were by now familiar to me. On this occasion, too, I discovered what perfect gentlemen the men were when faced with the surprising apparition of two new flower girls, who, tall as they were (Sophie was even taller than me), offered a sharp contrast to the small and delicate Frenchwoman, and called forth a number of friendly questions. It wasn't until the next day that we learned from our journalist friends how fortunate we had been not to spend the night in jail for selling flowers without any sort of license.

I made friends with a young immigrant physician in the Russian colony who had been accused of involvement in the assassination of Alexander II and sent to Siberia, where he spent four years in forced labor before finally being able to get away to Paris. Savély, strong as a tree (and able to pull nails from the wall with his shining teeth), introduced me to the whole circle of Russians. When, six months later, the hot summer sun began to be too much for us, Savély and I hurriedly escaped to Switzerland on a cheap holiday special. We climbed a small mountain near Zurich and stayed in a little hut on the meadow where we lived on milk, cheese, bread, and berries. Only on rare occasions did we go back down into Zurich to still our hunger for luxury at some hotel restaurant, carefully paying in advance for our double portions (once I ran into Wilhelm Bölsche from my homeland, as I had met Hartleben and Moppchen in Paris). A very small episode during our idyllic days on the meadow remains my strongest memory: we were walking barefoot one day—as we usually did upon the soft alpine moss—when we wandered across a slope into a field of creeping blackberries, without at first noticing them. In the fading light, we were no longer certain about the shortest way back, and every step we took, and every time we paused, we howled out in pain. We regained the soft meadow paradise with tears streaming down our faces.

During those minutes in the blackberry patch, something arose in me like a primal vision*—or a memory?—as if I had already experienced how one could plunge from the greatest happiness into Life, dreadfully abandoned and exposed. Another moment that suddenly occurs to me. While we were wiping the perspiration from our faces, and the blood from our feet, we forgot about our troubles as Savély said gaily: "We should be begging the blackberries' pardon—and not the other way round: because we trod on them with our feet, when we should have kissed them with our lips." Something within me responded, consoled: "Yes, isn't *that* misunderstanding the worst thing of all in the world?" Thus laughter and anger chased each other away, and left us free for new and daring adventures among the blackberries of life.

A few weeks later we were back in the whirl of the uniquely beautiful city, amazing people with our suntans, which were not yet fashionable in those days. From then until late autumn I made many new acquaintances, and was struck by many things, which I would not have missed for the world: but then the hour would come in which someone or something seemed to call to me in the night—and I had to leave. I've never been able to figure out rationally why or when it happened each time—regardless of how much I was enjoying my surroundings, open to them in body and soul. Something arrived uninvited in their place and was impatient to go. I wouldn't recall the night I returned to Germany clearly enough to tell about it, if it weren't for a letter kept by a woman writer who was a friend back then, which came into my hands a short time ago. It was written in Schmargendorf on October 22, 1894.

"It's been over three weeks now, since I arrived from Paris—surprising myself and everyone else, leaving secretly, without saying good-bye. And I arrived just as quietly, without sending word, in the middle of the night. I left my suitcases at the railroad station, rode out and walked along the quiet path across the dark fields into the village. This walk was beautiful and strange. Although I could see little, I felt autumn in the falling leaves and in the stormy wind, and I was glad; in Paris it had still been 'summer.' Everyone in the village was asleep; only the bright lamp my husband used to illuminate the books in the tall cases still burned. I could see his head clearly from the street. The door was on the latch, as always, and I stepped inside quietly. Our dog Lotte barked out loudly from the living room—she'd recognized my step. By the way, she's turned into a real monster in size and weight, and no one thinks she's enchanting anymore but us. We didn't sleep that night. When it began to get light outside, I made a fire in the kitchen, polished the sooty lamp, and slipped away into the woods. Thick morning fog still hung in the trees, and a spotted doe glided silently through the pines. I pulled off my shoes and stockings (which you can't do in Paris) and was very happy."

The only woman I was really close to in those years was Baroness Frieda von Bülow,* whom I had already known in Tempelhof. She was taken from me in 1908 by an all-too-early death, just as she was entering her fifties. During my Paris stay she had just come from her second sojourn in German East Africa, and stopped over with me, where her sister was awaiting her as well, the Sophie with whom I had sold Madame Zwilling's flowers. The next year she came to Russia to see me, visiting my mother and my brothers, among whom Eugen became a particularly close friend. Three of her own siblings met with violent deaths: two younger brothers and Margarethe von Bülow,* already a known writer at that time, who fell through the ice and died trying to save a drowning boy. Frieda was melancholy by nature, in spite of a manly strength of will and impulse toward life which had taken her to East Africa in her youth at the time of Carl Peters's success as an explorer. She liked to explain this mixture of energy and lassitude by the fact that she was a member of an old, exhausted family who would finally come to an end through their longing for subjection and self-sacrifice.

We also stayed together several months in Vienna*—in 1895—when I returned there for the first time from Petersburg. Having been in the Berlin literary circle, we were already familiar with the one in Vienna. I had exchanged several letters with Arthur Schnitzler while I was in Paris; he stood in the forefront here as well as far as I was concerned. Later I was sent off in other directions by him, strengthened. His *Liebelei* had just been a great success, and among those around him were Richard Beer-Hofmann, Hugo von Hofmannsthal—still quite young, in his hussar military uniform—and Félix Salten. Aside from personal visits, we joined them almost every evening in the cafés, for example in Grien-Steidl, and got to know the cultural life of Vienna in its most characteristic form. I was staying near St. Stephan's Cathedral, in a very good hotel, in two charmingly decorated but tiny rooms at the top of the adjacent building. The rooms, and the hours of conversation I spent in them, appeared in Peter Alterberg's first book, *Wie ich es sehe* (As I See It). If I had to compare the Viennese atmosphere to that of other major cities, I would say that it seemed to me marked by a confluence of intellectual and erotic life. What in other places distinguishes the man of the world from the professional or academic type is marked here by a charm and grace which lifts a "sweet young thing," indeed someone who is a sweet young thing and nothing else, into an elevated sphere of eroticism, while imparting to even the most serious devotion to a profession and one's calling a certain impulse, a mode of behavior which serves to blunt the edge of goal-oriented ambition. This leaves room for men to form friendships among themselves, in spite of their competition for love and honor, a form of friendship which seemed to me very unusual and very special. Arthur Schnitzler fit into this picture quite well: it was perhaps the brightest aspect in an existence which was, for him, tinged with melancholy. Perhaps, however, he would have been able to develop himself fully in a spiritual sense if he had been less divided internally, had his intellectual charm and grace guided him more insistently down one path—be it toward love or toward ambition.

Peter Altenberg stood a bit to one side—although not in the matter of friendship. When one was with him, one thought neither of man nor of woman, but of a being from some third realm. The well-known saying about him, "Mon verre est petit, mais je bois dans mon verre" (My glass is small, but I drink from my glass) is an accurate judgment, as long as one places the emphasis on "petit" and not on "mon": for what was new and exciting about Peter Altenberg's little texts depended upon the mysterious way in which he hindered the inner development of both sexes, turning their arrested infantilism into his own poetic specialty, something which was fully expressed in his own personal peculiarities.

Later, whenever I came to Vienna, I usually spent time with Marie von Ebner-Eschenbach,* to whom Fritz Mauthner had first introduced me. The last time was in 1913, a few years before her death, which I learned of from her niece, Countess Kinsky. I'll never forget the hours I spent with her—the peace and, how can I express it, the *substantiality* that emanated from her. When you saw her it almost seemed as if she was intentionally making herself as small as possible, as if she looked up out of her gray, infinitely wise eyes as modestly as possible, so that no one would realize what was sitting there before them: as if it would be best to keep that a secret. That which was so incessantly and intimately manifested in tone, word, look, and gesture. One gained from her both a sense of mystery and of revelation—preserved in the self-contained warmth of her inner presence.

The environs of Vienna are so beautiful that one is almost forced into the countryside, and both friends and society constantly met there. In the summer of that same year, 1895, I met with friends in Salzkammergut and in Innsbruck. I always needed forests, broad fields, and sun around me to fill the cup of experience to the brim—or even the mountains, in which I had spent so little time, apart from a few trips through Switzerland as a child with my parents. The following winter I was in Vienna again and in the summer of the next year I was in Kraxeleien in the Austrian mountains for the first time. I have a particularly vivid memory of a long trip from Vienna that a friend and I made on foot through Karnten across the Hohe Tauern pass toward Venice. On this slow and leisurely journey a brief but powerful impression was imprinted upon my memory. We had to reach the Rotgulden glacier before dark, but we had been delayed by a warning about a bull in rut in the meadows leading up to it. We took along a whole group of excited locals, with all sorts of strange weapons, to deal with the bull. For a few minutes, the bull was in sight—on the opposite side of the mountain, separated from us by a deep chasm, standing alertly in profile: the image of power and obsession, "godlike" in the old sense, and given the safe distance from which we were able to observe him, he made a deep and lasting impression. I for one was still thinking about it as we searched through the boulders upon the Rotgulden glacier, now alone in the darkness, asking one another if there weren't mountain huts hidden somewhere among them, as in the fairy tales.

The most impressive memory I have of the countryside was witnessing three springs in rapid sequence as I traveled from Italy, northward through

Germany. Never did the South penetrate my consciousness more triumphantly than on that occasion, when, in spite of a winter which had been like May, it still managed to turn into spring, without simply letting summer take its place. This gave the impression of something simply inexhaustible behind all visible appearances, which each season can draw upon, if it so chooses, and made me feel that if human receptivity were only more profound, more sensitive to nuance, the boundlessness of everything earthly would await us. Thus satiated, I was able to be fairer to the central European climate. It's easy to become annoyed with the phlegmatic weather, which is constantly having to start over again, wipe the rain and sleet out of its eyes, and urge the budding catkins on the branch to flower. I greeted the violets with joy, along with everything else which was, in the best sense, "sentimental": my heart was quiet, filled with patience, and therefore even more deeply delighted.

I can say least about the third turn toward summer I then experienced, the northern one I've loved since childhood. Awaited for so long, and so perfect in its brief unfolding, it announced itself brightly and insistently, not to be denied. When one hears the call of the cuckoo deep in the night, or the songs of fieldhands returning home, then one does not think of lines like "Hurry now, do something ere the too short summer's passed" but feels instead raised above time and transformation, beyond the quarrel of nights and days, of early and of late. At home I soon longed to be alone again, no matter what the season, and I had to work hard on my daily essays, as I had earlier on my theatrical reviews.* At most I would sometimes wander far across the fields, where, in snow or in the sparse leaf-green field, Frieda Bülow was living in the house of her relative the Baroness Anna Münchhausen-Keudell,* in two rooms filled with the most beautiful and distinguished pieces inherited from her family, and more recent exotica from East Africa. Early in 1896 we decided to spend some time together in Munich, where I met the second woman with whom I was to have a truly close friendship. We've remained close since 1896 (we're nearly the same age as well), and will remain so until the day we die.

Helene von Klot-Heydenfeldt* was from Riga on the Baltic and was living temporarily with her mother and sister in Munich. After reading Tolstoi's *Kreutzer Sonata*, a good book, she wrote *Eine Frau* (A Woman). She knew many Germans, and one year later she became engaged to the architect Otto Klingenberg. Long after that, having left Göttingen to spend a few months in Berlin, Helene Klingenberg's house became my home. Helene and Frieda differed from one another as a dark-haired young man differs from a blonde maiden. (Helene's Friesian husband and children were even blonder.) And

while Frieda's thirst for adventure took her into distant lands, Helene's fate—
she wanted a biblical text for an epigraph: "The Lord has dealt bountifully
with me"—seemed determined inwardly by the universal power of love: to
be a wife and mother. Frieda and I were different enough that we argued
constantly but fruitfully, a situation I was more comfortable with than she
was, since she would have liked for us to be alike in all things. Some deep and
hidden affinity must have bound me to Helene, which didn't stop me from
taking a completely different path than hers. It made no difference, because
her strongly loving nature took me as I was, without reservation, tolerating
me even when I seemed a demon.

In Munich* the communal life was not as extensive as in Paris or Vienna,
just as the broad and beautiful streets were emptier, as if they were calling out
for people to gather in them. Here one found oneself not among the native
"Munichers" but amidst all the German nationalities. Social life took place
in a few literary families and in the various corners of Schwabing. Among
those who gathered there—including Max Halbe, Frank Wedekind, the
Langen publishers, and later the Björnsons—I was most drawn to a country-
man of Helene's, whom she didn't know, however: Count Eduard Keyserling,
who was already going blind. When I visited Munich again years later, I was
extremely sad to learn that he was no longer living. Others, like Ernst von
Wolzogen and Michael Georg Conrad, I spoke with only in passing—
among the younger men I talked most often with Jakob Wassermann, whose
fine work *Die Juden von Zirndorf* (The Jews of Zirndorf) had already earned
him an excellent reputation. I became friends in particular with August
Endell,* an art dealer and architect, later director of the Academy of Art in
Breslau, who remained attached to me to the very end. It is sad that these
words must already serve as a memorial to that lonely and bitter, struggling
young man, who suffered from constant illness. I will always remember his
goodness and his friendship.

During one of the evenings we spent together at the theater, Jakob Wassermann brought a friend over to our seats to introduce him to us: it was René
Maria Rilke.

WITH RAINER

SOMEONE HAD BEEN sending me anonymous poems for some time, addressed to one of the so-called "royal homes" on Schellingstraße in Munich, where I had arrived at the beginning of 1897 to stay with Frieda von Bülow. Once Jakob Wassermann had introduced us— one spring evening at the theater*—I recognized the handwriting on the first letter I received after the performance as that of the author. Now he read other poems aloud to me, among them the "Christus-Visionen" (Visions of Christ). Some remarks in that first letter lead me to believe that I must not have liked them very much. Although some of them were supposed to appear in *Die Gesellschaft* (Society), and he sent others to me as well, we couldn't find them in later years, even with the help of the publishers at the Insel Verlag, and they have to be regarded as lost.

It wasn't long before René Maria Rilke became Rainer. He and I began to look for a place in the nearby mountains. Having moved out to Wolf-ratshausen,* we changed our little house again. Frieda had joined us in the first one; for our second place we were given the rooms over a cowshed at a farmstead built against the side of a hill. The cow was supposed to appear in the photo we took later—she didn't look out the window of the shed, but the old peasant woman was standing there, and just above the roof you can see the road leading back into the countryside. Above it all our flag is waving, made of rough linen, lettered in black, LOUFRIED. It was made by August Endell, who had quickly become friends with Rainer. He also helped us decorate our three connecting rooms by the addition of nice blankets, pillows, and household items. Toward autumn, my husband came for a while, along with our dog, Lotte. Jakob Wassermann visited us now and then, as did others. In our first place I studied Russian for a while with a man who came from St. Petersburg to visit me (I didn't like him much).

Although he had already written and published an amazing number of things—poems, stories, and the periodical *Wegwarten** (Chicory Flowers) which he edited—Rilke's effect as a young man arose primarily from his human qualities, and not from a sense of the great poet he would become. And this in spite of the fact that from the very beginning, in his earliest childhood, he had always felt drawn to poetry as his inevitable calling, and never lost this sense of mission. Yet precisely because he glowed with this dreamlike certainty, he did not overestimate what he had done up to that point; it simply spurred him on to renewed attempts. It seemed only natural that in his work with new techniques, his struggle with words, he would be caught up in emotional excesses as well—"sentiment" had to be called to the aid of what could not yet be fully expressed. The boundaries of such sentiment were set by his own nature: it remained, one might say, a technical necessity. For it emerged as well from the profound certainty of his own ability to create poetry. For example, even though Ernst von Wolzogen once addressed him humorously in a letter as "Reiner Rainer, fleckenlose Maria" (pure Rainer, immaculate Mary), there was no touch of feminine-childlike expectation in Rainer's nature, but instead a type of manliness: his own style of gentle but inviolable control and dominance. This was not contradicted even by his somewhat timid attitude toward outside influences or anything threatening, that is, to what was foreign. He felt this as something within himself he was meant to protect, something which had been entrusted to him, rather than some personal timidity. This attitude unified his spirit and his senses, allowing them to commingle: the human being merged with the artist in a full and untroubled way. No matter what part of him was stirred— it was a *single* emotion, which could not even conceivably be split, and which knew nothing of internal doubt, hesitation, or second thoughts, except in the still restless development of his own poetic gifts. Thus Rainer possessed what we call "manly grace" to a high degree, uncomplicated in its gentleness, and in imperishable consonance with all the expressions of his being. He could still laugh in those days, knowing himself enveloped in life's joy, innocently and without sorrow.

If, with this in mind, one thinks of the later poet, close to his goal and to the perfection of his art, it is abundantly clear why this was achieved at the price of the internal harmony of his personality. Something of this danger undoubtedly lies in *all* artistic endeavors, in the deepest sense, in such a rivalry with Life. For Rainer it was even more dangerous, for his gifts were turned toward the lyrical expression of the almost ineffable, to find words at last for the "unspeakable" through the power of his poetry. Thus it happened that his personal development as a human being and the unfolding of his artistic genius ran almost counter to one another in the end. The demands of art and of full personal development came increasingly into conflict as his works achieved a degree of reality so great that they excluded everything else. This tragic turn of events thus became more and more inevitable.

Years passed before all this became totally clear. That within him which longed to be poetry, gathered in increasing fullness and clarity; the weeks or months between the periods of rapture emptied themselves until they were nothing but a conscience-stricken waiting. It was during this period that I began to worry about Rainer. It seemed to me that any sort of work or simple activity would be better than that empty waiting filled with useless self-reproaches (he too was bothered by this more than anything else). We joked about the matter of finding some other activity for him, calling it "the post office clerk decision." But then we would cast aside all our cares again for years, since what seemed at times to be Rainer's fate, like the menace of illness, brought with it simultaneously a splendor of experience that called forth the most unprecedented hopes.

Although we met in a social setting, the two of us had long since developed a private life in which we held everything in common. Rainer shared our modest existence on the edge of the forest in Schmargendorf near Berlin. * A path through the forest led to Paulsborn, a few minutes away, past tame deer who sniffed at our pockets as we strolled along barefoot. Rainer often helped me cook in the little apartment, where the kitchen was the only place other than my husband's library that was somewhat like a living room; particularly when I was making his favorite dish, Russian-style groats, or also borsch. He no longer needed to be pampered, although he had previously suffered if even the slightest limits were imposed on what he wanted, and complained about his small monthly allowance. He would help me chop kindling or dry dishes in his blue Russian shirt with the red shoulders, then we would both continue quietly working in our separate studies. We were studying many things, but Rainer, who had been deeply involved with Russian literature for a long time, now worked hardest on the Russian language and national customs, since we were planning our long trip to Russia. * For a time this was tied to my husband's plan to take a trip through Transcaucasia into Persia, which, however, never materialized. Around Easter of 1899, we three left together to visit my family in Petersburg and then go on to Moscow; it wasn't until a year later that Rainer and I traveled more extensively through Russia.

Although Tolstoy's home near Tula was not our first stop, his figure was in a sense the gate by which we entered Russia. For if Dostoyevsky had first opened the depths of the Russian soul for Rainer, it was nevertheless Tolstoy who embodied the Russian as such—as a result of the poetic force of his descriptions. Our second visit to Tolstoy, * in May of 1900, didn't take place in his winter house in Moscow as did that of our first trip, but rather on the country estate Yásnaya Polyána, seventeen versts from Tula. He could be fully experienced only in the countryside, not in a city or a room—no matter how rustic it was in comparison with the other rooms in the count's home, nor how simple the lord of the house appeared, sitting in the overalls he had patched himself, working away at some handicraft, or sitting at the family table eating groats and cabbage soup while everyone else was enjoying some tasty dish.

Our strongest impression this time, tellingly enough, took place on a short stroll the three of us took together. After asking Rainer, "What are you working on?" and receiving the somewhat timid reply "Poetry," Tolstoy poured his scorn upon lyric poetry of any kind. We were unable to give our full attention to his lively diatribe however, because as we were leaving the farm, we came upon an absorbing sight. An aged pilgrim was approaching in the distance, bowing and gesturing in ceaseless reverence to our elderly companion. He wasn't begging, he simply greeted us, as many did who came for similar reasons: to see their churches or their holy relics. As Tolstoy walked on without noticing him, we strained our ears in both directions at once—but our eyes remained concentrated on each movement, each turn of the head, the slightest hesitation in the brisk walk which would reveal "*Tolstoy.*" The meadows of early summer were overflowing with flowers, taller and more deeply colored than one encounters anywhere but in Russian earth; even in the forest's shadow, improbably large forget-me-nots blanketed the somewhat marshy ground. And a memory as strongly accentuated as the colors of those flowers: Tolstoy, interrupting the lively and instructive flow of his words, bending down suddenly, cupping his hands—as if to catch a butterfly, lifting clusters of forget-me-nots and pressing them to his face as if he were drinking them in, then letting them fall carelessly to the ground. The words of the peasant, reverent and respectful, continued to flow from afar, fading into the distance; and in their unwillingness to ever cease, one seemed to hear: "I'm glad I had the chance to see you!" And I returned to the same words of thanks from the depths of our own emotion: "We're glad we had the chance to see you."

After this encounter, Rainer began to view every approaching peasant in the eager and exaggerated hope of finding in him a combination of simplicity and profundity. But in some cases he turned out to be right; for example once when we visited the Tretyakóvsky Picture Gallery* in Moscow together with two peasants. Standing before a large painting entitled *Grazing Cattle*, one of them remarked with annoyance: "Cows! We know all about them! So what?" The other reproached him with an almost crafty look: "Those cows are painted for you. So you'll love them, *that's* why they're painted. You have to love them, even though they've got nothing to do with you, you see?" Perhaps a little startled by his own explanation, the peasant turned with a questioning look to Rainer, who was standing beside him. And it was Rainer who provided the true epiphany: the way he stared at the peasant, the way the words were torn from him in his broken Russian: "*You know. . . .*"

And finally we arrived at the spot Rainer seemed to have been longing for: the people and countryside along the Volga—upstream, from the south to the north, where we landed beyond Jaroslávl. Here for a short while we could feel at home in the Russian Izbá (peasant's hut).* Disembarking repeatedly from the Volga steamer, we found it somewhere far inland—still new and smelling of resin, with its birch timbers, the bark unremoved. The young couple who had built it among others already weathered and blackened by smoke had entered domestic service because they needed cash. The inner room consisted of a bench running around the hut, a samovar, and a broad sack filled with hay lying on the floor. In the adjoining empty stall we found a second pile of hay, although the neighboring peasant woman guilelessly gave us to understand that the first haysack was spread out broadly enough for two. Was it but a few times that we disembarked from the Volga steamer? Weren't we guests of such peasants, and wasn't the peasant poet Drozhzhin* our host in his hut? Couldn't we fill whole books with everything we absorbed with such eager interest? Didn't we spend years that way? Were they really only days, weeks, scarcely months? But everything always returned to *one* hour and *one* Izbá: *we* were always the ones who sat on the stoop in the early-morning hours, the steaming samovar before us on the ground, merrily watching the curious chickens who scurried over from the neighboring log huts to visit us, as if they were coming to offer their eggs for our tea.

For Rainer, the "Izbá en route" symbolized a part of Russia's meaning, and the promise it held. Huts made of birch logs, cut at angles, in strong, solid peasant colors, leaving it to the seasons to fade or darken them. They were a "stopping place," a "place of rest," to draw one's breath—just what he longed for when we set out on our journey, and just what he needed in order to do what he had to do. A people lived here whose history had been one of oppression and misery, yet whose basic nature combined submission *and* faith: just as Rainer felt deep within himself an inner imperative which confidently embraced all the external events which forced themselves upon him. This people called their fate by the name of "God": no high and mighty power who lifted their burden, but someone near to them, protecting them, someone preventing any final destruction from drawing too near to this heartfelt intimacy—the Russian God of Leskóv, who "lives in the left armpit."* Rainer did not simply import this God from the historical realm, nor from the church, in his new surroundings; he wove his own most personal needs and devotion into Russia's history and theology, until it burst forth from him as a cry of need, as a song of praise, a stammering which became Word as never before—which became *Prayer.*

One should not be deceived by the fact that the God in his *Stundenbuch*

(Book of Hours) is not identical to the God he found in Russia; along with the attitude of pious trust in God's protection, the book also presents a reversal of this situation, one in which man becomes a God-creator, a God-constructor, who must now take *Him* under *his* protection. His devotion is not estranged here by presumption; instead it is so infinite that all emotions, from quaking humility to gentle tenderness, flow together in his piety, most intimately in the following poem, with its unprecedented and delightfully sweet tone:

> You have fallen from the nest*
> a young bird with yellow claws
> and staring eyes which sorrow me.
> (My hand is much too broad for you).
> And I lift a drop of water with my finger from the spring
> and watch to see if you thirst for it,
> and I feel the beat of your heart and of mine
> and both of us are frightened.

and not far on:

> We work at building you with trembling hands*
> piling one atom upon the other.
> But who can ever finish you,
> you great cathedral.

There is no internal contradiction here; no limit to his pious devotion, no poetry in him which does not spring from that piety: "God" creates himself in his poetry under the impetus of *all* human feelings; in fearless trust God is experienced as a harmonious and ordering principle.

Everything that rolls within us like a wave approaching the shore of conscious emotional expression breaks on that shore as *devotion* and *prayer*: everything that gathers as contemplation in the heart; everything that binds all ecstasy (even if it has a distant source, such as sexuality or reputation) in an unknown center. For what, even among "believers," underlies what we call God? It touches upon what is consciously available to us, yet is removed from our conscious motivations—it no longer seems like "us"; although "we" flow out of it and therefore are tempted to *name* it in the most concentrated form of its own being, to objectify it.

But "prayer"—as the discharge of the sense of Devotion—already presumes a high degree of inner need, inner celebration, self-abandonment or praise. When at this elevated level it becomes *poetry*, an instinctive artistic achievement, expressed with extreme power, something profoundly paradoxical occurs, reversing cause and effect: in this case the secondary effect, the *expression*, is no longer tied to the experience itself, but becomes an independent impulse toward the goal of—at least partial—relief and discharge of devotion.

The beginnings* of all this were already strikingly evident in the early stages of the *Book of Hours*, on our first trip to Russia. But it was the second journey that first brought the problem clearly to light, since it was then that our travels and the people we met allowed Rainer to devote himself fully to the "Russian" experience. Looking back on it, he complained bitterly that the profound impressions he received were expressed, for the most part, simply as "prayers." That, however, was because he *prayed them*; prayer and its realization were still congruent, a *single* reality which was already present in its completed form. The artistic effect as such, in whole or in part absent from the poems, was realized as never before within Rainer himself, in the extraordinary vision offered by his inner being in such moments—but always retreating before the anticipation of an anxious search for the *final* form which would *independently* confirm and establish the expression itself. He was torn between an impatience which rapidly transformed his impressions into images (which were in themselves a form in which he experienced reality), longing to kneel before each one until he had completed its poetic expression—and the opposing impulse not to ignore something else which was already at work within him creatively. Thus he would often find himself listening attentively, as if under a spell, in some quiet spot he found; *and* rushing past town after town, landscape after landscape, as if he were standing at the window of an express train, without any possibility of returning home. Even years later he spoke of gaps in his memories which could never be recovered, comparing them to our earliest memories of childhood; then he quoted these lines, softly and quietly:

See that he knows his childhood once again;*
the wonderful, instinctive things
and the infinite circle of dark rich legend
of his ominous early years.

This was tied to the secret appeal to "create his childhood again"; the desire to see it once more in a glimmering vision, in spite of everything which caused him to shy away from many of those memories. For beyond this dread, prior to all estrangement, earliest childhood still retained its original, self-nourishing security. The great impulse to the work he was yet to create had to emerge from *that* realm:

I believe in all which has remained unsaid.*
I wish to free my inmost pious feelings.

A time will come when I will do
instinctively, what no one ever dared.
If that's presumption, my Lord, forgive me. . . .

And if that's arrogance, then let me be
arrogant in my prayer. . . .

Although there may *always* be a certain competition when it comes to deciding the relative roles of man and artist in such matters, for Rainer, God himself was always the object of his art, the expression of his attitude toward the most intimate center of his own being, an ultimate anonymity beyond all conscious limits of the ego. And that at a time when viable images for "religious art" were no longer provided, indeed dictated, by a generally accepted belief system. One could put it this way: both Rainer's poetic greatness and his personal tragedy go back to the fact that he had to throw himself upon a God-creation who had become *nonobjective*. No matter how overwhelming the impulse to produce, to express, was for the believer, it still didn't impinge upon the all-powerful *fact* of the God who was embraced, who as such had no real need of him. Rainer's inner devotion and approach were unaltered by the lack of an object, but his task as an artist, as a shaper of forms, required him to reach deeply into himself, into the depths of his humanity: for if he were to fail in his task, it would threaten the very God whose objectification was entailed in his creative act.

Rainer's "anxiety" was his fate: not merely the anxiety of a gentle nature in the face of an object-loss in life, or that of all true natural artists as a result of a continual productive drive they cannot hold in check, but an *absolute* anxiety that one might be swallowed up by nothingness, and the fear that, irrespective of all our being, that which has its effect on us and everything around us would fall into that nothingness as well. Thus the man and the artist in him clashed as he came to grips with this "God"-oriented task: his humanity as the receptive living Being, his artistic nature as the active principle which was to attest to this Being in the creative act. Rainer thought of his artistic God-task, from the very beginning and later as well, as a seduction or temptation, striving toward heavenly heights which would, of necessity, tear him away from the deep, stable, underlying strength of the earth:

I was far away, where the angels are,*
On high, where the light dissolves to nothingness—
But God darkens deeply.

The angels are the final breeze
at his his very top;
to them it seems a dream
to flow through his branches.
There they trust in light
more than in God's darker power,
and Lucifer has fled
to join their company.

He is the prince in the land of light,
and his forehead is raised
so sharply against nothingness' great gleam,
that his face is burned,
and he must beg for darkness.

I quote particularly from the *Book of Hours* because it contains both early and late work. For this reason Rainer referred to the poems in conversation as "undatable," as he did to *Malte Laurids Brigge* (The Notebooks of Malte Laurids Brigge) and the Elegien (Elegies).

This assessment of the Luciferian principle characterizes the starting point for the developing concept of the angels in Rainer's poetry. A matter of great moment! Although the angels in the lines above are still innocent, seeming to gesture above them toward God, they nonetheless unintentionally reduce direct contact with him: like a vestibule from which one can't see past all the beating wings into the holiest of holies. And it doesn't stop there: even abiding in the realm of the angels depends increasingly upon the poet's productive power, upon the hour of grace it provides. Repose in God is deferred in favor of an audience with the angels. And toward the end this problematic concept is resolved in such a way that God and the angels become interchangeable.

One may follow this development along any of the lines of the picture as a whole. It is particularly clear in Rainer's changing use of the word *Armut* (poverty), which is also the title of the third section of the *Book of Hours*. For both the man and the poet, "poverty" originally meant keeping oneself free for what was essential in life, a refusal to become caught up in superficialities, a concern for the only wealth and precious possession which mattered, since

Poverty shines in splendor from within.*

Rainer's attempt to simplify his daily life, to avoid all claims and demands which might waste his time, reflected this attitude. But even at that time, between periods of productivity, the question was lurking: was some part of *his own being* unproductive, caught up in triviality and distractions? One still heard the beating of the angels' wings, who exist to sing God's praises, but now one stood in poverty among them: no longer embraced unquestioningly in God's all enveloping presence, where there are no rich or poor, but only the children of Being itself. *This* is what lends the hellish tones to Rainer's most terrifying images—his description of the poorest of the poor during his first stay in Paris*—even when he is portraying purely material suffering. Though he himself feared physical poverty that year, even that fear was simply a reflection of something within his soul which drove him to despair. It still has the effect of great and powerful poetry, even in smaller details (letters to me which were then incorporated in *Malte Laurids Brigge*), because in such passages those who are branded by poverty cry out in hopeless fear to a God who cannot love them. Projected into the midst of poverty, sickness, and filth, Rainer did not portray himself as a fellow sufferer, but instead depicted his own suffering, which finds frightened expression (in a letter) as follows: "I often long to say aloud, that I'm not one of them." His identification with everything misbegotten and rejected becomes an absolute part of his emotional makeup, in a manner which probably occurs only in a creator unable to create, that is, with the strength of an act of creation. Overwhelmed by these descriptions, I wrote to him in Worpswede how clearly they showed his creative power. If so, he replied, he must have learned "how to make things out of fear," out of the fear of death.

Against this background the spiritual salvation Rodin offered* Rainer is clarified. Rodin gave him a sense of reality unfalsified by subjective emotions and showed him how creativity could be fruitfully unified with life. His only rule and motto, "toujours travailler," allowed Rodin to "make things" with his eye upon the "modelé," without fearing them, without wishing to hide within them. In learning how to work in a direct and down-to-earth way, regardless of how he felt at the time, Rainer managed to incorporate daily life into his craft, into the technical aspects of his work, patiently persisting under the supreme command of art. Something within him had long since been urging him toward this goal: even in the circle of artists in Worpswede, through Clara Westhoff, Rodin's pupil, who first introduced them, before she became Rainer's wife, and before Rainer knew Rodin personally. Once he had moved to Paris, his anxiety first rose to a fever pitch, before his deepest desire was fulfilled: to move in with Rodin, to belong to him totally, a private secretary in external terms only, in reality a friend in a full and free exchange: it was actually through Rodin that the entire world of things was opened to him.

And not only the world of things: control as well over the misbirths of fantasy, the horrible, the disgusting, the demonic in all their distortions. Where his morbid sensitivity had previously caused him to succumb to anxiety, he now was able to maintain an artistic distance, even in this state of fear, freeing a neutral objectivity which had been trapped within him, so that he could now create as if he were unafraid. How did he learn this from Rodin's example and training? Rainer's neutrality toward the pure reality of what he observed cost him an enormous spiritual effort; everything had to be concentrated upon the object in question, and not upon himself. His emotions, held in check and thus in a sense emptied of feeling, would have gladly *revenged* themselves a hundred times over, so to speak, through debasing distortions, turning his accustomed exuberance loose in a negative fashion. From the moment this controlled state became possible, a new realm of pleasure was opened to him. A state of pleasure of which he was only half conscious at first—as in the immensely interesting depictions and exaggerations of Parisian misery. (It can't be denied that this self-imposed limitation in his creative freedom brought with it a danger as well: that in periods of self-debasement and disappointment he might include himself in an act of "revenge against the object.") In a late letter (1914)* Rainer referred to the artist as one who is not tied to the task of "solving things *within themselves*, but rather whose *purpose* is to absorb them in what he invents and feels, in things, in animals—, and why not?—even in monsters if need be." And one could add: in one's own "monstrousness" as well.

One senses directly how diametrically opposed Rainer's basic attitude—which alone created his God-symbol—was to that of Rodin, in spite of all Rainer's devotion to him.

It almost goes without saying that their personal relationship could not last forever, even if what brought about the change seemed an almost chance misunderstanding. In Rodin's case, his robust health and manhood solved the problem of how to keep art as his primary goal while leading a life of unconstrained joy and release, even allowing this to work to the advantage of his art. In Rainer's case, emulating Rodin's attitude and his life of creative activity presupposed such passive devotion, such an absolute upward gaze at the guiding master, that the major adjustment of his emotional exuberance in terms of a controlled calm was achieved precisely through a healing self-denial.

This even went so far as to influence the form of Rainer's God-symbol in the *Book of Hours*: the continuation of the book on the Mediterranean at Viareggio,* where he had fled to escape the horrors of Paris, shows traces of his attempted transformation. The dark fertility of God, still protecting the tender seedling, increases, so to speak, to a mighty mountain's weight, within which man is caught, stifling in the veins of earth—almost a repetition of Rainer's feverish childhood dream,* in which he is being ground beneath an enormous stone. And yet the cry of prayer, an appeal to God:

But if it's *you*: weigh down until I break:
let your whole hand fall upon me
and hear the whole of all my cries.

God's visage is now sterner, like that of the angels, like that of the master, who demands that one *accomplish* something. And the image changes once again: the mountain's weight, bearing down upon the fear and accomplishments of the children of man, presses forth *fruit*, as in the pain of childbirth. Pain—and death as well, if it occurs—is thus sanctioned, removed from the realm of incidental banality. Rainer's earliest longing is fulfilled:

Lord, give to each a death his own.

Death becomes a fruit of creation, an actual task to be fulfilled. But it is summed up instinctively in the meaning of being an artist: the absorption of life *in the work of art.*

As a result of his desire to actually *accomplish* something, Rainer was haunted by an increasing fear of death—particularly during those periods in which his productivity flagged—worried that some banal destructive force would take his life. His "own" death, as he wished it to be, included a note of consolation in that one was still oneself within it. Caught up in the desire for "accomplishment," Rainer never discovered, in spite of all his efforts, a perspective from which life and death could mesh: yet only this would satisfy his fundamental goal—to achieve a "total poverty" which submits itself completely, gives itself up absolutely, because it is so rich, having been absorbed into everything that is.

As an artist, however, Rainer achieved a permanent perfection of his abilities through Rodin. That's obvious to anyone who reads the *Neue Gedichte* (New Poems), which leaves the *Book of Hours* far behind, not to speak of the earlier poetry. But it wasn't just in his poetry that he attained technical mastery by substituting controlled neutrality for oversensitivity:

Rainer's great prose work, *Malte Laurids Brigge,* owes its origin indirectly to the Rodin period. For although it is always thought of as one of his most subjective works, this is in fact a misapprehension: in confronting himself as the subject of his art, he could view himself more objectively than he ever had before. Malte is not a portrait, but utilizes a self-portrait as a means of defining his own self more distinctly. Even where directly autobiographical material is used in Malte (but *not* anything from Malte's childhood), it's used in order to learn how to avoid Malte's fate in the very act of depicting it. A letter of 1911* from Duino Castle in which he reminisces about the book (I've already quoted it in the R. M. Rilke book), includes the following passage:

> Perhaps that book should have been written as one lights the fuse of a bomb; perhaps I should have jumped back as soon as I'd done it. But I'm still too attached to what is mine to do that. I can't bear extreme poverty, although that may well be the truly crucial task I face. It was my ambition to invest my entire capital in a lost cause; on the other hand its value could only be made visible by this loss, and so for the longest time, I remember, Malte Laurids's fate didn't seem to me so much a downfall, as it did a dark ascension into some neglected, lonely spot in the heavens.

One can only be moved by the courage and candid objectivity with which Rainer worked on this book, as if he were imploring the rapture of his own lyricism to clip its wings and stick to earth; and for that very reason when he did allow it sway, he wrote in pure joy, a joy which was at the same time new (as he told me in Paris, with an almost childlike satisfaction, while he was still at work on the book). As if the author's attitude toward Malte were a bit like that of the "God *who did not requite love*"* in the text. But he adopted this stance only to learn more about God and—to put it in the stark language of piety—his secret intentions for us. From that time on it was not being loved that was important, but one's own absolute devotion. The return of the prodigal son proved to be the misunderstanding of a religious impulse, which mistakenly sought what was its own, instead of turning its gaze away from itself and looking upward, where it could share in all abundance without even intending to. Thus the poorest become the richest, the humble are blessed and holy once more.

Prior to the late breakthrough in the Elegies and *Songs to Orpheus,* nothing stimulated Rainer more productively than the depiction of those who were *richest in poverty*: fate, more extraordinary than works of art, like women's fateful love affairs, which no matter how tragically painful they may be, nevertheless lead to total unselfishness as well as true self-possession. In the very first Elegy he calls them "those, you almost envy them, abandoned, whom you found so much more loving than those requited." (See the *Sonnette aus dem Portugiesischen* [Sonnets From the Portuguese], the 24 *Sonette der Louise Labé* [24 Sonnets of Louise Labé], the *Briefe der Nonne* [The Nun's Letters], etc.)*

During the years in which the Elegies were being written, when Rainer sent me bits and fragments, he expressed similar sentiments, praising men of action and lovers more enthusiastically than the singers who created art. As for example in a quatrain entitled "Fragment" from what would become the Sixth Elegy:*

How the hero stormed through the abodes of love,
lifted up by each of them, each beat of the heart meant for him,—
now turned aside, so soon so soon, he stood at the end of smiles: changed.

I recall, almost word for word, a conversation* I had with Rainer one summer afternoon in our garden, when, having completed his Malte project, he had decided not to write anything more, but instead to incorporate what would normally be his work into his approach to real life. We had been discussing how the typical lover often bases the strength of his love on illusions, and how the heart's creative power seems to gain in intensity and fertility, the less it appears to be legitimized by its object. Rainer broke out almost in despair: yes, creativity and creative power were eruptions *within oneself* and, like those lovers, one was manifesting the loftiest work of humanity! But what the artist created pointed toward a Being beyond the personal level, and it was from that realm that the artist drew his creative inspiration. If he were ever to lose that inspiration, into what abyss would he himself fall! For that *which was there*, knew nothing of him. It didn't need him: he alone needed *it*, in order even to know himself.

Against the background of such despair, one sees clearly, and with a shudder of certainty, how greatly Rainer longed for human experience, for *the revelation of life*, which, in spite of the perfection of his achievement, would go beyond the work of art, beyond the poet's word. Only there could that which was most deeply human in Rainer find a resting place, and peace. Everything depended upon that, until the next creative period. Thus his jubilation at the spontaneous breakthrough of the Elegies: "They exist—they exist!"*—not just as works, but as the mystery of existence itself, in which what he had created, and the substance of being, which enveloped him in its grace, were finally one. The unintentionally stern face of the *angel*, which looked down upon him so insistently, was thereby transformed into a faceless God, into whom the child of man could blend as he would into the face of all life. Within the productive moment they both remain a single, indivisible reality; that which cried out to the angel, who is not expected to heed our pleas, who can do nothing but overwhelm us with the demonstration of his terrible splendor, now becomes a resting in God, who, by his very nature, finds it impossible *not to heed our pleas.* *

From his youth on, Rainer found it particularly difficult to await the return of the next period of productivity because of his weak constitution: his *body* was not only upset by such waiting, but went into hysteria. Thus, a hesitant readiness for artistic action was replaced by morbid sensitivity, excitability, pain, yes even fits, which dragged his whole body along with them. Rainer referred to this in a joking way, but with a sort of grim despair, as his "displaced productivity," and to his body as "the ape of his spirit."* And from there it progressed into purely spiritual matters: he would be carried away, out of control, in an overly animated state which threatened to make him forget how ardently he clung to his *real* life, a state which he sensed later, or even at the time, was an "aping" of life. This was most painful to him when it involved the true blessings which fate had bestowed upon him, the kindness, goodness, respect, and friendship which surrounded him, as they did in such rich beauty and grandeur to the very end of his days. He complained most bitterly that he, the real Rainer, longed for and accepted even these blessings simply as narcotics, as distractions, enjoying them, using them, in a sort of self-deception, rather than blissfully allowing them to become a part of his own productive being.

It's my impression that Rainer's occasional flirtations with the occult* and mediums were also related to this morbid sensitivity; supernatural interpretations of dreams, influences from beyond the grave, were transmuted into images of abundant being and knowledge, with which it was his unfulfilled longing to identify. In good times he would bluntly reject such matters, deeply disgusted by them.

What disturbed me most was when traces of the torturing thought that he was only pretending also crept into his relationship to those younger disciples for whom he became a role model and a friend. He didn't just *seem* to be leading them or helping them—he *was*, yet in doing so he felt he was only projecting upon them what he wished in vain to achieve for himself. His intensity arose from the pain of such longing; just as his former notion that he would like to be a "country doctor" practicing among the sick and poor gained its attraction from the fact that the act of saving others would allow him to visualize, to anticipate, to believe in, his own salvation.

Rainer's whole tragic destiny is summed up in this tension between the exclusive grace of a creativity he considered to be holy, and the irresistible compulsion to imitate that state of grace, to "ape" it, to project it even when it was absent. This should not be confused with the relatively harmless way in which men who are deeply concerned with ethical questions or efforts for moral progress allow themselves to slip into the relief of pretense in their weaker moments, for which they are later sorry. In their case it's all a matter of taking stock of the improvement or degeneration of their soul. In Rainer's case there was something about his seriousness which was so remorseless that it went beyond the realm of the ethical—unless one were to elevate the commands and prohibitions of ethics to a doctrine of predestination. For the most frightening aspect about the unavoidability of Rainer's fate was that it didn't even allow him the chance of *repentance*. What lifted him up into a state of creativity, or sheltered him within its quiet depths, was no less a matter of the irresistible compulsion of fate than that which pushed him into false activity, or led him into the void of passive enervation. For this reason even early on he vainly sought to console himself by presuming that his basic nature was "prenatally" determined: stamped forever with all its faults, which in spite of how much he detested them, continued to affect him. This feeling was concentrated most strongly upon his mother. His harshest words on this subject, which pained him throughout most of his life, are contained in a letter of April 15, 1904, upon seeing her again after one of their longest separations. In the middle of a letter to me, he writes:

> My mother came to Rome and is still here. I don't see her often, but—as you know—every time I do it's like a relapse. Every time I have to see this lost, unreal, free-floating woman, who cannot age, I feel how much I've always wanted to escape from her, even as a child, and deep within me I fear that even after years of running and walking, I won't be far enough away from her, that somewhere within me there are still motions which are the other half of her vestigial gestures, fragments of memory she carries around shattered inside her. I'm frightened by her absentminded piety, her stubborn faith, by all the grotesque and distorted things she's seized upon, while she herself remains like an empty dress, ghostly and terrifying. And the fact that even so, I'm still her child, that within this faded, free-standing wall, some barely discernible concealed door was my entry to the world—(if such an entrance can lead in any other way into the world . . .)!

No matter how deeply personal this appears, it should not be taken in an *absolutely* personal sense, for the meaning of his judgment emerges precisely from the power of his exaggeration. He locates what he wishes to rid himself of in a suprapersonal, almost mythical realm. Many years later in Paris, after the three of us had spent some time together, he seemed totally disconcerted that I hadn't found his mother repulsive from the first moment I saw her, that she simply seemed overly sentimental to me. His own aversion was mixed with despair because he was forced to see *himself* grotesquely mirrored in his mother: his devotion as her superstition and hypocrisy, his spiritual creativity as her idle sentimentality. His objections to his mother were only a pale reflection of the deadly horror with which he regarded himself whenever what was most true and most blessed within him, like a ghostly empty dress, acted as if it were his mother—the eternal womb of the void.

When I imagine people contemplating Rainer's poetry—not just standing idly like people looking at pictures in a museum—I'm filled with awe by the thought of what lies behind their poetic effect: an effect of shared joy re-created. The thought that those who have shared that experience could scarcely avoid praising a life in which suffering and struggle have nonetheless achieved such heights of splendor: the splendor which has been brought to life for *them*. Yes, one could even maintain that the artist *himself* becomes the generous singer of praise for all the suffering which life held. Nothing is more certain than that Rainer achieved the joyous affirmation of his own despair in the celebration of the Elegies. In the mystery of poetic conception there is no denial of the relationship between the dreadful and the beautiful. * What occurs there, opaquely, takes place at the urging of a voice which may already be heard in the *Book of Hours*:

Let all things happen unto thee: beauty and terror.

Deep in the heart of anyone who saw it happen, a realization remains of how little could be done to alleviate Rainer's final loneliness, which his hand blocked from vision for a moment only, on the mountain's peak, shielding him from the abyss into which he sprang. Those who saw it happen could only let it happen. Powerless and reverent.

EPILOGUE, 1934

APRIL, *our* month Rainer—the month before the one which brought us together. How my thoughts turn to you now, and not by accident. After all, April includes all four seasons, with its periods of almost brassy winter breezes bearing snow, bright hot sunshine, and autumnal storms which deck the moist earth with innumerable buds in place of faded leaves. And doesn't spring tarry in such earth at all times, so that we know it's there before we even see it? It was from all this that the peace and matter-of-factness arose which brought us together, like something that was always there.

If I was your wife for years, it was because you were the first *truly real* person in my life, body and man indivisibly one, unquestionably a fact of life itself. I could have confessed to you word for word what you said in declaring your love: "You alone are real." Thus we were a couple even before we had become friends, and becoming friends wasn't so much a matter of choice as it was the fulfillment of that underlying marriage. We were not two halves seeking the other: we were a whole which confronted that inconceivable wholeness with a shiver of surprised recognition. We were thus siblings—but from a time before incest had become sacrilege.

Our spiritual union, ready and willing—to use your phrase—for all seasons dark and bright, was to be tested by the unavoidable circumstances of our daily lives, which made the poetic expression of our relationship problematic. But did we have the right to destroy what was written then as we did? In comparison with later work, it revealed so clearly your purely human features, the *solely* human qualities which were not sufficiently sanctioned by your ultimate sense of poetry to feel they were worth preserving as art. But many months later, in "Waldfrieden" (Woodland Peace) in Schmargendorf, as you wrote *Cornet** in a rush of inspiration, you were reminded of similarities to those earlier verses, which were no longer available for comparison, and which in any case may have lacked a technical mastery of the instincts of emotion.

Strangely enough, I couldn't appreciate your early poetry, in spite of its musicality (you consoled me back then by saying that you would repeat it so simply someday that I would understand it after all). The only exception to this—including the poems to me—was when you placed that one poem* in my room. I could have said the same to you, but of course not in verse. And was there not, whispering in *both* of us, something which eluded our grasp, yet which we "bore upon our blood"—and experienced to the depths of our physical being—something which penetrated both the most ordinary and the most blessed moments of our lives?

One year later, this poem found its place at my request in the *Book of Hours*:

Blot out my eyes: I'll still see you
Stop up my ears: and yet I'll hear you
Without feet I'll find my way to you
Without a mouth I'll still implore you.
Tear off my arms: I'll seize you
With my heart as if it were a hand
Tear out my heart: my brain will beat
And if you throw a torch into my brain
I'll bear you still upon my blood

I was troubled by the fact that I couldn't respond fully to the rapture of your lyric poetry in most of its forms. In fact, when I had to take a short journey from Wolfratshausen to Hallein in order to keep an earlier appointment, I was even displeased by the excesses of the letters with your pale blue seal that followed me daily. Until an unexpected pleasantry transformed it all into a lighthearted memory. You wanted to remind me of our little room on the ground floor, where you used to close the shutters to keep passersby from looking in, and only a little daylight would come in through the star-shaped hole in the shutter. When this lyrical postcard was delivered to me, filled in with black ink, bearing no message but the little star-shaped space left undarkened at the top—I immediately jumped to the delighted conclusion that it was the evening star in the darkened heavens, and was touched with reverence by such an authentic "René Maria"!

And yet—if the whole lighthearted reality behind it had been absent, the misunderstanding would not have been lessened. That's what we decided when I told you about it when I got home. We were thinking about *our* stars, which were neither poetic nor prosaic as they rose before us, or shined down upon us, and whose reality—blessedly joyful and thrillingly serious—could never be adequately expressed.

We crossed out a good number of lines with the blackest of inks back then; it was only during that summer that we gradually got out of the habit. Among those totally or partially destroyed, one half-poem still remained, decades later, in a faded Wolfratshausen envelope:

Then your letter brought me gentle benediction,
and I knew there were no distant places:
You come toward me in everything that's beautiful,
you are my spring wind, and my summer rain,
my June night, upon a thousand paths,
where no blessed one has ever walked before me:
I am in you!

You called the following year "our stay in Russia"—and it was, although we had not yet set foot upon it. And looking back it seems to me that this is precisely what made it magical. For it enabled us to immerse ourselves in everything we thought of as Russian: in detailed and precise study, in patient preparations, over which the expectation hovered—without any date yet being set—that we would eventually see it all first hand. It seemed as if we already held it physically in our hands. It made its way forcibly into your poetry, but at first as though lacking the weight of responsibility: in order then to receive the desired symbolic form—like a gift—beneath the Russian skies; to become the physical symbol of an inner rapture which cried out in you for release—a cry for "God" (to call it by its simplest name)—for a place, an image-space, in which the infinite is present in even the least of things, and where the poet's distress finds its expression in hymns, in prayer.

At first our experiences in Russia hardly needed forms of expression: they were discharged in the impressions themselves, and this often happened later as well. A type of lived myth arose in such cases, often triggered by quite common occurrences. What we shared could not have been described to anyone else. For example, what was it about that meadow in the evening twilight at Krestá-Bogoródskoye;* or the cart horse returning to his nightly herd,* with a punishing wood block around one leg; or the room behind the Kremlin* where we sat amidst the conversation of the mighty bells, although their speech was wordless, bells which—in Russia—don't move even when their tongues swing in their housings.

Such moments, shared by two people, often intensify the feeling that some event is approaching the soul externally—filled objectively, so to speak, with what would normally be supplied by an internal subjective receptivity. This gives to such impressions a sense of assurance and confirmation that is beyond compare. And this was no less the case because the basis of my reaction differed from yours: I felt a simple joy at seeing everything again, a happy replenishment I had been denied by my early emigration, which had cut me off from my Russian homeland for so long. For you the creative breakthrough, your turning point as a poet, was also a matter of something your whole being had been profoundly anticipating from the very beginning, something from which later events had only deflected you, turning you aside from that which was most essentially yours.

Many years later, in completely different circumstances, when you were in a state of despair because your were unable to write, you sometimes spoke of your efforts to attach a "mythic" or "mystic" significance to some object or something you'd see, as a means of numbing yourself, to escape your pain or fear. Then you would think of those experiences we shared as lost miracles, which nevertheless had once existed! They came to us so easily and naturally, not at all mystic, the most real of realities, which could only lead us home, again and again. I felt that in your joyful response, Rainer, when we had been traveling up the Volga for several weeks* and suddenly found ourselves about to board two different steamboats, and you said with such calm confidence: "Even if we had been on two different boats we'd still be going up the same river—for a single source awaits us both."

When I think of these things, I could spend the rest of my life telling us both about them, as if in this way, for the first time, the nature of poetry might be revealed—not as works, but as incarnation, not text, but body, and it is this which is life's "miracle." That which rose in you,* almost without intention, as "prayer," remained within the person at your side to the end of her days as an unforgetable revelation. It enveloped any person with whom you came in contact; it remained corporeal, disclosing at your touch how it partook of the divine; and the childlike, unselfish way in which you accepted it so trustingly ensured each day, each hour, its intimate perfection. Our time together was a cup filled to the brim with the desire to give each impression its due, or, to put it another way: it was an immensely festive and solemn holiday.

How little we cared at first whether the impulse to give creative form might come in conflict* with total receptivity to that which was to be expressed! Does someone praying worry about whether his prayer might seem more perfect if he has his hands folded correctly? Doesn't he hold God in his hands as surely as he holds himself, no matter how clumsy his gesture? The first time you gave up something "external" which was an element of your prayer to God, an element you wished to experience *fully*, because you were impelled "internally" to finish shaping the glorious remnants of something which had already occurred, your discomfort at having done so quickly fled, to be replaced once more by a peaceful sense of confidence. The next few times this happened you had an amusing thought, which we often laughed about. You said that if God could watch you at work, he surely wouldn't take it amiss, as we'd heard had been the case with Frau B., who felt that Herr B. wasn't giving her sufficient attention on their honeymoon—he had finally tried to pacify his insulted wife by assuring her that the only reason he paused now and then was to write passionate love poems for her!

But now a gradual change occurred, which caused our innocent laughter to fade. At first we thought the problem was physical—but it became increasingly clear that it was related to the conflict between hymnic experience and its expression in creative form. It was accompanied by anxiety, almost states of terror, in which the two competing claims could not be brought into balance, but instead became a ghostly tangle. I had my greatest fright once as we were taking our usual noon walk* through the magnificent acacia forest, and you found yourself unable to walk past a certain tree. At first you avoided the path completely, but later, when you'd got over that, you once reminded me of it, pointing to the tree: "Do you remember—?!" I glanced at the closest acacia and nodded, although it looked just like all the others. Your eyes widened in horrified disbelief: "—No, no! Not that one! This One!" And I could almost see the tree starting to turn eerie for you again.

Similar dangers arose if you failed to achieve a *complete creative form* for an impression. It was not disappointment, self-accusation, and depression which set in (as with the average, normal man), but an explosion of feeling which soon became immense, monstrous, as if you felt compelled to let yourself be overwhelmed, almost as in that blessed state when you were writing. You called it productivity displaced by fear, like some sort of desperate substitute for the formal controlling principle that had eluded you.

We completely forgot all this in the inexpressible joy and devotion of the weeks of undisturbed experience which followed, like those of the prayers in the *Book of Hours*. But then the periods of anxiety* returned, and the physical attacks. It seemed that what was trying to find release was no longer content with mere gestures of the soul, that your *body* was now voluntarily absorbing it, until it overflowed into pure convulsions. Horrified, you felt that unknown pathological causes were behind it all.

We didn't talk then about how one might transform the prayers into what became the *Book of Hours*—a work which bore the seeds of poetic fame: as far as we were concerned publication was ruled out in any case. But what needed to be done to rescue you from the personal conflict? To heal the breech between *devotion* to God and *testimony* to God? The most difficult aspect of the matter was that the poetic breakthrough, which led to such a direct confrontation with the immensity of its subject, forced you *simultaneously* to find a corresponding form of technical mastery, instead of allowing you—even if it took years—to seek such mastery in the everyday world, where objects of lesser import would have allowed you both the time and the leisure to accomplish the task of poetic expression.

We were already discussing then to what extent you should immerse yourself in the world, among people, in place of the symbolic realm in which you had intended to seize and celebrate the dream of the ineffable *directly*. But it wasn't until the end of our second stay in Russia that it became clear to me just how necessary that was. I had gone for a short visit with my parents at their (current) summer spot in the Finnish countryside when the letter* arrived in which you described yourself as almost depraved because your prayers had become so presumptuous. It's true that this was quickly followed by a second in a completely different tone, but it was written in that rapturous manner you had long since smiled at as "pre-Wolfratshausen," and seemed to me an inexplicable relapse.

I was even more worried by this because *my own* personal desires had been fulfilled by my renewed contact with Russia, and I was ready to face the unavoidable circumstances which reigned in my life with the necessary strength, and joyfully. What I needed had fallen into my lap *effortlessly*, while you had been deeply torn by the demands of your work. It had never been so clear to me at what profound depths *your* development to full maturity would occur. You had never seemed to me greater or more admirable than at that moment. I was drawn to you by the inner problematic which was weighing you down, and this effect never lost its force. Now it was necessary for you to enter into open spaces and freedom* as quickly as possible, to develop everything within you fully.

And yet—and yet wasn't I being torn from you at the same time—? From the reality of your beginnings, in which it had seemed as if we were but a single person. Who can fathom the darkness of our ultimate distance, our ultimate intimacy! Even in that concerned and ardent closeness, I still stood outside the circle of that which fully links a man and woman. And I remained closed off from all that remained, all that lived and grew, until the hour of your death, until my own.

I'm not trying to gloss things over. How many times I held my head in my hands back then, struggling to understand it myself. And how deeply disconcerted I was when, leafing through an old and tattered diary, which had as yet little to say about what I was experiencing, I read the nakedly honest sentence: "I'll be true to my memories forever, but I'll never be true to other people."

Once we were living apart, it proved necessary to stick to our vow not to continue by letter our habit of sharing absolutely everything, *except in the hour of greatest need.** For given my circumstances even *this* complete meshing of our lives was less feasible than it had been in past years.

The hour of greatest need descended upon you in Paris, as the heroic impulse toward "toujours travailler"* at the hand of your deliverer, Rodin, at first took revenge by transforming everything around you into vast and destructive specters—premonitions of which had already been in evidence in Russia whenever your creative impulses had been blocked. But in the midst of your anxiety you turned what frightened you into your own *creation* by giving it artistic form. Among other things from your literary estate I received a letter I'd written to you in which I can see how happy that made me. But even then I wasn't thinking about the *works* which now might follow. My deepest concern remained the healing of the split within you as a human being. And you were wrestling with your own conscience whether to give in to the legitimate desires of your publisher to bring out the *Book of Hours.*

The manuscript of that book, which was in my possession, became the occasion of our first reunion at Loufried in Göttingen, as we had christened it in memory of the inscription on the flag above our peasant hut in Wolfratshausen.

I can still see you lying on the big bear rug by the open door to the balcony, the shifting leaves casting light and shadows across your face.

Rainer, that was our Pentecost of 1905. The spirit arrived in yet another sense than you suspected in the storm of your emotions. To me it was like an Ascension of the poetical *work* above the poet as a *man*. For the first time the "work" itself—what it would become through you, and what it would require of you—seemed to me to be your rightful lord and master. *What more would it ask of you?* My heart skipped a beat as something in me looked forward across the decades to the still unborn Elegies.

From that Whitsuntide on I read your work on my own, and not just when I was with you. I opened myself to it, welcomed it as an expression of your destiny, which was not to be denied. And in so doing I became yours once again, in a second way—in a second maidenhood.

*   *   *

No matter where you tarried in the coming years, in whatever land, whether longing for the security of hearth and home, or longing even more strongly for the wanderer's total freedom, driven by the desire for change: there was no remedy for the homelessness you felt within. Now that we Germans have been confronted so strongly by the political question of a native land, Rainer, I sometime ask myself how much harm it caused that your own destiny included such a strong antipathy toward your Austrian roots. I can imagine that if you had loved your homeland above all others, and felt that attachment in your blood, it might have protected you from the despair of those periods in which you couldn't write, where the greatest danger was always that you would give up on yourself. There's always something sacred about one's native land, with its stones, its trees, its animals, and those feelings penetrate to our human core. And what good did it do when, in Switzerland, although you were already fed up with France in your Paris days, you almost claimed that country as your new homeland, speaking French, finding French friends, and seeking a new beginning in your work? Your letter still spoke of misery.* In spite of everything you were distressed and confused, ready to return home to your tower in Muzot. I can't really say anything about the lyric quality of your French poetry, since I'm unable to make fine distinctions in that language. But in my admittedly unjust opinion, some passages seem suspect: for example when you say of the rose "fête d'un fruit perdu"* (festival of a lost fruit). Is that just melancholy at work, or a joyful and blasphemous masochism? There is a photograph of you there which struck me like a blow to the face, and which I keep hidden away. When I first received it, something inside me cried out: didn't you *use* a foreign land beneath your feet, and writing in French, to talk yourself out of what was silently and secretly carrying you toward the abyss?

How could I do justice to such matters! I struggled with the meaning of your destiny myself, silently, and could come to no conclusion. I couldn't cease knowing that behind the poet crowned by fate, and the man who crumbled under that fate, an innate person existed, and that you *were* that person to the very end: a person who had confidence in himself because, far beyond himself, he trusted in something which sustained him so securely that it became his mission to bear witness to it in his poetry. Each time we met, we lived and talked in this *constant presence*, from which trust in you emanated, like a child whose steps could not go wrong, because they always remained on thoroughly solid ground. Then Rainer was there once more, and we sat hand in hand, inexpressibly secure, and the poetry which resulted simply wrapped another shining layer of that eternal security about you. I can never think back on this without hearing the words of the shortest poem* in the *Book of Hours*, which, in the moment of its conception (—oh, Rainer, that moment is forever etched in my mind—) seemed to me as if spoken by a happy and cheerful child:

I'm always striding toward you
    my steps almost a run
for who am I and who are you
    if our minds are not as one—

THE
FREUD EXPERIENCE

TWO VERY DIFFERENT experiences in life made me particularly receptive to Freud's depth psychology:* sharing the extraordinary and rare spiritual destiny of another person and growing up among a people who were naturally oriented toward the inner life. I won't refer here to the first of these. The second concerns Russia.

It's often been said of Russians—and Freud himself repeated it before the war, when his Russian patients were increasing in number—that as "subjects," whether healthy or ill, they unite two qualities which one seldom finds together: a simplicity of soul—and the ability to speak freely about things in individual cases, finding a means of expressing even difficult inner states and complicated situations. This has always been apparent in Russian literature as well, and not just in its great writers, but even in average ones (with some loss of clarity of form): a basic, deep sincerity speaks with almost childlike directness about ultimate human concerns, as if such things rise more immediately and more directly into consciousness from primal levels. When I think of people I came to know in Russia, I can well understand what makes them so easy to "analyze" today, and what keeps them more honest about themselves: the layers of repression have remained thinner, more flexible in their case, layers which in older cultures have been interposed between basic experience and its reflection in conscious mediated response. This helps us explain more easily one of the central problems of practical analysis: to what extent the infantile level within us all continues to *determine* our natural growth, and to what extent it often leads instead to a pathological regression, in which we fall back from a higher level of achieved consciousness into an earlier stage we had passed through.

Now psychoanalysis is, in its historical development, *practical therapy*, and when I entered upon my study of it, it had just become clear that the mental structure of a healthy person could be determined by an analysis of the states of an ill person, since in the latter case one could decipher, as under a microscope, things which remained almost invisible in the case of normal people. The analytical excavations had been carried out with infinite methodological care and caution, bringing to light, layer by layer, increasingly deeper levels of our primal being, and from the very first grandiose spadework of Freud* the indisputable results of the labor were confirmed. But the deeper one dug, the more evident it became that the subconscious of the healthy person exhibited the same qualities as that of the ill person: what we called "lust," "baseness," "vulgarity" and so on—in brief, all the things we were most ashamed of. Indeed even with regard to the motives* of our rational mind it was difficult to improve upon what Mephisto himself had said. For if culture gradually lifts us above this realm—through the exigencies and advantages of practical experience—it does so only by a general weakening of these drives, by a sacrifice of strength and intensity, so that a quite emaciated human animal stands at the end of the line, in comparison with which the unpruned creature without culture makes an imposing figure, almost like a lord of the manor. This cheerless prospect—scarcely more palatable for the healthy than for the sick, who could at least dream of being cured—undoubtedly drove even more people away from depth psychology, for it awakened in them a pessimism which, after all, resembled that of the hopeless neurotic whom analysis was supposed to cure.

If I am to add my own personal reaction to all this, I must first say that I owe something very important to the early psychoanalytic approach: the tendency not to allow oneself to be disturbed by general considerations about whether the end results are pleasing or not, to focus totally on the precise investigation of the object and the special case, whatever the outcome might be. This was exactly what I needed. My eyes, still filled with earlier impressions, thought they recognized in a more primitive people an indelible childhood we all shared at a deeper level and which—a secret treasure beneath all our maturity—was still with us. Now I was forced to turn aside from those impressions and instead devote myself in rational detail to actual human subjects. I had to do this to avoid the danger of falling into a blind enthusiasm, blind because it blocked one's vision: the attraction of an "agreeable psychology," from which there was no path to reality, but which instead allows us simply to wander about in our own imaginary pleasure garden.

I have no doubt that it was something analogous which created opponents for us, and sometimes caused disciples to defect—although for a variety of different reasons: this quite natural desire not to be left so totally adrift with regard to what one would most like to see answered, or perhaps more correctly: whose agreeable answer one already knows in advance. This will no doubt remain the case even when the most "scandalous" of psychoanalytic revelations have long since been rendered innocuous through familiarity. This also seems to be the justification when one tries to be perfectly neutral in discussing purely logical questions, yet nevertheless feels tempted, even in the so-called "academic disciplines"—unavoidably split into observer and object observed—to add a little personal spice to the results of intellectual labor, in order to make it a bit more to one's taste.

That was why psychoanalysis had to wait so long for its founder—for one who was capable of *wanting* to see on the path before him what others had always carefully skirted. He alone achieved a sufficient degree of impartiality (rather than some hard-won self-control, or a perverse attraction for the disgusting) to confront what was repulsive or offensive without allowing it to upset him. It was *sanctioned* as far as he was concerned by the fact that it existed and was there; which is simply to say that intellectual pleasure and scientific curiosity occupied such a major portion of his capacity for love, his desire for mastery, that for him the question as to where something might stand in terms of human values or judgments never even arose. It was precisely the purity of his unbiased attention (that is, the absence of a mixture of secondary motives and impulses) which resulted in his ruthlessly determined approach to knowledge, refusing to draw the line even at that which was respectfully hidden: and so it happened that someone totally comitted to logic, the complete rationalist, was the one who indirectly discovered the irrational. Thus he christened the new element he had discovered the "*un*conscious," emphasizing the negation in the name. The three modest letters which form the "nickname" in German ("Ubw" = Unbewuβte) always seemed unusually *positive* to me, a personal defense against obfuscation, against everything which might turn discoverers into inventors. *

Nothing clarifies Freud's approach more than his efforts to pursue psychological research to the point at which the unconscious, in itself inaccessible to the conscious mind, makes itself clear in *physical* terms, unwilling to bow to the censorship of our normal patterns of thought. No doubt the deeply shocked objections to the psychoanalyst's emphasis on "sexuality" arose, accordingly, from the fact that we who thought so highly of ourselves were reminded too strongly how much we have in common with everything which confronts our conscious inwardness from the outside; for the body *is* that part of the external which is unavoidably a part of us.

For it still seems to me that at the deepest level what upsets people is that they see themselves turned toward the *physical*, which is indeed part of man's existence, but by no means identical with the expression of the soul and spirit. The more we develop a sharpened sense of consciousness, the more inevitably an Opposite develops which can come only from the Outside, from an Other—and this is equally true of our own physical nature, which results in a fundamental lessening of its value for us. (The various ancient systems of metaphysics had things better in this respect. Inwardness and outwardness were not so irrevocably determined by a consciousness-determined Opposite, but were still subject to confusion with one another, as they are in the life of a toddler today.)

That was why Freud was so thoroughly disliked when he pointed out the significance of the infantile stages for our entire spiritual life. Not just the notion of pan-sexuality in children, which was so strongly attacked, but its identification as the ultimate source of nourishment of our entire subsequent development. As a result of which it becomes necessary to return to these beginnings in therapy: to the most *primitive* stage in individual spiritual experience, which becomes historically recognizable with the passage of time; to the *primal* level which always remains within us, even when we have achieved a full and healthy state of activity—no matter how much we like to think of that state as a "sublimation" floating above it.

Now Freud had simply taken over the word *sublimation* as part of his terminology (without thinking of the value concept that could all too easily be smuggled into it), and he too meant by it a diversion from a sexual goal. It called forth an immediate smile of understanding. Even so, it soon became one of his most powerful words (one of those which had to deal with all sorts of misunderstanding), according to which even the most forbidden sexual perversions, "in spite of their abominable effects," could be termed sublimations—in that, fixated at the infantile stage of sexuality, they remained diversions from the goal of physical maturity. For such diversions take place in the same realm where those sublimations which are valued *highly* occur (intellectual and spiritual accomplishments—social, artistic, scientific)—that is, at the still active infantile level. Up to and including the highest human achievements, in fact, the infantile is only a variant method of doing justice to the *primal situation* which unites us with the world-outside-us, bridging the gap which otherwise seems to separate us as individuals from everything around us. Even what we term "objectivity" rather than "love" is nothing but our conscious mind utilizing *its* methods in opening itself willingly to the unconscious, where we have never ceased denying individual isolation, insisting upon our shared roots with the cosmos. *That* is why we are so deeply concerned with our so-called "suprapersonal" interests, which is a marriage of our most intimate and instinctive personal desires with that which goes above and beyond the personal. *That* is why we "sublimate" things under certain conditions, that is to say, give up our crass sexual goals for them. Perhaps one could describe it thus: it is as if sexual goals too are only a sort of embarrassment on the part of the physically separate individual, an attempt to convince oneself that by uniting with another individual, one is in some way embracing the whole—while instead the other individual is more real to us only in the sphere of his physicality, and it is only in those terms that the marriage can be celebrated and be made fully and totally real.

It's only natural, then, for us to consider the most extreme examples of sublimation as responsible for the "more divine" aspects of our lives; for the word "divine" in some sense *always* stands simultaneously for that which is most intimate *and* that which transcends us most completely. But that itself is just a makeshift concept for the *sub*terranean, which we don't think of as earthly because that sounds too concrete, since it in fact transcends us, and in so doing expresses our being more strongly than the usual opposition of inner and outer. One cannot stress enough that the power of sublimation is directly dependent upon how deeply and securely it is embedded in this primal ground of the mechanism of our soul, and upon the degree to which this vital source affects what we do or don't do in our conscious lives. The more strongly inclined one is toward eroticism, the greater are the possibilities for its sublimation, the longer one is able to withstand the demands involved, without generating a conflict between the satisfaction of instinctual desires and accommodation to reality. *Such a person is in no sense an ascetic* whose desires are *weak*, and who tries to make a virtue out of necessity, nor someone atrophied by illness who finds comfort in the word "sublimation." It's not a matter of self-denying ascetics, but on the contrary those who even in the most adverse circumstances still realize their secret connection with those things which lie furthest from them, wielders of divining rods who sense the origin of springs beneath the driest earth—those who fulfill, not those who abstain—and thus are *capable* of abstaining for even longer periods of time because they know how close they remain to their inner home, their inner fulfillment. The crucial point is that they have not split themselves conceptually into body and soul, but instead gather themselves as human beings into a *single* vital strength—just as the jet of water in a fountain falls back into the same basin from which it rose.

It is with good reason that depth psychology requires that someone who wishes to become an analyst should first have submitted himself to the demands of its methodology, to the brutal honesty of an investigation into his own psychic makeup. The intellectual excavation which is to be undertaken on the living subject achieves its goal—both in research and in therapy—only through active involvement.

If there was often silly talk that the Freudians had formed a sectarian society behind the mere appearance of scientific legitimacy, such talk contained at least one tiny grain of truth: depth psychology could not be entirely divorced from a certain *manner of thought,* since it deals with material on the borderline between the conscious and the unconscious. And this in fact unites all psychoanalysts; this one aspect which is not "simply" a matter of knowledge, not mere science, reduces the importance of *which* analyst the student seeks out. In each and every one it is a matter of deepest responsibility to present his unconscious to his own self-analysis, just as he demands that the student offer himself for analysis as part of the learning process. One should not confuse this self-dissection on the part of the teacher (the analyst) with something done out of mere interest or pleasure. Instead it is a matter of a mastery of a most serious kind. It is the same struggle for the healthy subject as for the sick. It is for this reason that so-called "instructional analysis" often results in a personal renewal identical to that brought about by therapeutic analysis.

Thus there is indeed something in the situation of the depth psychologist which is normally excluded from the practice of science. A *touch of this general attitude* added to the total dedication of the scientist is of real value—in fact its *lack* can have the most disastrous results in the art of both research and therapy. The passivity of objective scientific research must call upon the help of an inner process in order to be fully effective. Honest and rigorous thought must be joined by the active involvement of the spiritual in man or the crucial material under investigation will simply be lacking. I put this rather strongly, since it seems to me that on occasion a lack of such emphasis has led to the presupposition that this is a sectarian activity.

There is yet another reason to remind ourselves of the actual behavior of depth psychologists, and that concerns the *founder of psychoanalysis himself.* For Freud's work, Freud's discoveries, are a result of the thoroughly human way in which he approached his research. His *initial* attention was focused only upon the path of his research, and he held to this path with a steely determination while *at the same time,* and to an equal degree, he opened himself willingly and without reservation to the final goal that awaited him at its end, although it ran totally counter to what he had expected. In sum, his method included an inner involvement which went beyond the aim of simple understanding.

In order to create psychoanalysis, its creator had to combine this twofold experience into a *single* achievement—not into two forms of analysis, but into a most personal synthesis. And it's time this was stated loudly enough to penetrate even the deafest ear. For this *synthetic* achievement is identical with his discoveries as such, with the inner friction between path and goal from which they were born. Only because of this does his achievement transcend personal assessments, wishes, or intentions—indeed from this point of view it is almost synonymous with the disappointment of hypothetical expectations, with a renunciation of what was anticipated, what had been surmised.

In addition to the overwhelming external opposition which made Freud's work such a martyrdom, in addition to the derision and scorn of his contemporaries, Freud also faced a *spiritual* struggle, in which he unwaveringly followed with all his energy only what he perceived, even when it ran contrary to his nature, yes even totally contrary to his taste. If one were to compare this with the sorts of sacrifices of life and limb made by explorers in their travels, it would be in terms of spiritual accomplishment through determination and a readiness to risk one's own skin—without worrying about what one would look like afterward. For Freud the thinker and Freud the man remain united in their personal influence in terms of that sacrifice. He would scarcely want to deny that he always hoped to see the biological sciences gradually accept and extend his own research, nor that he would regard it more as a pleasure than a loss to discover how difficult it was to gain access to the shy beauty of his "Ubw," which so many metaphysicians over the ages had allowed themselves to fondle in such a highly improper manner.

Everyone knows Freud as a personal rationalist in his writings, and not just in those passages where he draws theoretical conclusions—whether they are of a philosophical or antiphilosophical cast makes no difference—which he himself (although not always other authors) wishes to keep clearly separate from those which are purely psychoanalytical. He preferred by temperament either to incorporate assessments which could not be determined precisely and with certainty into some sort of rational perspective—or to set them aside with a shrug which said: "Don't take them too seriously."

To leave a thing undecided, instead of racking our brains in vain over inaccessible knowledge, is both the proper and worthiest duty of the human mind: a victory over the attendant desire to reduce everything to a common formula. But one could ask whether, given the single-minded emphasis on knowledge based on formal logic, and with the increasing ability to draw distinctions on that basis, that other desire might not increase almost instinctively, leading us to strengthen at least *this* unifying viewpoint more than is justified. By doing so we achieve, after all, the only sort of final summary possible—precisely *by means of* the undisputed rule of logical analysis and intellectual dissection. Is this not a form of self-revenge on the part of our pure, neutral, unconditionally abstract thought, as a result of its so-called "inhuman" abstraction? We cast the indestructible net of our *intellectual schema* over the limitless bits of reality which force themselves upon us: so that we can understand one another, in order to create a community in this world which is defined for us by the scope of our net (regardless of how any particular individual may feel about it, who after all simply throws his own thought, his own desire to know, over things in a similarly netlike fashion). And isn't this itself just an attempted *imitation* of that wholeness in which our feeling of life itself is rooted—a sort of veil we impose from above in imitation of the ungraspable primal ground beneath us, which we are unable to reach with our intellect?

Insofar as Man, a thing which has become self-conscious, conceives of himself at the same time as an Other, he simply reverses this situation by way of imitation: he symbolically turns "outward" the existential mystery of his own self. Our formal thought thus becomes a type of "symbolizing"—in order to come to terms with the ineffable by means of a reversion to language. Rationality would be the device by which we held out to ourselves the total synthesis of all existence: openly, but—as analysis.

At this point most people—by no means excluding scientists—decide to add certain things they consider necessarily true to their knowledge of those things which can be proved definitively. As if things would simply be too pessimistic if such a faithful optimism were not permitted mankind. Yes, as if we would simply wind up among the "dead," dissected, without body and soul, delivered up totally to Nothingness. Now Freud didn't simply reject such a view, he attacked it aggressively, out of inner conviction. And that upset people, insofar as it concerned man's nature, the needs and longings which lived most strongly in man. Freud's attitude can be explained by the fact that our weakness on this point—let's sum it up as the flight from physics to metaphysics—misuses the same intellectual tools we developed for use in the physical world. It was just at this point, which separates the two, that Freud came upon his discoveries, which up to then had remained hidden for the most part, largely because they were either denied all too quickly or because metaphysical presuppositions were prematurely interjected. What caused him to fight against this weakness, even to attack it aggressively, was the same earnestness, the total seriousness of the scientist who made no concessions, who relentlessly brought to light results he so little expected, and then would not tolerate any attempt to cover them up again. This should not be confused with the aggression of the convert, which corresponds to an impulse to teach or talk others into one's point of view (for example Nietzsche's "Stay true to the earth!" or any of his other proclamations).

The only thing Freud demands of us is that, at the decisive point, we show a bit of patience, that we bide our time somewhat in the service of our drive for knowledge, that we quietly hold to that honesty of thought which we have learned to use with such success in the face of external reality. Let us freely admit that Freud's approach places us among the physical objects! We should first admit to *that* part of us which makes us similar to all other things, before we turn our interest to how and to what extent we can effectively lift ourselves above it. For that "extra" quality which distinguishes us from everything we deal with consists precisely in the *consciousness* of that which allows us entry into the brotherhood of all things. What acts as a hindrance—and increasingly inhibits us in the course of our cultural consciousness—is the most stupid of all "class prejudices," which all too easily flees to an invented castle in the air in order to escape a primal ground shared with all other things. This ticklish spot, which has become raw or overly sensitive through our arrogance, will not be changed by even the greatest advance in our intellectual abilities, but only through a revolution in thought, in which knowledge is transformed into acknowledgment.

Since Freud was admittedly a rationalist by nature, and by personal taste as well, so that his disciples did *not necessarily* have to follow the "law that he followed," I want to stress again, as strongly as possible, something from my "Freud experience" which never faded from my mind or heart. Namely the degree to which it was his rational approach to scientific research which yielded the discovery of the *ir*rational at the end of the path he followed so unflinchingly; one might say it was such a splendid demonstration of false beliefs that it made a victor of the vanquished, *because* he had remained true to himself. Is this turn of events not a final act of compensation, in which the most mechanized Outwardness involuntarily finds its way back to a home in our most hidden Inwardness, where for the first time the words of Heraclitus about the infinite borders of the soul become fully true?

This dispenses with the most frequent objection to Freud's rationalism, that takes as its motto the time-worn quotation: everything transitory is but a parable—what's essential isn't. Oh, yes, that's true! But in Freud's case the parable was perfect.

GUSTAV V. SALOMÉ

AND HIS DAUGHTER

LOUISE

LOUISE V. SALOMÉ,
NÉE WILM

LOUISE V. SALOMÉ

(LJOLA)

HENDRIK GILLOT

LOU V. SALOMÉ, 1881

LOU V. SALOMÉ,
PAUL RÉE AND
FRIEDRICH NIETZCHE,
1882

LOU V. SALOMÉ

(STUDIO PORTRAIT)

F. C. ANDREAS AND
LOU V. SALOMÉ
(ENGAGEMENT PORTRAIT),
1886

FRIEDRICH CARL

ANDREAS, C. 1890

GERHART HAUPTMANN,

C. 1885

GEORG LEDEBOUR,

C. 1890

LOU ANDREAS-SALOMÉ,

1897

IN THE PAVILLION AT
WOLFRATSHAUSEN, 1897

RILKE AND DROŽIN, 1900

SIGMUND FREUD AND
HIS DAUGHTER
ANNA FREUD

FRIEDRICH CARL
ANDREAS, C. 1925

LOU ANDREAS-SALOMÉ,
1934

EPILOGUE:
MEMORIES OF FREUD
(1936)

WHEN, RETURNING HOME from a stay in Sweden, I stood before Freud at the psychoanalytic conference in Weimar in the fall of 1911, he laughed at my impetuous request to study psychoanalysis with him, for no one was thinking then about the teaching institutes which were later set up in Berlin and Vienna for the new generation. Then, when I visited Freud in Vienna after six months of preliminary study on my own, he laughed even more heartily, since I innocently told him that I also wanted to work with Alfred Adler,* who in the meantime had become bitterly hostile toward him. He agreed good-naturedly, on the condition that I wouldn't talk about him in the other camp or mention them in his presence. I adhered to this condition so strictly that it was months before Freud learned I'd left Adler's circle. But what I would like to recount is not related to any theoretical training, for even the most fascinating training would not have diverted me from what was contained in Freud's discoveries. When one considers what he "found," the most brilliant theoretician would not have managed to shift my attention from it, nor would those discoveries have been lessened had Freud himself developed a misguided or incomplete theory about them. He considered theories—and many were still being developed at that time— as an unavoidable form of communication with his colleagues, and when they formed in *his* mind, they naturally reflected his scientific and personal character, the precise clarity of his chosen manner of thought. But if I attempt to describe what it was about his way of thinking that led him to his discoveries, he would no doubt laugh at me yet a third time, for that would be no easier than pinning down the specific quality inherent in the hand of the painter or sculptor. And his approach focused *upon something*—namely on the momentary expression of a living individual: with a gaze for which nothing was ever so isolated or so momentary that it did not open itself to him, revealing itself as a total expression of human nature. Instead of merely thinking about things—no matter how profoundly or creatively—Freud showed a willingness to concentrate his attention on the exact, precise drives to which we are subject by nature as limited human beings, aspects which can be revealed and discussed only by this method.

On one of the first evening meetings of the study group (where a female member had been included for the first time the previous year) Freud indicated by way of introduction that we would be speaking with total and open frankness about matters which might be somewhat shocking. He added, as a pleasantry—and with the special touch of delicacy of feeling he could show on occasion: "as always, we'll be complaining about how hard we have to work weekdays—with the difference that now we have a Sunday among us." I often felt the word "Sunday" fit him as well, and his gaze, which I've already described in terms of the rich material it revealed: no matter how repulsive or shocking that material seemed. For me there was always something Sunday-like behind the weekday business. Freud, in what was no doubt one of his own moments of disgust, expressed surprise that I was immersing myself ever more deeply in the study of psychoanalysis: "since the only thing I do is teach people how to wash dirty linen."

Of course we all were familiar with ironed and mechanically pressed linen in dresser drawers before Freud. But what one could learn from soiled linen, whether it was one's own or a total stranger's, was not just the nature of linen, but something about nature in general, something of value in itself because it was transformed into experience.

Thus even when the most repulsive and shocking matters were laid bare, the gaze was not directed at those things in themselves. Once when such matters were being discussed, Freud—although he was no longer laughing at me—said in amazed disbelief: "Even after we've talked about the most terrible things, you look like Christmas is coming."

Among my memories of our last meeting—in 1928—in the garden of the little palace in Tegel, nothing stands out more vividly than the image of the brightly colored beds of hothouse pansies, which had been transplanted in full bloom, and now awaited the coming year beneath the falling leaves of a well-advanced autumn. It was truly restful to gaze upon their splendor, the infinite variety of tones of dark red and blue and bright yellow. Freud picked a bouquet for me before we left on one of our many trips into Berlin, which I wanted to combine with a visit to Helene Klingenberg.

In spite of Freud's difficulties speaking and hearing, we were still able to carry on conversations of the unforgettable kind we had prior to his long years of suffering.* On such occasions we sometimes spoke of 1912, my year of psychoanalytic study, when I would always leave a note at the hotel so I could be located in case Freud had time free. I would come to him as quickly as possible, no matter where I was. Once, shortly before such a meeting, Nietzsche's *Hymnus an das Leben* (Hymn to Life) had come into his hands: the *Lebensgebet* (Prayer to Life) which I'd written in Zurich, and which Nietzsche had set to music in a slightly revised form. Such lines were not at all to Freud's taste. Given his own sober and clear-headed prose, he could hardly be expected to welcome the enthusiastic exaggerations which an innocent and inexperienced young woman had easily enough allowed herself. He read the final stanza aloud in a merry voice, filled with good-natured friendliness:

> Centuries in which to think and live,
> Let all your content be their gain!
> If you have no more joy to give,
> At least you still grant pain.

He folded the poem and tapped it on the arm of his chair: "No, you know, I can't really go along with that! Just one persistent cold dragging on would be enough to cure me of such wishes!"

We came back to this that fall in Tegel as well: did he recall our conversation of so many years ago? Yes, he said, he remembered it quite well, and even what we talked about afterward. I don't know why I even asked him that question: the knowledge of the terrible long years of suffering he had gone through raged within me—years in which we all had to ask, each and every one of us, what more could be demanded of human strength. And then something occurred which I didn't understand myself, something I was powerless to hold back, that crossed my trembling lips in rebellion against his destiny and his martyrdom:

"That nonsense I wrote back then, just because I was filled with high spirits—you lived it!"

Upon which, shocked by the openness of my words, I broke into loud and uncontrollable weeping.

Freud didn't reply. I simply felt his arm around me.

BEFORE THE WORLD WAR
AND AFTER

IN THE LATE AUTUMN of 1902 we moved to Göttingen, where my husband had been named to a professorship in Persian. * Among other things, this fulfilled our longing for a truly rustic life, since the area north of Göttingen was much more promising in this respect than the environs of Berlin. Just when we were becoming a bit desperate in our search for something outside the city, we came upon our little half-timbered house in the middle of an old orchard on Rohnshöhe, like one of those miracles that solve everything in a fairy tale. It was still so isolated in those days that young foxes even appeared once at the end of the long garden.

Being so close to nature always seemed to fulfill my life anew. No matter where I had been, over the course of three decades, when I returned home the season at hand always seemed to have gathered to its full upon this patch of land, as if it sprang from the very earth itself. I developed a special habit. Each time I'd been away for a while, I would take early-morning walks— scenic strolls so to speak—to see things again, to check the impressions I'd received against what had happened in the meantime to the trees and bushes, to everything which had disseminated spring, or celebrated fall: eternal change amidst eternal constancy. I tested the extent to which the complications of human experience stood up to that which makes nothing of its own being, and yet is so self-evidently real.

In the first spring after we had moved, I was forced by deteriorating health to take a trip with a friend who was a doctor. The fruit trees were just starting to bloom. A huge old pear tree (just last year a storm toppled it at last) thrust a branch covered with white blossoms through the window deep into my study. It almost seemed a sin to leave it behind. But I told myself that next year it would return with the same shimmering spring beauty: and wouldn't you know—the next year the tree didn't bloom. It had flowered too pro- fusely, and had to skip a May. This explanation did not, however, lessen the impression this experience made upon me.

Many windows looking outward, and the sun coming into the house through them. Both of my rooms upstairs were like a bower, surrounded by broad-limbed lindens which offered a green curtain against the dazzling sun. In late autumn, when the first storm winds drove the leaves from branches, they let through a flood of new light as if by way of consolation. My walls, which I had covered in a deep blue-gray material, began to fade, but they never really looked bad. The basic, neutral tone simply seemed more selflessly offered up to the willfully bright colors of the Russian peasant embroidery and other souvenirs of my past. Of course one didn't dare move anything to a new spot, or even straighten it: the patch behind always peeped out in its original deep blue-gray, keeping faith with what had been. Thus Heinrich Vogeler's etching "Love,"* which he had put there himself, and which was actually a portrait of Rainer, stayed on the main wall. But I'm still opposed to constantly altering our rooms to suit our current mood, or the changing times. (Rainer often went too far in this respect, involuntarily confusing an external change to suit the mood of the moment with what were inner preoccupations—thus allowing himself to be mistakenly lulled into such action.) Rainer loved my rooms, and not least because of the strong patches of color behind the furniture and the pictures, which seemed to offer hidden paths back into the past: like little gateways into an imperishable world.

The two large bearskin rugs which dominated the study came from Willy Brandt's dangerous hunting expeditions in Russia. They were surrounded by simple pine bookcases. But it was never much of a library, even before my husband's death, after which I threw a few of my own things in with the sale of his books. I had refrained (and properly so) from adding any new books to my collection right from the start, so that my husband could build up his own library, which was both a professional necessity and a great pleasure to him. The basic stock of books from my girlhood had been left behind in Russia: our great writers, German and Russian, as well as the books I studied in semisecrecy, some of which (Spinoza for example) I had obtained with some difficulty in exchange for jewelry I'd been given. But the major and annoying reason for the miserable state of my library was the following: that the thickness or weight of books caused me such problems when I was reading them lying down that I made a practice of tearing them into sections, and never bothered to have them rebound. And then I've always tended to lose them or to give them away too, particularly those that meant the most to me. And I'm afraid there's a special and somewhat foolish reason for this: a contempt for paperback editions published in the thousands, because they are unsuited to their content; as if by all rights the contents should stand before our eyes as an independent intellectual and spiritual entity, with no relationship at all to paper.

In 1904 I made our little house the setting for a story, *Das Haus* (The House),* in which—with ages, backgrounds, and personal relationships altered—I portrayed only people I knew extremely well, even Rainer in the figure of a young boy with happily married parents; and with his permission I also quoted a letter he had written to me. But even before that I relieved my spiritual homesickness for Russia by writing *Ródinka,** which I would like for people to have read, because I was able to say something about Russia in it. The other things I wrote were written more or less just to be writing, they were important to me for the process involved, and remained somehow a necessary part of my life. I kept my stock of manuscripts in a safe at the bank, and would take something from it only with the most "ignoble" of motives, for the disgraceful purpose of making money by publishing it—and how reluctantly I did so! With the exception of essays of the most varied sort, which I scattered about in the world without ever collecting them. I wrote them partly because they involved topics near to my heart at the time, and partly because I was spurred to do them in the first place by financial difficulties.

I have to confess something strange in all this: when I wrote scholarly essays I felt strengthened, as if I had been doing something feminine, whereas in the case of anything poetic, the activity seemed masculine; that's why most of my feminine characters are seen through the eyes of a man. The reason for both reactions stems from my childhood and early youth: for in the case of scholarly work, in which I was trained by my friend, the feminine principle of my love for him was active, while, since he opposed everything that stirred my imagination, I could only escape into that realm through an attitude of masculine defiance. Given the fact that human endeavors are so deeply rooted in the unconscious, it is hardly surprising that this aftereffect did not actually cease until well into my later life, around the time I turned sixty.

I often succumbed to the strong temptation to spend the winter months in Berlin, where Max Reinhardt* had invited me to attend rehearsals for the Kammerspiele (Chamber Theater) he was founding. The experience made such a strong impression on me that even my other relationships with him, and the intellectually rich circle around him, took second place—and that says something.

I'm not thinking here of the controversy over Reinhardt and whether he deserved praise or blame, nor even about the premieres themselves, but about his unique qualities as a practicing professional, just as what will last about him is not a tradition or school, but the unique impression of his work (which was allowed to develop so freely because *Edmund* Reinhardt took care of all the financial matters). It seemed to me that the true point of genius in the Reinhardt who dreams, opening himself so passively to poetry, as a great actor opens himself up to a work of dramatic art, is a tremendous *presence* which allows him to control the performer. An actor who struggled with timidity, and more often than not shy in society as well, Reinhardt was completely transported while directing, in a manner which alone explains his extraordinary endurance and vigor: he embodied an almost indistinguishable combination of a dreamer's will *and* an almost brutally forceful one. One of my strongest memories is of a moment in which even the most extreme brutality was not repellent: when Agnes Sorma in *Ghosts* listened to her son's confession, choking back her sobs, without catching the exact tone that Reinhardt was demanding, the rehearsal ended in general exhaustion. As she left the stage the overstrained woman broke out in a fit of weeping: at that moment Reinhardt jumped up, raised his arm, and cried out excitedly: "That's it! That's the tone I want!" At which point she had to "rehearse" her tears again.

I was left with the following impression of Reinhardt: while poetry is generally communicated first by the sound which expresses it, it often seemed here as if it were lifted directly from the head of the poet, in that it was expressed through the act of directing the living person by means of *willpower.* The dream element and the impulse of the will combined into an expressive effect, breaking forth in a quite personal way to make visible that which was to be created. Premieres alone, no matter how brilliant, can't give any real impression of this—except perhaps for the actors, who, however, are busy with their acting. At any rate it says a good deal when I emphasize that everything else I received from Max Reinhardt, the impressions and the relationships with the circle around him (and how rich they were, when I merely think of the names Kayssler, Bassermann, Moissi, Gertrud Eysoldt!), pales in comparison to the impression of his own performance as a director.

I also experienced something totally different when Stanislavsky's troupe passed through,* whom I knew from Petersburg, and whom no one enjoyed more passionately than Reinhardt. In their case the company director is, to a certain extent, replaced by the *the will of the group,* since all the actors come from the same economic class and educational background, something which has been largely missing from the theater until quite recently. The Russian nature made it even simpler: but I often thought such a principle, such a coming together, should, in itself, make possible a new basis for the theater—arising from a general and profound human need; not simply theater as private aesthetic pleasure. But Stanislavsky was deadly serious about the technical aspects of acting: "One hundred rehearsals per performance!" he decided, and Reinhardt sighed with longing: "If I could only do *that*!" I got to hear about such matters from the Russians as a result of various invitations, and from Harden, who was a master at concentrating the confused babble of Russian and French conversation upon the points of interest to him. Our walks together from the Hotel Unter-den-Linden, where the Russians were staying, to his little villa in Grunewald, were splendid continuations of the evenings. Back then we always understood one another; it wasn't until the World War that I became completely estranged from Harden the political writer.

Many trips took place during the winter months in Berlin; to Norway, Sweden, and Denmark—but without meeting Rainer when he was staying there in the summer of 1904, due to something silly I did without thinking. I knew that he was staying in the south of Sweden with friends of Ellen Key, and on my way through Copenhagen I'd sent him a picture postcard of my hotel, with a little mark above my window. When Rainer received it, he made a special trip over to see me, and of course I was already gone. We had both known Ellen Key* for about the same length of time, and I went on my third trip to Paris—in 1909—with her. We met Rainer there, who was then Rodin's secretary. Ellen Key was so kind to me that she even bore my dislike of her books with good humor, even though she threatened me: "You ox, next time I'm not going to visit you in Göttingen, I'll just keep right on walking till I get to Italy." She enjoyed visiting us as much as I did visiting her in Sweden, in her place by Lake Vetter, once for the whole of late summer.

Rainer and I just missed one another a second time without knowing it, after he had been living in Duino and I was spending some time in Sistiano at the conclusion of a southern trip:* we later enjoyed imagining what it would have been like to run into one another unexpectedly on an early-morning walk on the beach. What seemed far more important, however, was the fact that no matter how long it had been since we had seen one another, whenever we got together again—whether at my home, or at his in Munich, or some other place—it seemed to us as if we had been walking along the same path all the time, approaching the same goals, almost as if a secret, unwritten correspondence had overcome our separation. No matter what had happened in the world at large in the meantime—we always reached the meeting point together. Our personal reunion was itself nothing less than a celebration of this fact, lifting even our cares or sorrow into a state of spontaneous gaiety.

I visited Spain as well, long before Rainer did. But when I entered San

Stefano I was so shocked by a bullfight that I fled the country, preferring to stay in the Basque district in France (Saint Jean de Luz). As the years passed I not only enjoyed traveling, but became even more open and sensitive to external impressions. Things no longer merely served as a decorative background (as even Rome had) for what was happening inside me. I opened myself in a new way to impartial joy, and gained an insight into the world. Paul Rée, who first brought me to a state of true cheerfulness, soon found me so increasingly lighthearted that he was in the habit of saying that at this rate I would still be kicking up my heels as an old woman. Later people assumed that's what my youth had been like too, and on more than one occasion this led to an amusing misunderstanding: during a desultory conversation in a mixed group of people someone maintained loudly that he was sure, many years ago, he'd heard that I disappeared somewhere every spring and fall, only to return totally rejuvenated. In a serious tone of reproach I told him I hoped he would defend me from such false accusations in the future, since I had *never* held to any particular season.

I didn't always choose the same friends as traveling companions; different lands and peoples called for different modes of experience; and I also needed to withdraw into seclusion now and then. Compared with travel today, where oversea journeys are common, mine covered but a small portion of Europe; I was never attracted to the extreme western part of it. My longest trip south went through Bosnia, Herzegovina, Dalmatia, Bulgaria, Montenegro, and Albania, into Turkey via Scutari. The people of what is now called Yugoslavia brought a true deluge of memories—as if the Russian people had been released from their oppressed state into happiness and freedom. The formality of the Turkish authorities made no difference, people were nice to each other. I've seldom seen anything as lovely as the tall, dark-blonde women, who offered such a strong contrast to the heavier Turkish women with their clumsy gait (at least in those days!); and seldom such charming ragged children in the street: their movements seemed atuned to beauty, as if by some ancient tradition. Their whole system of gesture seemed colored by it: whether it was bareback riders racing down the slopes in their native costumes, or people crouching quietly beside the water. (Doing their wash or saying their prayers, their gestures showed the same controlled form.) We often passed an aged beggar, crouching in the grass, who, in spite of his outstretched hand, looked like some kindly old prince, so that we were not at all surprised the next time to see him pull out a blue enamel cigarette case with the other hand, and offer it to us.

Everything seemed more Oriental than in Russia, more ancient and untouched: over a year later Rainer and I had a lively discussion about this, as if we shared the same memories. What had attracted Rainer to the religious life in Russia seemed to color everything here in an even more profound and authentic form: perhaps more mechanical, if you will, but precisely because of its age, its "ossification," it was more effective; without requiring that one harbor similar convictions. Even in the Russian church service, and more so in the Armenian, this more hardened form is effective; it holds out, as it were, an empty silver bowl to the stranger, into which he may place his own brand of devotion. This is also true of the Islamic faith, which therefore fits in easily alongside the Greek Orthodox ritual. When all one has to do is remove one's footwear upon entering the mosque in order to join the pious stillness of those who stand or sit in silent prayer upon the beautiful rugs, one is irresistibly drawn into a state of inner spiritual communion.

I recall an impression on my first night there, which gave me a sense of the nature of their religious devotion. Our windows opened onto the tumult of a narrow street, in which the cries of shopkeepers, the grating of passing carts, and the braying of donkies all vied to create a general uproar, when suddenly there was a moment of utter stillness, as if the cosmos were holding its breath; it was almost like being cut off from nature itself. Even the braying donkies fell silent. From the minaret of the mosque, which thrust into the darkening sky like a pointing finger, came the cry of the muezzin: "Allah Akbar." Rising thus from the hearts of all living creatures, in fear and longing, echoing upon the margin of light and dark, one did not stop to think about the idea behind it, but simply joined in universal devotion; just as at night, before the gray of morn, the same cry penetrates the sleeping mind like a proclamation of the rise and fall of life.

My last trip—1911—was to St. Petersburg and Sweden. On the way home from Stockholm I traveled to Weimar with a local psychotherapist, where the Freud Congress was taking place that September. One year later I was in Vienna,* and after that I didn't undertake any further journeys unless they were connected with Rainer, or Professor Freud, or business.

After the war had drawn a line between the present and those years of innocent travel through various lands and peoples, they seemed in retrospect to have formed a separate stage of my life, in which what was foreign and what was familiar merged naturally, filling me with joy and trust—reduced now to memories, and only visible from the distance of those fifteen years, since 1914, in which I've become another person.

In the place of various exchanges with old and new acquaintances, I drew closer over the years to a few congenial companions. In the still somewhat limited circle of friends around Freud in Vienna, I found myself taken into a group which seemed to me, given their goals, like a gathering of brothers and sisters. For me it had the same beneficial effect in some ways that Paul Reé's circle had: in fact it was like a return to comfortable naturalness I had shared with my brothers—in spite of our differences we were all born of the same parents. Even coming from all ends of the earth, we found ourselves with everything in common.

Most of them took part in the war. Professor Freud, who had three sons, and his son-in-law, in the field, once wrote to me,* alluding to my generally high opinion of men: "Now what do you have to say about brothers?! And can even you, with your cheerful disposition, ever be completely happy again?" Torn between warring nations and at war with myself in my profound loneliness, I could only answer no.

War as a man's affair, as typical of men: how easy it is to think that things would be different in the world, if only women ran it. How often one weighs that dream, rebelling against our immutable human nature: for doesn't it seem as if we can almost see her, towering over the borders of all struggling nations like a huge monument: the figure of *maternal endurance*, bending over every fallen soldier, over every mother's son? And yet our eyes mistake themselves in raising the invisible to such clear and concrete meaning. It *is* not what it seems. For the maternal, from whose corporeality Mankind arises, is not simply a matter of eternally *enduring* what happens to each of her sons, it's also a matter of the eternal *repetition* of that which threatens the life of each of them. To be a mother necessarily involves the most passionate partisanship in both love and hate—a stubborn intolerance and destructive rage whenever that which she has brought into being is involved, a part of herself she has released which is nevertheless inalienable. The maternal transmits its devotion and its brutality alike to every child, the inexorable limitations of our kind.

No matter how deeply we long for peace, each of us knows in his heart that life in its fullness presupposes a readiness to do angry battle against everything which threatens us. Therefore fundamental pacifism of even the most sincere and high-minded kind is always suspected, with some justice, of being a bit too coldly rationalistic; for whenever such a purified distillation of rational thought and emotional control wins the upper hand, that passionate partisanship which identifies with the object under attack is sadly lacking.

There is really very little difference in this respect between primitive, more savage, ages and our own more civilized one, proud of its culture, which on the one hand has been able to develop more efficient weapons and increasingly lethal modes of destruction, and on the other hand busies itself morally with treating and healing the wounds it inflicts on the enemy. We wage war because we are already at war within ourselves: one could hardly imagine any two forces more strongly opposed to each other, nor more fiercely struggling for space, than the two levels which inhabit our own nature. Mankind engages in such a double life, emotional and rational, that one would hardly think it was one and the same person who was inevitably involved. Except that as man reaches a higher level of development, a third possibility sets in: to arrange things so that the two get along (as enmities among nations are laid aside after a war), even if there are always occasional cases in which one momentarily overruns the other. We turn to such cultural methods in order not to tear ourselves apart in internal war. Of course this results in a sort of involuntary *masking*, concealing and confusing—and not only on the outside, covering our countenance, but also turned inward, behind the face, toward our own soul—something which is hardly possible for a more naive, simpler mankind, still in touch with its own basic instincts. But in strongest contrast to this, such times also allow us to experience more primal stages, tearing men open to reveal a level from our ancient past— rending us more deeply than any other fate. From what those who returned from war recounted over a year later, one gathered that it was a gripping revelation of something they had never known before. It was "comradeship," a fellowship in shared experience that went far beyond friendship or family, uniting them in a totality, a self-same being, as if a time once more existed in which mankind was unified and strong, prior to its separation into individual consciousness. Those who were in the war seem also to have experienced an hitherto unknown relationship to *nature*, which went beyond the practical, aesthetic, or emotional guides by which they normally lived.

One would think on the basis of such reports that it would be possible to see this renewal among the utterly devastating changes wrought by the "powers of fate upon friend and foe alike." Particularly in comparison to those nations which had been spared by war, who—as did we in times of peace—knew of such matters only indirectly, like a story heard secondhand. Such abysmal experiences of the greatest horrors of reality surely carry with them enormous human value, since in confronting themselves and that reality, human beings learn the true nature of both: only when the right to hide things from oneself has been abolished can one truly experience life.

The dozen years which followed the war were only its continuation, in spite of all efforts to bring it to an end. In my case the Russian Revolution had separated me permanently from my family and the land of my birth even prior to the official close of the war. The revolutionary upheaval there could only be preserved by the continued use of power.

During and after the war my involvement with Freudian depth psychology, both as scientific study and as therapeutic method, increasingly occupied the whole range of my personal life.

Nothing was more warlike than the ruthless manner in which psychoanalysis revealed the tensions which rage within us, down to the very foundations of our soul. Nothing took us so far beyond a state of war—two human beings a foot apart upon the borderline of peace—as the mutual exploration of the basic nature of the human soul.

What happened then? A stranger simply entered the room, was received without love or hate, was calmly introduced to the work at hand—and was exposed to something more overwhelming than anyone can imagine who has not experienced it firsthand.

The years passed, age thinned the ranks of my contemporaries as the war had thinned the ranks of the young—and the stranger stayed.

Rainer died in the final days of 1926; my husband on October 4, 1930. Soon after that I tried to say what he was like in a rough sketch—with only his friends and disciples in mind. Later I attached it as an epilogue to what appeared in the following year, my own uncontrollable *memories* of life, which in an increasingly forceful way, simply told themselves to me: those human repetitions of what is fading away, catching up with us, not totally by accident it seems, only in old age, as if they had to come a long way to demonstrate to us how imperishable they are.

All that aside, the personal life of the individual is far less important than we like to think: within which particular existence it fell to us to test happiness and pain. The least of lives, the most apparently insignificant, may prove inexhaustible, while the most splendid and successful ones may fail to reveal a comprehensible whole to the human eye.

Existence remains for us a picture puzzle: and yet we too are included within its open secret.

F. C. ANDREAS

A MAN OF consequence seems larger-scale than what we all-too-easily call the average man. There is room for the *whole* person, with all his inner contradictions, and all his needs. What we call talent often arises from an internal drama in which these opposites are reconciled only with the greatest of effort. A *balanced* personality—in some sense the goal of all humanity—can in fact be achieved only by reducing our human possibilities in the interests of an easy inner peace. Otherwise such balance remains a simple utopian ideal, modeled on the non-human realm of flora and fauna, against which we measure with envy our own continuing complexities.

In human terms, we view the distinction between a primal level of thought and self-consciousness as analogous to "primitive" and "civilized" societies, although the latter is simply a continuation of the former, since even the highest form of consciousness rests on primal ground. We refer to this dichotomy as European and non-European (in spite of the high level of development of earlier non-European cultures), or we think in terms of directions: generally northwest as opposed to southeast. In the final analysis, this opposition represents a general insoluble ambiguity of the human condition. To experience this antithesis intensely as an individual, however, results in a life both richer and more difficult, one in which talents and needs are often at odds. If an individual is *born* into such conflict, the gifts he receives are inevitably intensified, and the elements may take revenge upon each other. Indeed, this condition becomes characteristic of the total personality. This comes to mind whenever I think of F. C. Andreas, who found himself, for better or worse, caught between the two, although I realize how one-sided such a summary of his personality is, revealing but one trait of his character. Nevertheless, since I was too close to him to paint a full portrait, I will offer this sketch.

Friedrich Carl Andreas was, by birth, a product of the confluence of East and West. His grandfather on his mother's side was a highly-gifted North German physician* who emigrated to Java and married a beautiful, gentle, and lovely Malaysian. His mother married an Armenian who lived in

Isfahan. He was a member of the royal line of the Bagratuni, and, as was customary in Persian feuds, the defeated family changed its name, in this case taking on the Christian name Andreas. Little Andreas's father moved to Hamburg when the boy was six years old. At the age of fourteen he sent the youngster to high school in Geneva, where he showed a burning ambition, proving to be a passionate student of languages, and music. He pursued Oriental Studies at various universities in Germany, specializing in Persian. He graduated from Erlangen in 1868, then spent two years in post-graduate study in Copenhagen before he was called home by the outbreak of the Franco-Prussian War. At the end of the war he went to Kiel to continue his study of the Pahlavi language and script, which he did not complete until 1882, since he had been sent in the meantime as a member of an expedition to Persia. Although this was fully in accord with his wishes, and provided him with experiences and personal impressions of the Near East which reinforced his studies, it also revealed the tension between the goal-oriented European within him and that part which wished to experience life at leisure, without worrying about the passing of time, as if he were *returning home*. The gift fate had thus provided in such a friendly and surprising way proved to be a problem. He was late catching up with the expedition—which was already underway—having been held up in India where he had been making valuable discoveries and observations, which, however, had nothing to do with the purpose for which he had been sent. They were angry with him, and partly as a result, misunderstood his first shipments from Persia and demanded that he return home. The straw that broke the camel's back was a hate-filled emotional outburst in his official reply, after which he continued stubbornly working away in Persia *without* any financial support from the government. His stay in Persia lasted six years, most of them spent in bitter poverty. He was finally forced to return home by eye trouble he developed while deciphering inscriptions in bright sunlight. He managed to scrape along as a private tutor until he received a professorship at the newly founded Institute for Oriental Studies in Berlin. But this soon came to an end as the result of intrigues which made it appear as if Andreas were not fulfilling his professional duties in this case either, duties which consisted of training diplomats and businessmen with a practical interest, rather than teaching young academics. But in fact his dismissal was unjustified, since his class consisted entirely of research-oriented students of the sort he was born to teach.

The primary danger such external misunderstandings revealed was an inner tension in Andreas, for even when he was allowed to pursue his research as freely as he wished, he ran into a second problem. It seemed to him that the path of rational proof was inherently endless—one could never complete the journey so to speak—compared to intuitive, almost visionary, evidence offered to him by the objects of his investigations.

Precisely because he was so overly thorough, tracing everything in the minutest detail, and thereby attaining total mastery of his field, it seemed impossible for him to give due justice to his talent for intuitive evidence. He could never *finish* anything; the final product always fell through the crack between these two tendencies. Someone who had a grudge against Andreas once said quite accurately: "In the Orient you would have considered your husband a *wise man.*" But he didn't picture himself in a tent beneath the southern sun, conveying wisdom to young disciples. Instead he thought of himself solely as an explorer on scientific expeditions, following the paths of Occidental learning, with his eye firmly fixed on a strictly scientific goal. The two sides of his nature were not inclined to be reconciled. Each made the sort of total demands characteristic of his strong temperament. Even later, after his difficult years, this situation remained unchanged. After Andreas had received the chair in Göttingen for Persian and West Asiatic Languages,* he still failed to publish the results of his research. They remained working notes, still *in progress* so to speak. Strictly speaking, such results are never really finished, even in their published form. They can always be enlarged upon and improved, made even more convincing in terms of broader and more profound analysis—if one wanted to devote one's whole life to the undertaking. The combination of ultimate thoroughness and the gift of intuitive insight into overall relationships which was Andreas's greatest strength in scholarly research could never be officially evaluated, since he could never bring himself to publish something merely for *practical* reasons. Thus the most valuable part of his intuitive vision remained internal, a personal experience, although each minute detail of his work, each small point of his argument, pointed toward a whole, and indeed illuminated that whole.

There was *one* area, however, in which these two opposing methods of understanding were effectively combined: this strange mixture of the visionary and the academic found a sure response in those with similar scholarly inclinations—in students who were ready to work. Those students absorbed his meta-scholarly vision in the very process of their academic training. The fact that Andreas had to spend fifteen of the best years of his life without worthy students (giving language lessons to Turks in Berlin instead, for example) was almost a crime. Only in Göttingen did he experience the pleasure of developing a following among the most gifted of those who attended his lectures—a following unlike that accorded to a mere teacher, or even a teacher who was also a friend. His students were the field in which he sowed the wealth of his knowledge—with a precision and thoroughness which were his alone. A colleague of his, who had known him since his youth, said to me after my husband's death: "Once anyone attended his lectures, he had them in his hands—they were true to him forever! But how truly he devoted himself to them as well!"

Andreas's former students almost effaced his death for me. I don't mean by their mourning, nor their condolences, nor their regrets—they restored his image to me with such living force that he seemed only now fully real. One of his favorite students told me how, after having returned from years of military service, he felt out of touch with academic life, since he no longer felt impelled toward scholarly studies, and he could no longer recall the substance or methods of scholarship. "Attempting to rebuild this inner world by study seemed to me hopeless; but I only had to remind myself how it had been with Andreas . . . the first time and afterwards . . . , how he looked as he spoke, how his words flooded over me, threatening to drown me in their fullness, so that I thought I would never be able to comprehend it all, although the best teacher I'd had up to then had told me: 'Now you're far enough along that you can work with Andreas.' And as I remembered this, I found again what I'd been seeking, something which was far more than mere book knowledge, something which couldn't even be taken down in notes, since Andreas always was searching in new directions, discovering new territory with his students. This living experience was still whole within me, and carried me forward into the future."

His students synthesized the personal and the scholarly elements which remained at odds within him: what seemed self-evident *and* what required infinitely detailed scientific proof. The overall impression he made upon students was summed up by one of them as the most "magisterial" he had ever experienced; Andreas was utterly immune to external attacks, secure in the knowledge of his expertise, and in his lack of all ambition or desire for public fame, his inner freedom.

The way in which Andreas taught his course (not at the university, but at home, in his study) also allowed his purely personal side to find expression. The students would gather in the evening, at the edge of night, so to speak, and were in no hurry to leave, just as Andreas himself, who never went to bed before four in the morning, made no real distinction between day and night. The spirits thus engaged were fortified either with tea—which he made himself with Oriental care—and cakes, or with wine and cold cuts, according to the nature and theme of the subject at hand.

Whatever happened to his students happened to him. During his early years in Göttingen he managed—with great effort—to find financial support for one of his students to join an expedition to Persia. I don't think I ever saw a look of such radiant joy on any face as I did on his the day he came home and told me about it. Only in *that* moment were the sufferings he had endured as a result of his own unfortunate expedition finally wiped from his mind.

And yet in spite of the profound satisfaction he gained from such scholarly community, his dual nature persisted at the deepest level of his being. It remained *latent*, like a potential tragic flaw—although only indirect hints of it appeared now and again; as when one of his students began working on his own—a student he had chosen, supported, and loved precisely because he was so talented and productive. This student proved to be much better at conforming to the *practical* needs of his profession than Andreas ever had. Andreas instinctively transferred to his student's work his *own* uncertainty about whether a topic had been adequately treated, whether it *should* actually be published: an uncertainty as to whether the endlesss ramifications of the subject they had studied together had been covered completely, or if instead true understanding had been sacrificed to the pressures of time and in the interests of personal ambition. But who can say whether this distrust was not essential for Andreas—almost a hygienic necessity—in order not to begin to distrust the tension between his own two inner methods of working: a spontaneous and self-evident awareness—*and* a strictly scientific approach to inherently infinite material which could never be definitively covered. His great fear was always that of a dilettantism which assumes that it comprehends the whole only because it is ignorant of the details. In his latent hostility toward his favorite students, this fear intersected with the opposite fear of not having fully conveyed to them the wealth of his own knowledge before the sorrow of being parted from them. That did not lessen his devotion to them, it deepened it profoundly and painfully. Once, in our younger years, Gerhart Hauptmann expressed my husband's capacity for love perfectly: "how fierce and how gentle."

One cannot ignore the dangerous side of this tension within Andreas. At times it could overburden him, make demands upon his strength which resulted in an inner restlessness. Because he could not look back upon finished and completed work, his weeks seemed to lack Sundays, and as a result this hale and hearty man could suddenly look harried and exhausted. It reached the point where I didn't share things with him which might have distracted him, even though he would have found them interesting (and what didn't interest his lively mind!). This situation also led to his perplexity with regard to simple professional duties which were tied to deadlines and required a constant if superficial attention. In such cases he tended to give Caesar more than his due, but it was such a strain that he never performed such duties quite adequately. And struggles with this sort of detail affected him so directly that it could seem like a blow of fate. Throughout his life he was pained by what he had failed to accomplish in his younger years, and the wrongs he suffered in his German homeland as a result. I remember asking him once, on behalf of someone who wished him well, whether he would provide a biographical sketch for an encyclopedia. My husband was standing at the time, pouring himself a cup of tea. He didn't answer, but his tanned face turned white, and his eyes bored threateningly into the opposite wall, as if the poor fellow asking the question were standing there, already a doomed man. He set the teapot down quickly, because his hands were trembling. The banal reason for setting the pot down was obvious. But I had the impression that he wanted to free his hands.

But these are minor matters compared with what we usually call letting oneself go, or lack of self-control: he was equally capable of that on occasion, in an equally extreme fashion. He was generally prey to such outbreaks when his whole nervous system was on edge for some reason, and something would happen, perhaps not even touching directly upon him, which would serve as a welcome pretext for the release of such feelings in the midst of the quiet order of things. One was almost more shocked by his reaction, perhaps unfairly, than one was by what had caused it.

A small episode from the early years of our marriage seemed to me characteristic: we had purchased a huge Newfoundland as a watchdog, and one summer night my husband slipped through the garden into the hall to see whether the dog would sense it was his master or think he was a burglar, since he was naked, an unfamiliar state as far as the dog was concerned. Andreas, however, moving with stealth and care, his face a study in concentration, so resembled a stalking predator that—it's hard to put it into words—they were as alike as two mysteries. He became so wrapped up in the inner drama of the animal, in the question of "for" or "against," that he apparently wasn't playing anymore, but seemed to have surrendered to his own twofold wish: for indeed he always wanted new companions to both love and protect him. The dog, in a state of extreme tension, came out of the whole affair with flying colors by reacting to both needs: he *growled* threateningly, but *backed up.* My husband, pleased as could be, laughed aloud, whereupon the dog leaped up to his shoulders and received a joyful hug.

Many people admired his reserve, his restrained manner, a slightly closed impression, in spite or because of his inner interest in others. For example when his close friend Franz Stolze,* who accompanied him on the expedition to Persia, talked about the years they'd spent together, as one does when the subject is so interesting, Andreas generally remained taciturn. One sensed that he thought of them as intimate memories, rather than of general interest, as if even a superficial discussion were something of an indiscretion. And not only the aspects which had caused him suffering, but the good times as well, which stirred him too deeply. But then there were times when he would reveal parts of that experience, like jewels, to his friends and students: the evenings with the viceroy, about his servant, his horse, his fox terrier, which he was sad to have to leave behind, and his chameleon. Here's how one friend recalled such evenings: "When, toward morning, I became too tired for any further real work, but had not yet been granted permission to leave, the conversation would go on. Once he read to me the quatrains of Omar Khayam* in Rosen's translation; it wasn't like being *told* about Persia, it was like a scene beneath the Persian sky. Oriental wisdom flowed from the verses, they spoke of love and wine, and were imbued with joyful spirituality and their own special tenderness." Or: "In addition to our ongoing sessions, in which no subject was ever presented as fixed and unchanging, everything, even the apparently formal rules of grammar, became a living part of the Orient. Behind the rational scientific conclusions one still felt the flow of life upon which they were based—an unspoken, pulsating life, which made each word and all the accompanying rules of pronunciation and declension a part of the real world."

It seems to me that the "full reality" of the spiritual in those from the *East* has remained more directly visible than it has in the case of the *Westerner*, for whom "idea," "ideal," and "ideological" still refer to something above or below the human level (except for the Goethean love of the Orient and of Nature,* which is *Both* at the same time"). The spiritual is given a form of expression which is *physical*, and the sensuous gains a meaning beyond itself. This explains certain things about Andreas's special nature, in which the "spiritual" and the "physical" were indissolubly united. His students know how often he answered questions of hygiene in detail before or after the course, as if they were a part of the subject matter. And although he was totally careless about his own health or appearance, his physical state—his unblemished body, bathed and anointed with an Oriental seriousness— commanded a respect equal to any other aspect of his person. One might say in jest that if his body did not actually *manifest* the intellectual realm, it was irrefutably at home there, its presence assured in a mysteriously existential and spontaneous manner. I'm always reminded of a little poem by Matthias Claudius (which my husband knew, perhaps from his childhood in Hamburg), which he never quoted without an overtone of sly joy which seemed to stem from *his* own self-certainty and self-presence, which neither the one-sidedness of love's darkness nor of intellect's brightness could undermine:

Seest thou the moon above?
We see but half of it
And yet it's round and beautiful—

The line between youth and age was also less clearly drawn in Andreas's case than one would normally expect; they were less separate and sequential. I hardly know whether he was more self-possessed or more impetuous when I first knew him; for if he was *completely present,* it was through a presence which had a timeless aspect—which included a yet invisible part of a whole which was "round and beautiful." I imagine it was this which some people, including those who barely knew him, referred to as his "charm." In spite of the inner tension from which he suffered, he exuded a sense of undeniable presence, up to the end of his life at age eighty-five, as he passed into timelessness without a thought for death or approaching dread, like a preoccupied child. When he was very old I sometimes thought that even if he hadn't led the life he did, with such natural devotion to extraordinary things, but instead had been a monster, a criminal, a glutton, yet still remained so full of life after so many years, with such a good and joyous heart, so capable of both anger and tenderness—truly, he would be vindicated, and pleasing in the eyes of men.

What I say of him here can do little more than touch upon the memories of those whose goodwill already surrounds him; I realize this as soon as I look about the rooms in which he lived, where even the most ordinary events speak eloquently of him, make visible his form.

Or I look out the window toward the orchard, and see him walking at day's end. It's early twilight on a summer evening; soon he will lie down to rest. His mind will still be wrestling with the problems he's been working on so tenaciously and joyfully, oblivious to everything around him. But what one could actually see was quite different: walking with an animal's caution, he awakened the blackbirds with a few notes in imitation of their song. They replied softly, falling into sweet conversation; as did the rooster in the henhouse, who having fallen fast asleep, was awakened by his call, and seized by ambition, tried to outcrow the stranger.

The imitator of blackbirds and roosters did so with a facility and understanding that matched his abilities at the desk as a student of languages: in that moment the experience was as important to him, and as revealing, as one offered by a gathering of his peers.

WHAT'S MISSING
FROM THE SKETCH
(1933)

THE ELEMENTAL AND intimate* do not declare them-
selves openly. As a result, what is truly essential remains unsaid. If it
is not expressed in positive terms, however, it may still be avowed in the
negative: its boundaries may be sketched by means of its gaps and omissions,
its empty spaces determine its outline.

What I wish to speak about happened suddenly, in a very personal hour,
in the midst of a journey. It arose from a misunderstanding between me and
the friend of my youth, Paul Rée; as if an obstacle were thrown beneath a car
traveling along at full speed, wrecking it.

There had been ample external obstacles, but we had undertaken our
journey in a state of carefree contentment; wherever it led, it would be our
very own path.

The misunderstanding arose from the fact that I took a step on another
person's path, without being able to tell the full truth about this step to my
friend,* for the sake of the other person.

Paul Rée, who found nothing harder to believe than that someone might
love him, saw this step as proof of a separation which had already taken
place internally and drew his own consequences, eventually even including
hate.

He did not suspect that I never needed him, before or after, as badly as I
did at that hour, never needed his friendship as much. For the compulsion
under which I took the step I could never take back separated me not from
him, but from myself.

Only someone who knew my husband intimately and fully, who loved
him intimately and fully in character and nature, can know what the word
"compulsion" meant in this case.

What brought about this compulsion was the power of something irresistible to which my husband himself succumbed. Irresistible because it did not begin by manifesting itself with the force of an instinctual desire, but simply appeared as an unchangeable *fact*. So too its full expression did not take the form of persuasion, but instead incorporated itself in the figure of my husband, in his entire physical presence. There's no point in trying to describe this to anyone who didn't know my husband; it's something I never saw in any other human being. It is almost a matter of indifference whether one compares it with colossal, powerful forces, with the unrestrained actions of huge animals, or to the effects of the most delicate, helpless creatures, like a little bird one cannot bear to step upon, whose trusting reality no one dares deny.

It is revealing, however, that these imprecise comparisons are instinctively drawn from the realm of creatures.* One realizes the limited nature of all human measure.

In my case the impression was not influenced by any state of feeling at the time which might have overcome my willpower, as for example a strong erotic attraction; it was, on the contrary, clearly of a different order. For my reaction was not that of a *woman*: I remained as *neutral* in this respect as I had toward the companion of my youth.

But in that case the reason lay in something which, no matter how subtly it manifests itself, cannot fail to differentiate the feeling of even the deepest friendship from that of love: because the senses are aware, more faintly or more strongly, of a *physical* alienation. That was not the case here, neither in the beginning, nor in the course of the coming decades.

There are other inhibitions which might have had an effect: inhibitions familiar to so many women, which are nowhere more clearly delineated and analyzed than in the discoveries of psychoanalysis. However, the experiences of my later youth show that this too was not the case.

At first my husband thought, as anyone in his place might, that these were "girlish ideas, which in time would pass." And by time, he meant the whole of life—yes more than that: for it even excluded death, which my husband simply didn't consider in the robustness of his being.

This *challenge of the totality* of life concerned me far more that the particular question at hand, which I myself couldn't really answer. I was still filled with sadness at the departure of my companion, whose acceptance into our bond had been made a condition of the marriage—one which my husband had finally decided to accept, not even deterred by this in his determination.

When one considers how much older and more experienced he was than I, and how much more naive and childish I was than other young women my age, his faith and his unshakable certainty apppear almost monstrous.

However neither of us knew me very well, or much about my real "nature"—or whatever we call that part of us which dictates our actions without our prior knowledge. Whatever girlhood views I had, or whatever beliefs I might have harbored after serious and thorough consideration, had no *basic* effect upon my decisions. I would like to illustrate this difficult point with an example from a totally different area, one which I've already discussed in my earlier "memoirs": my departure from the Church. It was not an act of defiance, nor one of fanatical adherence to truth. I struggled rationally against the impulse, which was causing my parents pain and would result in public scandal; I even considered myself guilty, in an almost moral sense, of overexcitability in the whole matter. But in fact it was not I who made the decision, but a nightly dream, in which I heard myself cry out loudly "No!" during the confirmation ceremony. Not that I feared, upon waking, that I would actually do so in the end; instead it was a matter of finally realizing how totally impossible it would be to force myself to do what was asked of me, even for form's sake.

What we consider to be our motivations or judgments, no matter how carefully we work at weaving the web of their relationships, prove in certain circumstances to be as insignificant to us as the gossamer strands between two branches, which are blown away by the slightest breeze.

One's life can be changed by that sudden realization.

It rose suddenly before us, although the moment passed in silence. We never brought ourselves to talk to one another about it.

One afternoon my husband stretched out beside me on the sofa, where I was lying sound asleep.

Perhaps on an impulse he had decided to catch me by surprise, to conquer me. At any rate I didn't wake up right away. What seemed to first wake me was a sound; a weak sound, but one of such strange vehemence that it swept through me as if it came from an infinite distance, from some other star.

It was accompanied by the sensation that I didn't have my arms beside me, but somewhere above me. Then my eyes opened: my arms were near a throat. My hands were encircling the throat, and choking it. The sound was a rattle.

What I saw, eye to eye, close before me, unforgettable throughout my life—was a face—

* * *

Later it often occurred to me that on the evening before our engagement, I could have taken on the deceptive appearance of a murderer.

My husband carried a short, heavy, pocketknife on his evening walks home to his apartment, which was some distance away. It was lying on the table where we were sitting. He picked it up calmly and stabbed himself in the chest with it.

As I rushed down the street, half out of my mind, searching from house to house for the nearest doctor, those who were hurrying along with me asked what had happened. I told them someone had fallen on his knife. While the doctor examined the unconscious man on the floor, a few words along with his look made clear his suspicion about who might have been wielding the knife. He remained in doubt, but treated me discreetly and kindly afterward.

The knife had slipped in his hand and the blade had partially closed, so that the heart had been spared. At the same time a triangular-shaped wound had been inflicted, which made the healing process slow and difficult.

That wasn't the only time we stood at death's door, finished with life, having set our family affairs in order. We were both filled with the same perplexity and despair.

Of course these were hours, moments, far different from the rest of our experience. We were bound by so many common inclinations and interests. In general—it seems to me—the value of this is overestimated. Of course it builds bridges, gives pleasure, and leads to shared work, but just as often it simply glosses over personal differences and disparities, rather than allowing people see one another clearly and thus to draw together even more profoundly.

My husband's areas of academic expertise were totally beyond my knowledge and comprehension. But even had I been as close to him in this regard as one of his favorite students from the later period, and talented in that direction, it would only have displaced my activities into peripheral areas and deceived us until the next irresistible hour of our separation. But external circumstances also kept us occupied. My husband's position in the Institute of Oriental Studies in Berlin offered him absorbing and interesting work. Since this professorship was intended primarily to train diplomats or industrialists with their eye on Asia, it was of course inevitable that it required only a portion of his scholarly abilities. His colleague and friend Rosen, who left the institute to join the diplomatic service, becoming an ambassador and later foreign minister, said with a smile that it was too bad my husband's position only called for him to offer milk, and forced him to hold back on the rich cream.

But in fact the situation was quite different: my husband attempted to skim the cream from the milk! Or to put it another way: by including in his purely scientific studies that which would flow back into life and strengthen it, by means of the study of tribes and dialects, he offered a concentrated form of milk which was never merely academic.

He had the good fortune to find a few suitable students, among them Solf, who was devoted to him throughout his life.* The position itself, however, was spoiled and became impossible for him, precisely because he was only allowed to offer—milk.

All of this was part of his basic nature, as natural as breathing itself, rather than the result of some external tension or avoidable misfortune. And yet it included the elements of a disastrous fate. It was as if what drove him most strongly must inevitably founder upon the perfection it demanded. As if what was vital to him in life was pushed into the realm of the impossible by the limitless nature of each single realization. As if "absolute" and "relative" were so intertwined that they mutually canceled out any given result.

Perhaps it was something of this sort which lent such direct and suggestive power to the expression of his nature and will. Perhaps a part of this hidden tragedy was expressed in his forcefulness, his ability to compel—like a subjugation by that which was most real, and never to be realized.

So I fitted easily into the life which seemed necessary for him to achieve his goals. I was also prepared to leave Europe, when it at first appeared that we were going to Persian Armenia in the monastery region of Echmiadzin. Our external life-style too was determined more and more by my husband: like him, I strove for simplicity in food and clothing, and for a radical relationship to air. In spite of my northern upbringing and habits, I dedicated myself willingly to such changes and remained true to them throughout my life. And there was one area in which we were quickly in agreement, which opened the same doors to both of us: the *world of animals*. This world of the not-yet-human, which so profoundly reminds us of what lies beneath our own humanity, of a simpler and less complicated life no longer in our reach. Our attitude toward individual *animals* was as similar as our attitude toward individual *people* was usually different.

In contrast to my husband's single-minded and fierce devotion to his work, my readiness to adapt was furthered by my lack of aims and ambition. I couldn't even have said what I considered essential and necessary in life, perhaps for the very reason that it was not required for my daily cares and needs. It almost seemed to me as if anything one touched *correctly* would lead one to the center of things. In addition, I was secretly resigned to the fact that—no matter what I did—I had literally nothing more to lose. The difference between my varying behavior now, and that of my earlier youth—not just toward my companion in those days, but toward all the companions around us—consisted in the fact that *then* the question of whether or how far one might wander along a path with another person remained a relatively harmless one, which could be answered in spirit, while *now* such a question never even arose—in the face of the indissoluble responsibility I had assumed.

On the other hand this situation granted me total autonomy to develop my own intellect and spirit. This task took on a life of its own, became an affair of earnest and longed-for solitude. It did not actually concern our life together and its problematic aspects for me. There was practically none of what people refer to as give and take in our relationship. So the years, four decades in all, brought with them no blending—but also no reduction of that which developed separately in each of us. Even long after we were elderly people, I so seldom came to my husband with anything which concerned me deeply on a daily basis, that I might as well have been coming from Japan or Australia—and when I did, it was like visiting a strange and distant part of the world I'd never set foot on before.

One can hardly make such a situation comprehensible to someone else, and yet it would be a mistake to think of it solely in terms of *distance*, a distance which indeed increased over time. A scene from the last year of my husband's life may clarify this. During the late autumn of that year I spent almost six weeks in the hospital with an illness, and since I made it a habit to continue my psychoanalytical sessions from four p.m. on each day, my husband received permission to visit me at three: the official visiting period was thus limited. Sitting across from one another like that was something completely new to us. We had never experienced the standard family evenings "by the cosy glow of the lamp," nor did we disturb one another when we took a quick walk, so the present situation was highly unusual, and we were delighted by it. It was a matter of cheating the minutes, of stretching time as the daily bread by which one lived was stretched during the war. Each time we saw one another again it was like a reunion of two people who had returned home from a great distance. We felt this, and a calm serenity descended upon the richness of those hours. When I finally returned home, the "visiting hours" simply continued, and not just between the hours of three and four.

✳   ✳   ✳

Among those in the literary and political circle which formed shortly after our marriage, we met a man whom both of us found striking and likable. * The first time we met I missed his name, as often happens, nor did he hear mine. The next time we were introduced I noticed that he was examining my hands very closely, and I was just about to ask him what he was staring at, when he asked roughly: "Why aren't you wearing a wedding ring?" I laughed and told him that we had forgotten to buy rings, and now we'd decided just to leave it that way. But his tone didn't change. He almost hectored me: "But you have to!" Just at that moment someone asked him teasingly how he had liked the "summer breezes on Plotzen Lake," where he had just finished serving time for lèse-majesté. I couldn't help but find it funny that I had been scolded about social mores by this same person, but he remained in a bad mood, while up to then he had been talking quite animatedly.

Later we quickly became friends, and after a few weeks, on the way home from a meeting we had attended, he declared his love, and added, as if to excuse himself, something which left me at a loss: "You're not a woman: you're a girl."

The shock of this inconceivable knowledge so overwhelmed me that neither at the moment, nor later, could I be sure of my own attitude toward this man. It's not impossible that I had similar feelings about him; yet to the extent that such feelings were developing, even subconsciously, they were held back by a second, equally strong shock, perhaps even stronger than that experienced by the most virtuous married woman who unexpectedly finds herself beginning to fall in love. For how weak the bonds of sacrament or society seem in comparison with the *indissoluble* bond created by my husband's character and nature, which would not admit of the slightest loosening.

I was soon subjected to *this* shock as well, which we had worked our way through even before we were engaged, when we took our "eternal vow." The excitable state of my husband, who wasn't blind, and yet preferred blindness, insofar as he would rather simply stab the other person to death rather than talk things over with him, was the determining factor. And this led to an involuntary feeling far different from that of love toward this man on my part: namely the frightened desire to flee, before which I was helpless, which transformed our days and nights into painful torture. My friend's efforts to help me during the increasingly rare hours we spent together, in willing friendship, and with a refinement of sentiment which enshrines him forever in my memory, meant salvation from an almost unbearable loneliness. But things didn't stop there: the fears and concerns he had for me intensified his own emotional state immeasurably, torturing and pressuring me a second time, when I had already been rubbed raw.

I learned twenty years later that the strength of his hate matched that of my husband's. Deeply worried about the effect of political oppression on my relatives in Russia, I sent him a brief, sealed note, in which I asked for his help and advice. He recognized my handwriting on the envelope, which bore his name and "Member of Parliament." The note came back marked "refused."

The end of it all was that I gave in to my husband's demand never to see my friend again.

The actual meaning of this experience for our marriage soon became clear: it was not humanly possible to go on as we had in the past. There still could be no talk of divorce. It was typical of my husband's way of thinking that this was not based on any future hopes, nor in the expectation that something had gone wrong in the past which might now be corrected. He was simply fixated on the idea that our relationship was a given, incontrovertibly *real*, in spite of all that had happened. I'll always remember the moment at which he said: "I can't stop *knowing* that you're my wife."

After painful months together, interrupted by periods of separation to escape our mutual solitude, a new arrangement was settled upon. Nothing would change externally: inwardly everything would. In the years to come I traveled a good deal.

Once, at a moment in which I was deeply moved, I asked my husband: "Can I tell you what's happened to me since then—"

Quickly, without allowing me to draw a breath to say another word, he replied: "No."

Thus a deep and inviolable silence arched above us and what we shared, a silence from which we never emerged.

In spite of my husband's peculiar character, his reply must have had something typically masculine about it, no matter how varied the circumstances may be in which such utterances are made. Years later a friend gave me a similar answer. I hadn't seen him for a long time, for perfectly innocent reasons, and since he seemed to misunderstand the situation, I offered to explain it to him. After a moment's silent thought, he replied firmly: "No. I don't want to know."

Since we tended not to socialize, we didn't know how people felt about us. Perhaps, given the way the world is, people thought that my husband was unfaithful to me, or I to him. Who would have guessed that at this period of my life I would have happily bestowed a wife, or the best, most loving, most beautiful mistress, upon my husband, in a true Christmas spirit? Our mutual silence would have concealed anything that might have happened, and I never ceased wishing that for him.

As for me, the previous storms and struggles which had so brutally checked my growing longing may have actually played a role in the fact that when love did come, it came to me quite quietly and naturally.*

Not only without feelings of guilt or rebellion, but as something blessed, which would make the world perfect and whole: not just a world perfect for oneself, but a world perfect in itself. Like deeds which occur with the eternal approval of something far higher than our own opinions, which we simply receive passively.

Therefore one shouldn't even attempt to compare and measure the *greatness* and *permanence* of true passions: whether they last a lifetime and are incorporated into all practical matters, or whether they may be repeated. One can feel such passion as a splendor beyond all understanding and still be aware, in all modesty, of one's own inadequacy, because in such cases the individual traits of love can be more clearly distinguished and judged, both objectively and subjectively. But we know so little about the mystery of *all* love, precisely because we are necessarily limited to the purely personal— because we understand it only in those terms. The entire area of the all-too-human, as well as that superhuman realm we so passionately seek, is entangled in the evaluations and judgments of something no human heart has ever fully revealed to the human mind.

Thus nothing remains for the mind to exercise itself upon except the most mysterious of *physical* consummations, which are merely exposed thereby to banalization. Isn't this similar to the bread and wine of the sacrament, which prudently becomes the food and drink of the body, in order to *exist*?

For us, a human being in love, regardless of the exalted state of both his spirit and his soul, remains a priest in his robes who has but a dim idea of what it is he's celebrating.

My husband's professorship in Göttingen came late, but he remained active for over twenty-five years, since even his retirement didn't markedly change things. The main body of his students, and colleagues from other countries who worked with him, remained at his side. Once he was nearly offered a professorship in Berlin, but it failed to materialize because an essay he was working on would have had to have been readied for publication more quickly than my husband thought was proper. The entire affair of the automatic pressure one was under to publish added a degree of annoyance to the pleasure of his work. He also fell prey to the natural tendency to blame some external hindrance or other whenever he missed a deadline. One result among others was an intense and almost infinite hatred for the owner of the tavern across the street from us, from which the sounds of a gramophone drifted (if only faintly) in our direction. I often thought of the humorously intended words of his oldest friend and colleague, Professor Hoffmann in Kiel, who visited us shortly after our marriage: "Perhaps if Andreas were threatened with torture, we might be able to get a publication out of him— and perhaps not even then: writing itself is such a torture for him." For the only way to complete an essay is to give up on the full and perfect expression of that which permeates one's life to the very core.

In this regard, I can't help thinking about the impression the German war effort made upon him, all patriotic passion aside: the impression of simultaneous ecstasy and exactitude, of being lifted by the transporting power of emotion and of unparalleled thoroughness in execution, never overlooking the smallest detail. His admiration sharpened the sense of his own personal problem. He was at a loss to see how the two tendencies could reinforce one another instead of getting in each other's way.

But in his case it was an unresolvable tension, embedded in his very nature, an arena in which the two quite different worlds into which he was born faced each other. And the most bitter thing of all for him—insofar as he could have done it—would have been to artificially resolve the apparent tension by sacrificing one for the other. Nothing would have devastated him more than to have to pretend, for the sake of some short-term goal or success, that he had indeed truly completed an essay which still cried out in him for a broad and timeless total permutation of its relationships.

Although the drawbacks of this attitude are clear, one should not overlook the fact that it infused him with a wondrously youthful quality, which he never lost. Whatever was at work within him always had something of the future about it; not just of a future which was both blessed and condemned to occur, but one from which all sense of mere time had disappeared. If that caused him to be, by turns, uncertain, restless, exhausted, relaxed and idle, it also rejuvenated the innermost expression of his being with a power almost unknown to me. Even when he was quite old, the effect was not lessened by the fact that his shoulders stooped, or that he didn't hear so well, just as his white hair made him more impressive, and his dark eyes seemed even more penetrating, in spite of the blue irises of old age, as if now they needed more than just the black to shine.

I remember his seventieth birthday in great detail. He was not prepared for the official celebration offered by his colleagues and friends, since the confusion of the times had prevented such occasions on his sixtieth and sixty-fifth birthdays. The party actually got him out of bed, since he had been up almost till dawn, but with what inner presence he stood among them then. In a spontaneous response to their congratulations and their open reverence—including a gentle reminder from the current chancellor of the university that they still expected him to give them what only he could give—in response to all that he developed with passion and conviction an overview of what he felt still remained to be accomplished in scholarship in general. He foresaw in the coming decades the beginnings of a cooperative approach in the philological disciplines, following the example of the natural sciences, and one could tell that he was personally witnessing this, guaranteeing it, as something which would inevitably occur over the course of time. People smiled meaningfully at one another here and there, others had tears in their eyes. And surely neither he nor anyone else was thinking of the expectations they had had of him, expectations which remained unfulfilled—and which in a higher sense, perhaps, could never have been fulfilled.

I was always aware of his inner state, but it never became a topic of conversation between us. I can think of only two occasions over the years when we even touched upon it. This habit of not facing each other directly, turning aside so to speak, remained peculiar to us; nor did other aspects of our relationship to one another alter or develop over time. The basis of our relationship remained simple and unchanged. Added to this was the fact that my own activities were private in nature, insofar as what stirred me in witnessing the lives and actions of others was not something suitable for repetition, and moreover any major distractions could easily hurt my husband. The total freedom we each had to be ourselves was also something we both experienced internally as something *shared*. One could perhaps call it a simple respect for one another, in which we concurred, something which gave us a feeling of security and possession. For no matter how busy he was, my husband always had a wonderful sense of one thing: whether and to what extent the other person was happy and at peace. One proof of this made a deep impression upon me. I had started to write a story, something that was out of character for me by then, since I'd completely given up the habit of writing once I started working with psychoanalysis—and the overload of the two types of concentration had totally absorbed me. When I was finished, I laughed and said, with a somewhat guilty conscience, that I must have been very hard to be around, and quite worthless, during all that time. To which my husband replied almost in jubilation, with a shining face I'll never forget: "You've been so happy!"

There was more than simple goodness in the joy he felt, no matter how strong a role that played as well. The ability to *share in another person's joy*, the most striking feature of his nature, always meant understanding the other person as someone like him: an understanding of the essential primal ground they shared. That's what lent him the powerful, convincing expression he achieved: the expression of a *reality* which he saw. And even today, in spite of the fact of death, to which he never paid any attention, with which he had nothing to do, this expression is carried on in me: every time I come to the deepest part of myself, it's as if I confront this shared joy. Would he not perhaps have said—because, in spite of everything, he was right about the two of us?

Was I overpowered by what he said back then because it arose from an ultimate truth?

I don't know. I'm sorry, forgive me: I don't know. But such joyous moments seemed to know for me.

So I experienced my memories of you not merely as something past, but as something which at the same time was walking toward me. It was not a funeral rite, it turned into a lesson of life.

BIBLIOGRAPHICAL NOTE

The books of Lou Andreas-Salomé appear in the order in which they were written:

Im Kampf um Gott by "Henri Lou" (Novel), Leipzig-Berlin: W. Friedrich, 1885.

Henrik Ibsens Frauengestalten (Literary criticism), Jena: Eugen Diedrichs, 1892.

Friedrich Nietzsche in seinen Werken (Philosophical criticism), Vienna: Carl Conegen, 1894.

Ruth (Short story), Stuttgart: Cotta, 1896.

Aus fremder Seele (Short story), Stuttgart: Cotta, 1896.

Fenitschka. Eine Ausschweifung (Two short stories), Stuttgart: Cotta, 1898.

Menschenkinder (Collection of novellas), Stuttgart-Berlin: Cotta, 1899.

Ma (A portrait), Stuttgart-Berlin: Cotta, 1901.

Im Zwischenland (Five stories of adolescence), Stuttgart-Berlin: Cotta, 1902.

Die Erotik (Monograph), Frankfurt a.M.: Rütten & Loening, 1910.

Drei Briefe an einen Knaben (Three letters to a boy), Leipzig: Kurt Wolff, 1917.

Das Haus (A Family Story), Berlin: Ullstein, 1919.

Die Stunde ohne Gott (Children's stories), Jena: Eugen Diedrichs, 1922.

Der Teufel und seine Großmutter (Dream play), Jena: Eugen Diedrichs, 1922.

Ródinka (A Russian memoir), Jena: Eugen Diedrichs, 1923.

Rainer Maria Rilke (Memorial volume), Leipzig: Insel-Verlag, 1928.

Mein Dank an Freud (Open letter), Vienna: Internationaler Psychoanalytischer Verlag, 1931.

UNPUBLISHED:

"Der Stiefvater" (Play in three acts).

"Die Tarnkappe" (Play).

"Jutta" (Short story).

PUBLICATIONS FROM THE LITERARY ESTATE:

Lebensrückblick (Looking Back), Zurich: Max Niehans, and Wiesbaden: Insel-Verlag, 1951.

Rainer Maria Rilke/Lou Andreas-Salomé (Correspondence), Zurich: Max Niehans, and Wiesbaden: Insel-Verlag, 1952.

In der Schule bei Freud (A year's diary), Zurich: Max Niehans, 1958, Hans Huber Verlag, Bern, 1968, and paperback edition with Kindler Verlag, Munich.

Sigmund Freud/Lou Andreas-Salomé (Correspondence), Frankfurt a. M.: S. Fischer, 1966.

Friedrich Nietzsche, Paul Rée, Lou von Salomé (The documentation of their encounters), Frankfurt a. M., Insel-Verlag: 1970.

ABOUT LOU ANDREAS-SALOMÉ:

Elisabeth Heimpel: "Lou A.-S." In: *Neue deutsche Biographie*, Vol. I, 1953.

Gertrud Bäumer: "Lou A.-S." In: *Gestalt und Wandel*, Women's portraits, 1939.

Hans Jürgen Bab: *Lou A.-S* (Literature and personality), Berlin dissertation, 1955.

H. F. Peters: *Lou: The Life of Lou Andreas-Salomé* (see Afterword).

Rudolph Binion: *Frau Lou: Nietzsche's Wayward Disciple*. Princeton: N.J., 1968.

Ernst Pfeiffer: "Lou A.-S." In: *Handbuch der deutschen Gegenwartsliteratur*, Munich, 1965.

Also see the Notes and Afterwords in the first five books listed from the literary estate, all edited by E. Pfeiffer.

The photographs in this book are all from the literary estate of Lou Andreas-Salomé. The picture of the older Lou was taken by the editor toward the end of 1934.

AFTERWORD

LOU ANDREAS-SALOMÉ wrote the "Sketch" (Grundriβ), as she liked to refer to her memoirs in conversation, while she was in her early seventies, in 1931 and 1932. Several sections were later rewritten. As a "Vorwort" (preface) to these ten chapters she offered the following note: "A Sketch of a few memories from my life—omitting several which insist upon their right to solitude." What she meant by this is at least partially evident in "What's Missing From the Sketch," written a year later, in 1933. Only partially, however, even though the title implies that everything missing from the Sketch has been included. This epilogue (which Lou A.-S. was unsure about adding to any published version of the Sketch at the time) did expand on the chapter she had written in memory of Friedrich Carl Andreas by its revelations about the enigma of their communal marriage. But it did not enlarge in similar fashion on the chapter "With Rainer" which, although delving more deeply into biography than the memorial volume for Rilke of 1928 (and reinforcing its perceptions), did not shed any additional light on the personal nature of their relationship. Only in the following year, 1934, was "April was *our* month, Rainer—" set to paper, which, although not expressly intended as part of the Sketch, nonetheless ends the "solitude" of this most personal memory, revealing the full nature of her experience with Rilke. Here one should understand "experience" in the broad sense Lou Andreas-Salomé intended for it in her chapter headings.

If one understands the word "experience" as referring simply to what an individual experiences or even to mere egocentric sensation, the sense of the word in *Looking Back* is almost the exact opposite. Here the ego is simply the unavoidable perceiver of something "fundamental" which is of far greater dimensions, which constitutes life and yet excedes it. The portrayal of the *first* "experience," that of God, makes abundantly clear that what is here called experience can be assimilated and fully comprehended only over the course of a lifetime.

Not until old age did a retrospective view provide her full insight—not only in terms of distance and breadth but also in an increasingly profound relationship to what was fundamental about life. And only this receptivity allowed "experience" after "experience" to emerge—and empowered her to report on her life as a whole. Lou Andreas-Salomé would never have been moved simply to provide an overview of her life, with its wealth of human encounters, emotional experiences, and insights. A special blessing of her advanced years was her ability to analyze experiences as "they descended toward the heart of life." One got the impression in her presence that even the most distant wave of experience, arising from the depths, would finally break upon the shores of her advanced years, reaching her once more, only to ebb away again. Unlike the simple memories of the elderly, everything was as fresh to her as on the day it occurred: it was now a part of a single present moment.

It almost goes without saying that such an "experience of life" is religious in nature—understood in the broadest sense as the experience of being guided by some basic source. The extent to which this influenced her daily life can be illustrated by something Lou Andreas-Salomé said in her later years: "Whatever is going to happen to me, will happen. And I never lose the certainty that arms are open behind me to receive me."

Looking Back is thus not so much a self-conscious effort of reflection as it is the composition of a life which was "telling its own story," and of course desired a discerning consciousness in the listener. A unique autobiographical form was thus created; one which reveals itself fully to the reader only in a retrospective view of the whole, by perceptive cognition, by "seeing through" each individual experience as well as their connection to each other. Even the word "Sketch" in the German subtitle "A Sketch of a Few Memories From My Life," if one understands it as an "outline of what is fundamental about life" tries to convey this sense of "seeing through" the individual event or course of events to the mystery of life itself, as well as the relationship of all such events to what is fundamental. An experience proves itself to be an "experience" in the present sense by the very fact that it can be included in the Sketch. Since they are not simply random, the number of such "experiences" is clearly limited. Such an "outline of what is fundamental" could occur only in a philosophical sense, in which the most personal experiences and the experience of life are one.

Instead of opening with the traditional tender and mysterious images of early childhood, the memoir begins by focusing on the crucial theme of the "God Experience" (a title normally more suited to the final chapter of a life story). But the experience of the divine figure and its disappearance is not a simple childhood memory. Similarly, the "Experience of Love" (which also brings to mind later stages of a life story and some kind of summary of such experience) is something other than just girlish love. The invisible outline of the extinguished image of God, having set an ever-present measure for this life, fashions the young love for Gillot into a "model for love," valid for each and every other such relationship. And this outline, whether in incomplete fragments or as in the guiding light of the stars, may be discerned above each subsequent experience. What has become invisible is reflected in the absolutely unconditional friendship with Paul Rée, as well as in the indissoluble yet limited bond with F. C. Andreas; and also in the consummation of love with Rilke, in that the "real" can *not* be held on to forever. It is also to be found in the "Experience of Russia," which is not just the experience of a homeland. One becomes aware of the mysterious, almost dramatic unfolding of the effect from one "experience" to the next as a hidden law which is more compelling (particularly for the one living through the experience) and more difficult to grasp than "the law that you followed" (Goethe, "Dämon"). Outside the personal realm (Gillot-Rée-Andreas-Rilke) the most distinct reflection can be found where one least expects to find it: in her encounter with depth psychology in "The Freud Experience," which can be fully understood only in terms of her earlier "God-experience": the delighted acceptance of the discoveries and talents of a "rationalist by nature," the acceptance of talents of a distinctly unintellectual nature. It is only there that—to stay with the metaphor—the outline of the invisible that first revealed itself upon the heavens, so to speak, completed its full circle—how else could it have been a divine outline—at the "base," thereby including the darkest earthly kingdom. We must remember that it is a divine outline which has become invisible and faded away that determines and encircles "experience" after "experience." The question is obvious: whether an outline which remained visible, a God believed to have a shape, would have accomplished what it did by vanishing.

In place of, or in conjunction with, such a visual approach to analyzing the unusual nature of *Looking Back*, one can also attempt a direct philosophical interpretation, for it is unmistakably not only a religious but also a philosophical document. And, in both respects, it is an original and exceptional text one must first learn how to read. Such an investigation would, however, be immediately confronted by the unusual fact that Lou Andreas-Salomé utilized the concepts of "experience" and "sketch" in this "raw" form, so to speak, in depicting her life, and that she did not organize her portrayal systematically according to these or any other concepts. She adopted the often-misused word "experience" without hesitation, and she was not in the least bothered by the increasingly limited and diametrically opposed meaning the word gained in the course of her usage. She neither tried to develop nor work with a "concept" of experience. The interested reader, however, will realize that a critique of the concept of experience which focuses, for example, on its "subjectivity," on "possession," or on "mystery" will find no confirmation in what is expressed here. Even more so than in the case of the word "experience," the word "sketch" is used in a nonphilosophical sense, without presuppositions, in spite of the fact that she means it to carry weight. At first, it clearly indicates that certain recollections serve to delineate the fundamental aspects of her life in a way similar to the "floor plan" of a building or the "outline" of an academic discipline. The meaning of the word "sketch" must embed itself deeply enough in the reader of these memoirs for him to understand it as the "outline of a foundation" (Umriβ eines Grundes) and to construct a connection in meaning between the "experience" and the "sketch," retaining the original implications of these two words. Furthermore, they also serve as a warning against limiting the world of Lou A.-S. in terms of *any* concrete, conceptual definitions. For no particular philosophical orientation or hard-and-fast view of life would have allowed Lou Andreas-Salomé to depict her life truthfully, and, at the same time, portray the truth of life itself. At least, not without betraying its mystery, the sense in which it is a gift. This freedom from the constraints of predetermined concepts is also clearly reflected in the differences among the individual "experiences"—differences in form as dictated by the subject matter. These may be roughly characterized as basic "meditation" ("The God Experience"), personal "confession" ("What's Missing From the Sketch"), explanatory "treatise" ("The Freud Experience"), and straight-forward autobiographical "report" ("With Other People").

Two comments need to be made about the text of *Looking Back* as it is presented here. One concerns the length. The total text goes beyond the original "Sketch of a Few Memories of my life," even including "What's Missing From the Sketch," through the addition of "April was *our* month, Rainer—" to the chapter "With Rainer" and by adding "Memories of Freud" to the Freud chapter. Both of these latter additions are taken from handwritten memoirs which are located upon the infinite plains beyond that shore from which Lou A.-S. looked back upon her life. They are distinguished from the conceptual plan of the rest of the memoirs as well by their tone of simple celebration in the face of life. It seemed appropriate to include the memories of Freud because the personal element of the relationship (which was not just about psychoanalysis) was, by the very nature of the chapter, somewhat slighted. And the recollection "April was *our* month, Rainer—" is a part of any complete "sketch" of the encounter "With Rainer," which simply did not wish to relinquish its "right to solitude" at that time. The original plan of *Looking Back* clearly excluded such intimate and personal revelations. It was only when Lou Andreas-Salomé found the appropriate form that she was able to convey what was to be said while simultaneously protecting it. She accomplished this by no longer writing for a reader, but rather as if speaking to a quiet, receptive listener in a conversation rich in memories and farewells.

The second comment concerns the style of the memoirs, which is that of the elderly Lou Andreas-Salomé. Its development, from the characteristically clear and direct language of the young Lou to the late style with its apparently loose, yet strangely appropriate combination of the most disparate elements, can be easily traced in the various texts reproduced (both in the main body and in the notes) from all phases of her life. Lou A.-S. once remarked in conversation that, while "writing" (which she also enjoyed as a physical activity), she was always in a hurry to get to what was crucial. This hurry (which was not the same as being rushed) is already noticeable in her style during the early and middle years: the next sentence is always ready to receive the baton of thought from its predecessor and run with it; one sees it in the very movement of her language. It's a spoken language, embodying her person and her personality. In her old age, one notes the lack of classical style, and an expressive fullness which is still not quite baroque, achieving a unity of thought and life which is totally concrete and concentrated, a unity, therefore, of form and content. Yet in spite of this sharp contrast to her earlier manner of expression, it may be noted that this later style too is still a spoken one (hence its tendency to the abstract and the "inorganic" in expressing thought). It is uttered in a joyful hurrying toward what is important and not, so to speak, for its own sake. The following illustrates how little attention Lou A.-S. paid to "formulation" and literary tradition even in her later years, when working at her desk. From time to time, a sleepless hour granted her (as though purposely placed there during a night's rest) an insight she had been patiently struggling to achieve for some time in vain. This insight then gripped her in words of dense meaning which even the well-deserved sleep which followed could not extinguish. With a peculiar questioning and trusting shyness, as though unwrapping a gift of inestimable value, she could later recite these same words to her visitor, as though repeating them to herself, words which had been spoken in the joy of being at one with language (and which were now, so to speak, spoken in a personal style which suited her age), and these same words would often find their way into her written memoirs.

In her later years then, it is the act of speech which underlies her language. The joyful urge to get to the point, the "directed" quality of her style still remains. Age here is not ossification, however; it is lively abundance which does not isolate itself, but retains an openness in its gestures and expression, in the unity of receiving and giving gifts. And so, the hurrying-to-arrive is really a moving-about-within-riches. These riches are found in those passages of simple narration which stand in delightful contrast to those determined by logical thought. This wealth is intentionally reflected in the happy glow or sorrow of the eyes which had seen the memories. More than anywhere else however, one recognizes these riches in the way she moves in the intellectual arena. Her personal language reaches a boundary—a quite different border from that of the formulaic (in which the rigidity and repetition of the formula becomes a sign that the most internal of possessions have become impossible to express). The distinguishing feature of *this* language in her advanced years can be characterized more as a tendency to abbreviate in code, in that the eye which sees the flash of meaning seems to be ahead of language, and language can only try to catch up as quickly as it can. In any case, the language of her advanced years is controlled by the immediate involvement of memory and not by distanced observation from the sidelines.

There is a notation in pencil, dated November 1934, at the conclusion of "What's Missing From the Sketch": "All of this is written too quickly, because my eyes no longer dare wait for anything." Partially for this reason, Lou Andreas-Salomé did not revise the texts for later publication. The task of editing has been aimed only at producing an accurate text, and, where the text had fallen into disorder or become disrupted, at providing a careful reconstruction. A personal note must be added to justify the manner in which the text was prepared for publication.

Approximately two and a half years before her death, in 1934, Lou Andreas-Salomé presented me in advance with the gift of her entire literary estate for "whatever I chose to do with it." This bequeathal was what mattered to her; everything related to it, from the perusal of the individual writings to the possibility of publication of certain texts, was, in accordance with her wishes, a matter for me to decide after her death. As different as the perspectives are with which one views a text, whether as an editor or as one simply trying to understand it, our communal journey through the "Sketch," and our joint musings about the linguistic expression of certain passages, gave me guidelines for the critical approach I later took.

In the summer of 1935, realizing the possible fatal consequences of impending surgery, Lou Andreas-Salomé bade farewell to my friend Josef König and me—we had been friends of hers in her later years. She perceived the time which remained thereafter as an additional gift. What she said to each of us at this farewell, "Everything was good, every part of it," uttered retrospectively about her life, indeed existence itself, in summary, remained her good-bye to us. She knew herself to be "in the throes of death" even before we recognized the signs. In the last weeks of her life, she received us in turn almost daily for short visits. She once remarked that, in the "Sketch," "people (would) encounter each other." She had several chapters read aloud to her: "I want to know how I put it then" and "Yes, I would still say it that way today." When I began to read to her, she might say, "I seem to be so distanced," but then she would immediately begin to talk about the matter at hand with complete clarity. In the same strangely alert yet fuzzy condition (of which she was fully conscious), the thought came to her, borne out of the distance she felt from herself: "I've worked my entire life, worked and worked—and what for, really? Why did I do it?" What echoes from this question was not doubt about the meaning of such intellectual work but rather amazement at its factual reality, and an inability, not perceived by her as painful, to decipher its very meaning. At the very end, pulled by the waves of the final sleep, she lay with closed eyes, almost the same as she always had, and wanted to be told of everyday activities. It was as though she were still tasting small pieces of life. In the midst of this she said: "If I let my thoughts wander, I find no one: only [and this was certainly added for our benefit] you are here" and also: "The best is indeed death."

Lou Andreas-Salomé died on the evening of February 5, 1937, at the age of seventy-six in her home in Göttingen. The cause of her death was uremia. Her wish to be laid to rest, after cremation, in the garden of her home could not be granted. The urn with her ashes is buried in her husband's grave in the Göttingen city cemetery.

—Dr. Ernst Pfeiffer
Göttingen, August 1951

AFTERWORD TO THE
NEW EDITION

A DECADE AND a half after the death of Lou Andreas-Salomé, *Looking Back* was published in 1951 with Max Niehans in Zurich and Insel in Wiesbaden. Another decade and a half has passed and a second edition now appears, published this time by Insel in Frankfurt am Main. The publishing house of Max Niehans no longer exists. Anyone who rereads such a book fifteen years later can judge whether the quiet work of time has acted as a "leveler" or has thrown the subject into sharper relief. But time's effect on *Looking Back* cannot be gauged solely by considering whether or not the book has stood the test of time. *Looking Back* was the first publication from the literary estate of Lou Andreas-Salomé. In the meantime, the correspondence between Lou A.-S. and Rilke has appeared, as well as her diary, *In der Schule bei Freud* (In Freud's School), and her correspondence with Sigmund Freud. Therefore, at least the sections about Rilke and Freud in *Looking Back* have awakened increased objective and critical interest, since the documentary publications are now available.

There are also changes in the text of the book itself. The new edition is not identical, word for word, with that of 1951, but it is no less authentic.

A few years ago, the editor acquired a second manuscript of *Looking Back*. It consists of typed pages with corrections and insertions, but is composed mostly of notes in pen or pencil; some were quickly jotted down and then clarified, whereas others were carefully developed in detail. All in all, it's about the same length as the previous manuscript without the chapter "What's Missing From the Sketch" and has been loosely bound by Lou A.-S. This working manuscript, which shows clear signs of constant revision, was obviously intended (after a clean copy was made) to be the copy text for the book.

Yet Lou A.-S. continued to work on this clean copy of the manuscript as well. She replaced typed pages with handwritten ones, added here and deleted there, all without consulting her old manuscript in its various versions. The manuscript in this form (which Lou A.-S. had not reviewed totally, but which she felt was complete) was the basis for the 1951 edition. The two manuscripts are not two different versions of her description of her life, nor do they represent two contrasting phases of work. They are, rather, the result of a single process.

There is also no temporal distance between the two manuscripts. It appears that most of the notes were made mainly after the death of F. C. Andreas. The chapter "F. C. Andreas," the last one in the old manuscript, bears the handwritten date of 1931. It is followed chronologically by "What's Missing From the Sketch" in 1933, "April was *our* month, Rainer—" in 1934, and "Memories of Freud" in 1936. The latter two were added to *Looking Back* by the editor to complete the chapters "With Rainer" and "The Freud Experience." The tone and content of all three of these above-mentioned memoirs contrast increasingly with *Looking Back*. The Rilke recollection is written as though the chapter "With Rainer" did not exist, and the same can be said of the relationship between "What's Missing From the Sketch" and the chapter entitled "F. C. Andreas."

The previous edition had posed various difficulties for the editor. Since Lou A.-S. preferred to completely rewrite something she had finished rather than revise the earlier version, she frequently lost sight of some things which had already been more accurately conveyed. Chance occurrences caused other problems. It was, therefore, not only justified but also necessary to make use of all extant versions to clarify the text. The leeway this afforded in producing a new copy text was limited, however: the point was only to clarify the final thoughts of Lou A.-S. about each topic, which sometimes included returning to her earlier formulations or emphases. Errors and misunderstandings which arose on the part of the editor in the course of his work on the first edition were also eliminated in the process.

The Afterword to the first edition, such as it is, has not been changed. The Notes were reviewed and supplemented by several important documentary additions.

—Dr. Ernst Pfeiffer
Göttingen, October 1967

AFTERWORD TO THE PAPERBACK EDITION

WE BEGIN WITH the fragment of a letter Lou Andreas-Salomé wrote at the age of fifty-four to Baroness von Gebsattel (who was at least two decades younger than she), since it may reveal to the reader its ultimate relationship to the later perspective of *Looking Back*.

Victor Emil von Gebsattel met Lou A.-S. in September 1911 at the Psychoanalytical Conference in Weimar. His acquaintance with Rilke was the basis for the personal contact. After approximately a year, he wrote the following to her: "Appearing before many, transforming yourself endlessly, you will always imbue the strongest and most intrinsic potential in others with the power of flight. And you will do so out of pure passion for the fullness of each individual's life, forcing each person beyond his habitual limits, in a cool and calm enthusiasm."

This impression of continual transformation supplements and substantiates the statements Lou A.-S. makes about herself, occasioned by the pain of the war, the "World War," in the letter fragment which follows:

[She had apparently just mentioned Hendrik Gillot:] he [showed me] that the way out of myself was like an entrance—an extension of the boundaries of my own physical body, slightly overflowing into the sphere where inner reality continually receives the world as a gift.

This probably is related to something else as well—namely that all along (probably since the time of fairy tales), everything *external* seemed to me to have a mysterious character—as though extending too far beyond and above us in its grandeur to be purely and simply embraced. That is why it seemed so far removed from us, something "external," our counterpart. Everything material, tangible, and objective instantly becomes a kind of sham and, although our view of them changes with time, it never really diminishes. The end result is that the most natural gesture toward the smallest particle of the outside world is imbued with a quiet reverence for what is "inside."

I'm well aware how much of this sort of optimism (which basically is more than that) might be attributed to the God of my childhood. But actually, it only shows the deeply irreparable nature of the instinctive way I have looked at things.

I have a particular reason for talking about this, however: it's only from this perspective that I can actually tell you about these five months, and my internal experience of the war—and I can tell you, with absolutely no exaggeration of any kind, that I have not suffered so intensely since childhood. To be sure, I don't have the same feelings about it now as when I last wrote you, and now we would soon find ourselves in agreement about your views. Just as the enthusiasm was fueled by recrimination, so too the hate is not truly real; for all nationalities involved, the whole thing rests on a demonic foundation, just as you say. And it is precisely here that an even more evil dissolution of reality takes place: all of human experience becomes ghastly, lurid, and eerie, and *that* is where I find the war and its reality (made all the more crass by its own forced intrusion) to be the most gruesome.

By using the phrases "most gruesome," and "all of human experience becomes ghastly, lurid, and eerie," with reference to the historical situation at the time, Lou A.-S. was neither talking directly about nor trying to clarify her inner and (opposing) image of "grandeur"—which, for her, is embedded in materiality. But even the phrase "from this perspective" shows that this spontaneous reference is actually an attempt to define the word "gruesome" fully by opposing it to an equally sublime concept. In *Looking Back*, Lou A.-S. writes that denying reverence to the last cosmic dust particle would be tantamount to "murder" in her eyes. This same principle applies to the inner human essence; when it becomes ghastly, lurid, and eerie, "murder" occurs—in the same, absolute sense of the word.

Now we turn to the two books about Lou A.-S. which have appeared in the last decade. They raise an obvious question: To what extent can they be reconciled with her own words in *Looking Back* and with the letter fragment already quoted above? The books are: H. F. Peters's *My Sister, My Spouse: A Biography of Lou Andreas-Salomé*, New York, 1962; in German translation, *Lou: Das Leben der Lou Andreas-Salomé*, 1964. And: Rudolph Binion, *Frau Lou, Nietzsche's Wayward Disciple*, Princeton, 1968.

The two books differ greatly in quality—and both represent extremes. The book by Peters, a model of pseudoscientific method, doesn't miss a single opportunity to go astray—as biography (which sees itself as sexography), as psychology, with regard to every kind of fact, and with respect to everything which one calls tact. The editor (whose position makes criticism difficult) felt it necessary to reveal the misuse of documentary materials: "Die Historie von der Lou" (The Story of Lou), *Neue Deutsche Hefte*, May/June 1965.

Rudolph Binion's book, a labyrinthian and exclusively psychoanalytical investigation, would not be considered here had it not addressed itself to personal matters. Many statements made about Lou A.-S. and the editor, and allegedly verified, reflect a deep distrust of them and of what they have said and done. Lou A.-S. is suspected of continuing to revise and thereby falsifying *Looking Back* after certain portions of it had been completed and the editor "certainly did some more." (This fabrication is refuted in the *Nietzsche-Documents*, p. 413ff.) Lou von S. is said to have misidentified letters in her Nietzsche book (which she had dedicated to Paul Rée: "To Someone Unnamed in Faithful Memory"); she supposedly represented letters by Nietzsche to Rée as having been written to *her*. An entry by Lou von S. in her *Stibbe Nestbuch* (Stibbe Village Diary) during her time with Nietzsche in Tautenburg is interpreted by Binion as though Nietzsche (Nico) had told Lou von S. "fairy tales": "And perhaps she took their sessions over her notebook for story hours with Saint Nick. . . ." (p. 91) There can be no doubt that such wild interpretations, intensified by a constant and pervasive suspicion, also surface in the psychoanalytical realm. (Clarification of the "Village Diary" passage in *Nietzsche-Documents*, p. 446f.) The editor, whom Binion accuses of creating editions "all deftly annotated to her [i.e., Lou's] greater glory" had supposedly undergone analysis with her "to the extent of eliciting a colossal transference." But analysis was never considered a possibility by either Lou A.-S. or him. Originally she had made the suggestion of conducting a *training* analysis with him—solely so that he could analyze a sick friend of his instead of her doing so. But she then discarded the idea in order, as she said, that she remain just a friend. Binion never understood that the editor was pushed to the point where he had to protect himself—on the one hand, by Binion's indisputable talent and on the other hand, by the increasing, almost extortionate, pressure of his demand "But I must" (in conversation). Insofar as possible, while remaining true to his duty as sole editor of the literary estate and sole means of access to that estate, he provided Binion with the working materials he requested, even going above and beyond the call of duty in lending him unpublished transcriptions which he himself had not even read. Binion's book is not only an investigation; it is, as its structure already indicates, a demonstration, with predetermined results.

The text of *Looking Back* was reviewed again and the notes (which had already been enlarged in the second printing of the 1969 edition) were expanded in individual cases. Ursula Schenk assisted in adapting the details concerning Nietzsche from the *Nietzsche-Documents (Friedrich Nietzsche, Paul Rée, Lou von Salomé: The Documentation of Their Encounters)*.

—Ernst Pfeiffer
Göttingen, Autumn 1973

NOTES

The epigraph is taken (by the editor) from *Dank an Freud* (Homage to Freud), p. 14.

1. *we will later refer to as our first "memory"*: While composing her memoirs for *Lebensrückblick,* Lou A.-S. wrote, in the early spring of 1931, her Open Letter to Professor Freud, *Mein Dank an Freud* (My Homage to Freud). Her unique view of our origins (first glimpsed in this chapter) may become more comprehensible if the reader compares the consciously free portrayal here with the one so closely tied to theory in the Open Letter, and the "yearning to return home to the maternal darkness" (of which Lou A.-S. speaks on p. 38 of the Open Letter) with the "yearning to return home to unity with everything that is" here. A remark Lou A.-S made in conversation illustrates both her similarity to and difference from Freud: "He deserves the credit for reestablishing the human being's unity with everything that is a part of life, and he does so not intuitively but rationally. From the very beginning, the difference between us was clear: he would have preferred to release humans from this dangerous connection with the One, whereas I sense that power even in its false location in the pathological."

Yet another comparison comes quickly to mind: with the message of Rilke's Eighth Duino Elegy about "The memory, as if that for which one strives, had once been closer." "Everything here is distance, and there everything was Breath." The elegy also goes on to speak of "that openness," which only the animals, the (nonhuman) "creatures" can perceive "with all their eyes." This "openness" can be related to Lou A.-S.'s "sheltering" (if such a summary expression may be permitted), not in order to look for influences but rather to explain the particular perspective in *Lebensrückblick.*" The word "Zurückrutsch," used several times by Lou A.-S., is a vividly feminine German form of the Freudian concept of "regression," the "return of the libido to earlier stages of development."

4. *in my little story* Die Stunde ohne Gott: from the book *Die Stunde ohne Gott* (The Hour Without God) and other children's stories, published by Eugen Diederichs in Jena, 1922. She remembered the details again, when she was "already approaching old age" in June 1919 during a stay at Henry von Heisler's house in Höhenried. Written shortly thereafter, the story begins with the country servant's farfetched tale of the mysterious couple in front of the miniature house and the increasingly penetrating questions of the child. After this, the small girl's life with God unfolds in all its immediacy and, even considering all the poetic transformations, is very close

to her memories. For example, God's appearance "in broad daylight" is mentioned: "In the entire apartment, there was only one room which admitted only one person at a time and offered only one chair. In this room, she (little Ursula) was allowed to do exactly as she wished, and this included locking the door. The lock, of course, was not meant for God." The second visit of the friendly servant introduces the second half of the story and with it, the catastrophe: "What the servant himself can't explain, he, who has seen everything from the beginning—no, human beings just can't know such things. . . . How in the world is it possible that she forgot that? To ask God, who knows everything? Not just now, but back then—who are they, this strange couple, who seem so familiar?—The name, she wanted to know the name of these people! And now she lies there, listening."

In the diary from the long Russian trip she took with Rilke in 1900, one finds the first (extant) memory of her earliest childhood: "And finally everything becomes a dream. The largest and the smallest things flow without distinction into one another, maybe all of life is already there but who will disentangle it. . . . Finally, at the very end, I see myself as a very small girl, in bed in the evening with two dolls next to my pillow—one doll is made of porcelain and the other of leather and wax. I see myself telling God the nicest stories instead of saying my evening prayer." And one of the last notes from Lou A.-S., from February 1936, begins with this recollection: "When I think back to my earliest childhood experiences, I almost instinctively see myself at night, telling God stories before I fall asleep" and tries to expand upon what she says here in *Lebensrückblick*.

7. *quite different external impressions to one another*: This whole passage is illustrated by the portrayal of this imaginative process in the children's story *Das Bündnis zwischen Tor und Ur* (The Alliance Between Tor and Ur) which is the third story in the book *The Hour Without God*. There is a passage at the very beginning about "the little girl" Ur[sula], who likes to "attach her thoughts," everything she has imagined, to "things and people she encounters." "One used many people for this, whereas a few real, nonimagined ones to play with would have sufficed." In order to develop her protagonist completely, she adopts suitable impressions from the "successive people" she meets "until an entire bundle of people coalesces into one single individual." For example, she adds the quality "Grandfather" to the boy Tor(wald), her playmate, by utilizing the impression of someone she had met—a shy old man who was glancing about fearfully. When Torwald notices this tendency to fantasize, he yells (just as the "little relative" of Louise von S.): "You're a liar!" Ursula then remembers that once, when she had fantasized another episode, she drew the amazed reproach: "You invented that!" And it was then that she resolved "not to add one jot." The remark (p. 7.): *Perhaps something of this habit carried over into later life when I began to write short stories* also means that Lou A.-S., as a storyteller (like little Ur), had the peculiar tendency and ability not only to re-create multiple forms from one human "model" but also to portray this person at a different age from the one she knew him to be. (The figure Balduin in the novel *Das Haus* [The House] has

traits of the young Rilke—the one she imagined him to be before they had even met; see the note to p. 108.)

7. *"O bright Heaven overhead"*: Lou A.-S. recalled this poem for the first time at the end of the long Russian trip as "originating many years ago during a bright night in Rongas [Finland]." In the first version as she remembered it, in the diary, it is somewhat different and has one extra stanza.

8. *"Turn away from half measures"*: Three lines from the fifth (penultimate) stanza of Goethe's poem "Generalbeichte" (General Confession) from the cycle *Gesellige Lieder* (Convivial Songs). The stanza reads: "Willst du Absolution/Deinen Treuen geben,/Wollen wir nach Deinem Wink/ Unabläßlich streben,/Uns vom Halben zu entwöhnen/Und im Ganzen, Guten, Schönen/Resolut zu leben (If you wish to give/ Absolution to those faithful to you,/We will follow your lead/And strive ceaselessly,/ To turn away from half measures/And be resolute in living/Wholly, fully, beautifully.") Nietzsche took this rule of life from Giuseppe Mazzini, whom he met in February 1871. From this time on, this thought became almost a motto for him and his friends.

9. *confirmation instruction with Hermann Dalton*: Dalton's attention was drawn to Louise von S. during a presentation of his regarding God's omnipresence (one cannot conceive of a place where He is not) when she remarked: "Oh, but one can—in Hell." Dalton asked to see her after this; her departure from the Church touched him personally.

11. *Illogical as it may be, I must confess*: This last paragraph, written in pencil, was added to the chapter later (probably around 1936). Lou A.-S once remarked in conversation that she would "have liked to express the One Thing [which was to her] of sole importance, in a kind of sermon." Perhaps, as she added, because she had "begun her writing" by putting together sermons for Gillot. Once, in a contemplative mood, she lamented the "loss of God" as her "disaster."

12. *living person took their place*: Hendrik Gillot, 1836–1916, clergyman at the Dutch mission in St. Petersburg. Gillot was at the time the most important non-orthodox Protestant minister in the city. Since he was a member of the mission and not subject to any of the reformed Protestant church governments in Petersburg, he was relatively independent in his pronouncements. Hermann Dalton, who gave Louise von S. confirmational instruction, was one of his theological opponents. In Holland, Gillot had published the book *De geschiedenis van den godsdienst* (The History of Divine Worship, According to the Liberal German Theologian Otto Pfleiderer), Part I, Schiedam, 1872. One of young Lou's textbooks was Pfleiderer's *Religionsphilosophie auf geschichtlicher Grundlage* (Philosophy of Religion on a Historical Basis) of 1878. Gillot preached mostly in German, especially in the winter. In

the summer, when the upper classes either resided in the country or traveled, he used Dutch more often.

Seventeen-year-old Louise von Salomé was persuaded by a relative (the one from whom the following quotations are taken) to listen to one of Gillot's sermons. As soon as he entered the pulpit, and gestured and spoke in his own characteristic way, she knew immediately that she belonged to him: "now all loneliness is at an end," "this is what I've been looking for," "a real person," "he exists," "I must speak with him"; what he said was not a motivating factor. She inquired about his apartment, wrote to him that she would like to talk with him—but not because of religious qualms. She stands waiting in his study, "her hand pressed to her heart." Standing in the doorway, he says: "Have you come to see me?" and opens his arms. At first she continues to visit him secretly; they work—with such diligence that she once faints while sitting on his lap: "It was impossible to do wrong." After a longer period of time, Gillot tells her that she should tell her mother (her father had died shortly before, in February 1879). She follows his instructions so literally that she goes straight to her mother, who was entertaining company at the time and announces: "I've just come from Gillot." Her mother cries. Frau von Salomé receives Gillot. Secretly listening, Lou hears her mother say: "You bear the responsibility for harming my daughter" and Gillot answer: "I *want* to be responsible for this child." From then on, she is allowed to visit him freely; the work overtaxes her health; "I had to follow him, he was He— then ceased to be, when he misjudged me" (with his marriage proposal); "Even today it is as though it were yesterday, I could still write in this 'present moment' as I had written then." (This account is taken from conversations with Lou A.-S.)

From letters written in response by an older, understanding female relative of Lou von S. (from October 1878 to June 1879), one can recognize the emotional course of events: the loneliness of the girl, the danger of a "rift" between her and her mother over basic internal differences, and the decision to leave the Church: "so, the die has been cast! What kind of battles you must have fought before you came to the decision and its execution; and then these storms! . . . You say yourself that you sometimes feel as though you were in a desert." The mother also confides in this relative: "It really amazes me that the first (and so totally unexpected) storm has passed without my feeling ill. I needed all my moral strength to keep myself going. Then, as so often in my life, I definitely felt how powerful God's strength is, even in a weak person, when one trusts him completely. My patriarchal faith is no longer fashionable, but I am happy that I have it! You say that Lyola is suffering too in sympathy with my own soul, but I don't believe that because she would have done everything differently from the start and would prove it to me by her actions. You ask me to treat her lovingly, but how is that possible with such a stubborn person who always has to have things her way in everything. . . . Lyola believes that it was a lie and a crime to be confirmed by Dalton against his conviction, but I know in other matters that things were not handled so scrupulously." Something of the relationship with Gillot and the struggle with him can be seen in the letters from this relative: Frau von S. decides (probably in April 1879) "to see Gillot, to consult with him about your instruction and the confirmation in Holland. . . . That he does not limit his instruction to religion and preparation for confirmation is to me completely understandable, given his whole being and will." "How terrible the battle must have raged within you before you capitulated completely." "How difficult this yielding must have been, especially for you; I know you so well! But that you did it, is, in my opinion, neither 'wrong' nor a 'disaster.' Since things are the way they are, then we must feel at peace and look upward in trust. You say so yourself." Several aspects of Gillot's character are also mentioned: his ability to look right through a person so that one feels "totally undressed . . . how he must suffer from the contradictory feelings which rage within him . . . but what willpower this man must possess!"; his "terrible thoroughness" is emphasized, as is the danger to Lou's health: "You say that mental work won't harm you, that it is better than fretting." The topics that Lou von S. at first developed for Gillot pertained more to the history and philosophy of religion, whereas later they tended more toward the philosophical. Gillot gave her systematic instruction in philosophy; in particular, they read Kant together in Dutch. In later conversations with Nietzsche and Rée concerning the classical modern philosophers, she proved herself to be the most well-read. Whether defending her ideas or attacking others, she played off her knowledge (which she had deepened during studies in Zurich) successfully against the "more advanced" views of the other two. Lou A.-S told about this with amusement.

14. *my trip to Zurich*: This occurred in September 1880. The confirmation in Holland took place the previous year. The words of confirmation: "Fürchte dich nicht, denn ich habe dich erlöset: ich habe dich bei deinem Namen gerufen, du bist mein (Fear not, for I have chosen you, I have called you by your name: you are mine)" is from Isaiah 43.1. Lou von S. also made Gillot conduct her church wedding with F. C. Andreas, held in the church in Sandpoort (Holland) where Gillot had confirmed her. The wedding took place on June 20, 1887. (The engagement was announced on November 1, 1886.)

14. *a tale I wrote ten years later*: According to a note in the manuscript, *Ruth* was first written between December 23, 1893, and February 6, 1894, in Schmargendorf, originally with the subtitle "Ein Portrait." It was published in 1895 by Cotta in Stuttgart. In the story, Erik is a teacher and Ruth one of his pupils. No direct encounter was incorporated into the fiction. The "surprising turn" (via the marriage proposal) is portrayed in the last pages: "I wanted to lead you out of the world of fantasy, in which you dreamed, into the world of real life. . . . [Even] if I must destroy the fantasy world which has become deeply rooted in your heart. . . . It seemed to her as though she had to call to someone far away—to call Erik to save her from something, someone unknown. But it was he—it was indeed he—who stood there before her."

15. *to leave Zurich to be taken south*: Beginning approximately September 1881, Lou

von S., accompanied by her mother, visited various health spas (for example, a cold-water sanitarium) without success. In January 1882, her mother "took her south."

15. "*When at last I lie upon the bier*": This poem, "Todesbitte" (Deathbed Request), was incorporated by Lou von Salomé (using the pseudonym Henri Lou) into her first novel, *Im Kampf um Gott* (Struggling for God), which was published by Wilhelm Friedrich, Leipzig and Berlin, in 1885. The poem was revised as if a man were speaking to his child.

20. "*Indeed, I love you life, as friend*": Lou von Salomé also incorporated "A Prayer to Life" into her novel *Struggling for God*. And there she chose the form which Nietzsche had given the poem because it becomes "more solemn with slightly longer lines," but it also retains (except for inconsequential deviations) the more powerful final lines of the first version and their rhyme: "To live for centuries, to think / Wrap me in your arms again, / If you have no more joy to give, / At least you still grant pain." Lou von S. gave Nietzsche "A Prayer to Life" in Tautenburg in August 1882 and he then set it to music in Naumburg. According to an 1887 letter to his sister, the music had originated earlier. The composition appeared in 1887, with Gast's help, as *Hymnus an das Leben* (Hymn to Life), written for a mixed choir and orchestra. It had already been "reworked for a four-voice choir" by Professor Riedel, the president of the German Musical Society, in September 1882, according to one of Nietzsche's letters to Lou von S. from that time. The 1887 version has the concluding lines: "Centuries in which to think and live / Let all your content be their gain! / If you have no more joy to give, / At least you still grant pain." Nietzsche did not indicate the name of the librettist in the score, but he did in *Ecce Homo* (1888) when discussing the origins of *Zarathustra*: "It should be expressly stated here, since there seems to be a misunderstanding about it, that the text is not mine. It is the amazing inspiration of a young Russian woman whom I knew well at that time—Fräulein Lou von Salomé. Whoever grasps the meaning of the last words of the poem will know why I selected it and admired it: they have grandeur. Pain is *not* a valid argument against life! 'If you have no more joy to give, at least *you still grant pain. . . .*' Perhaps my music also has grandeur in this passage." Lou A.-S. claimed that for her the end of the "bombastic" poem expressed her desire to embrace life totally, "robbed" though it was by the loss of God. For him, Nietzsche, Lou A.-S. continued, the poem's conclusion was an expression of his *amor fati* (willing acceptance of whatever fate decrees). See Freud's comments, p. 105.

22. *Even when our ninety-year-old mother died*: See the note to p. 28.

22. *The oldest of them, Alexandre, or "Sasha" . . . filled with energy and goodness . . . a wonderful sense of humor*: In a letter concerning her brother's devastation at the death of one of his children, Lou A.-S. characterized his humor as follows: "But one thing I knew and had always sensed: that this ability to *see* joy, to *look beyond* annoyances,

lay not only in taking pain and sorrow lightly, brushing them off easily, but also in the deep *need* for happiness—which springs from a deep sensitivity to pain." The death of this brother on February 20, 1915 ("He was my security") prompted Lou A.-S. to postpone her meeting Rilke in Munich for weeks. For information about the *second brother*, Robert, see p. 27. The *third brother*, Eugène, was highly thought of as a doctor, especially in court circles. His lengthy suffering and death on May 4, 1898, aroused unusual sympathy; Lou A.-S. has described the "private" nature of his character in Dr. Trebor in the first part of the posthumous novel *Jutta*. For more information about the *father*, Gustav von S., see the notes to p. 33.

27. *loosely associated with the Cadet Party*: the Constitutional Democrats ("Kadetten" [Cadets], named in jest after their abbreviation KD [CD]), who tried to work toward a true parliamentary system in the Duma (1905). After the March Revolution of 1917, they declared themselves in favor of a democratic republic.

28. *Our elderly mother was also spared*: Lou A.-S. says in a letter about her mother (probably written in 1898) that she never really knew her mother well "because I did not have in Mama a natural friend. Rather, I always opposed her, attaining through struggle everything which a mother with a totally different nature might have *wanted* to give me. Only *afterward* did I see her clearly and without bias, and then I *loved* her for her strength, loyalty and *great* nobility." A diary by Louise Wilm (her maiden name), kept in the days before her marriage to Gustav von Salomé in December 1844, indicates how this woman thought and felt—her declaration of love, her religious self-examination, and her solemn vow to overcome her own weaknesses through devotion. "My darling child" is the heading used in later letters to her daughter. Louise von Salomé, born to a sugar manufacturer in St. Petersburg on February 7, 1823, passed away without suffering ("of a cold," Lou A.-S.) on January 11, 1913.

33. *My father was sent to St. Petersburg as a young boy*: at age six. He was born in the Baltic provinces on July 24, 1804. His father died young; his mother came from a German-Baltic family. Letters written by his siblings to the young officer Gustav von S. indicate that he had brothers named Carl, Fritz, Alexander, and Georg (he had a total of nine brothers) and one sister. Lou A.-S. kept letters from the young colonel concerning the Polish uprising until the last years of her life. The golden brooch (a small saber) which Czar Alexander II had had made for Frau von S. carries the (translated) inscription: "For bravery, service, honor, and glory," "For the assault on Warsaw 25/26 August 1831." Lou A.-S. remembered that General von Salomé had also, in his position as privy councilor, conducted military inspection tours. His wife was known throughout her life as "the Little General." His death on February 23, 1879, was also said to be "wonderfully easy."

33. *spoke German almost exclusively*: As already mentioned, the father's siblings had

German, or at least non-French first names; they wrote their letters in German (as he did, at least to his wife) and the letters of little Louise (Lyola, also Lyolya) as well as those of her siblings were also in German. The mother called her husband Gustav; his name is so written (Gustav Ludwig) on Louise's baptismal record when he was already privy councilor. All the godparents had German names. It was only during Gustav v. Salomé's career as an officer that he became so fluent in French (the ruling social language) that, according to Lou A.-S., he was better versed in it than in German.

35. *larger one which was to follow, where I learned next to nothing*: the reformed Petrischule (St. Peter's School) (secondary-school level), where Louise von S. finished school, in the end as an auditor.

35. *Naródniki*: The "people's party." More a movement than a political party. Begun after the abolition of serfdom in 1861, it was composed of intellectuals who espoused the cause of the lower middle class and in particular the peasants and farmers, whom they idealized (theory of "Peasant Socialism"). They were at their height in the 1870s and once again, to a lesser degree, at the turn of the century, disappearing in the October Revolution of 1917. Many students were members. The circle around Sófia Nikoláyevna Schill, with whom Lou A.-S. and Rilke had contact in Moscow during their long Russian trip in 1900, was more independent than the others. It offered "courses" for young workers and peasants who hungered for "education" and "truth." Lou A.-S. writes in her diary about the "liberal Moscovite enlighteners of the masses."

35. *our relationship to the former emperor*: Lou A.-S once remarked that her father had supposedly been close to Czar Nicholas, who reigned from 1825–1855, in part perhaps because the summer house of the general's family was in Peterhof, the summer residence of the czars. (Nicholas II relocated it to Tsárskoye Seló [now Pushkin] for security reasons.) The story goes that when the czar rode by, her younger brothers often stationed themselves there to salute him.

35. *Vera Sassúlich*: In the summer of 1877, the governor of St. Petersburg, General Trepov, had a political prisoner beaten because he had not saluted him in the courtyard of the detention prison. As a result of this, Vera Sassúlich, who came to the general as a petitioner, shot and severely wounded him during an audience on January 24 (February 5) 1878. The defense attorney, Alexandrov, won an acquittal. Friends took the would-be assassin to Switzerland for protection from potential persecution. A number of terrorist attacks followed the attempt. The *Erinnerungen* (Memoirs) of Vera Sassúlich were published in Moscow in 1931. Alexander II was killed by a bomb attack on March 1 (13), 1881.

36. *stay in Paris in 1910*: Impressions from the first visit to Paris, from spring to

September 1894, are recounted in the chapter "With Other People." The second trip, with Ellen Key in May 1909, was actually taken because of Rilke, who was living in Paris at the time. The trip referred to here took place in the winter of 1910.

36. *shortly after the Azéf tragedy*: Minister of the Interior Pléve had smuggled the informer Eugen Azéf into the ranks of the social revolutionaries. Azéf's primary function was to tell police about planned assassination attempts on the czars, but he was also to keep them informed of terrorist activity in general. Many conspirators were arrested based on his denunciations and several were executed. Occasionally an attack was allowed to succeed to protect his cover. He had a diabolical nature and more than once betrayed the police to the conspirators. This double role was not discovered until 1908, when Vladímir Búrtsev went before a disciplinary committee of the social revolutionaries. The social revolutionaries did not exist until the creation of the Duma in 1905. With the phrase "after almost a century of action," Lou A.-S. is referring to the effectiveness of the revolutionary movement in Russia in general.

38. *the brutal asceticism of the Skoptsý*: One of the secret sects, in existence since ca. 1770, which demanded self-castration of its followers in anticipation of the Messiah.

40. *The two trips we took together to Russia*: See the notes to p. 70.

42. *"Old Russia"*: Written in Finland, the "Nachtrag" (Afterword) to the diary of this trip contains the poem "Volga," entered on August 13, 1900, as well as "Du heller Himmel über mir" (O Bright Heaven Overhead) and a poem "Wiedersehn." The poem "Altrußland" (Old Russia) was not written, according to Lou A.-S., until the "Rußland" (Russia) chapter was written. The main body of the diary, written in Russia, closes with a poem, "Mein Land, das ich so lang versäumte" (My Country, Which I Have So Long Neglected).

44. *a March evening in Rome, in the year 1882*: "On a January evening" in the typescript. The confusion probably was due to the fact that Lou von Salomé and her mother arrived in Italy in January: "It was in the first days in January as, tired and sick, I came to Italy . . ." she recalled, looking back on New Year's Night in 1883. Evidence exists of visits to Malwida von Meysenbug in February. Paul Rée had stayed with Friedrich Nietzsche in Genoa from February 4 until the trip to Rome via Monte Carlo. The exact date of the meeting with Paul Rée can be determined from a recollection she penned on March 17, 1888: "Today, six years ago, I met you."

44. *von Meysenbug's*: Malwida von Meysenbug (1816–1903) was a daughter of Karl Ludwig Georg Philipp Rivalier, a courtier in Electoral Hesse, of Huguenot heritage. In his youth he had been a friend of the prince, who later raised him to nobility and made him a baron. Malwida von M., who herself had been involved in republican-

revolutionary actions around 1848, was exiled from Berlin in 1852. In London, asylum for emigrants in those days, she met the Russian revolutionary writer Alexander Herzen (son of Prince Yákovlev and a Stuttgart woman) and the Italian freedom fighter Giuseppe Mazzini, among others. After Herzen's death, she adopted his daughter Olga, with whom she had spent the winter of 1861/62 in Italy. Her *Memoiren einer Idealistin* (Memoirs of an Idealist), which concluded with her 1860/61 stay in Paris and first meeting there with Richard Wagner, were published anonymously in Stuttgart in 1876. By spring 1882, the third edition had already appeared. As a "Nachtrag" (Afterword), she published in 1898 *Lebensabend einer Idealistin* (The Twilight Years of an Idealist), a loosely connected collection of memoirs and observations. At the laying of the foundation for the Bayreuth Fest-spielhaus in 1872, Malwida von M. met Friedrich Nietzsche among Wagner's acquaintances. In 1876 she invited Nietzsche to spend his sabbatical vacationing in Italy as her guest. He suggested that his friend Dr. Paul Rée "accompany" him. Malwida rented Villa Rubinacci in Sorrento and stayed there all winter, from the end of October 1876 on, with Nietzsche, Rée, and a law student from Basel named Albert Brenner. Rée prepared his book *Der Ursprung der moralischen Empfin-dungen* (The Origin of Moral Perceptions) for publication; Nietzsche worked on *Menschliches, Allzumenschliches* (Human, All Too Human). Malwida von M. had not known Rée previously. In *The Twilight Years of an Idealist* she writes of Rée as "a very dear friend [whose] strictly scientific and realistic point of view she did not share, [despite her] high regard for his personality [and her] recognition of his kind nature, which could be clearly seen in his selfless friendship with Nietzsche." Rée's way of looking at things supposedly "gave [Nietzsche] an almost childlike pleasure." Several excerpts from the journal letters he wrote to her after his stay in Sorrento are published in the book. She called him Paolo.

44. *young Paul Rée*: Paul Rée, born to the owner of a Junker's estate in Bartelshagen in Pomerania on November 21, 1849, was thirty-two years old at the time. His actual home, the Junker estate Stibbe, in West Prussia, was purchased ca. 1868. Succumb-ing to his father's wishes (despite his own interest in the field of ethics), he studied law in Leipzig. As a one-year volunteer, he fought in the Franco-Prussian War and was wounded at Gravelotte. He was awarded the doctorate in 1875; his dissertation was entitled: "TOY KAΛOY," notio in Aristoteles ethicis quid sibi velit. In that same year he published a small book of aphorisms: *Psychologische Beobachtungen* (Psy-chological Observations, From the Literary Estate of . . .). His more personal relationship with Nietzsche came as a result of this book (Nietzsche's first letter to him is dated October 22, 1875), although they had met two and a half years earlier in Basel: "A friend of Romundt has arrived for the summer. A pensive, talented, Schopenhauerian by the name of Rée" (Nietzsche to Erwin Rohde, May 5, 1873). Among the theses he defended in his dissertation was that the conscience could be explained in terms of historical development: "Conscientia non habet originem

transcendentalem"; his pessimism with regard to human affairs is expressed in the thesis "Progressus moralis nullus est in rebus humanis." There are definite thematic connections between this thesis and his *Die Illusion der Willensfreiheit, ihre Ursachen und ihre Folgen* (The Illusion of Freedom of Will, Its Causes and Its Results), published in 1885, as well as with his book *The Origin of Moral Perceptions*, which had appeared in 1877. He tried to prove the first thesis in a "Prolegomena" he had originally intended as his dissertation to qualify for university lecturing: *Die Entstehung des Gewissens* (The Origin of the Conscience) in 1885. His final philosophical work, *Philosophie*, appeared as *Nachgelassenes Werk* (Posthumous Work) in Berlin in 1903 with the prefatory note: "My earlier writings are the immature works of youth." This text is even more extreme than his previous ones in its almost splendidly one-sided and radical treatment of earlier themes. A letter from Rée, dated Nov. 1897, on his relationship to Nietzsche, was added by an unnamed editor, and contains the following critique: "I was never able to read him, however. He is brilliant but lacks ideas. . . . Everyone acts out of vanity, but his conceit is pathological, morbidly provoked. If he had been healthy, it might have caused him to produce something great. But as a sick person who could think and write only on rare occasions, and who feared that he was no longer going to be capable of work at all, as a person who wanted to attain fame at any price, this pathological vanity produced only sickness. In many cases, there were brilliant and beautiful thoughts, but the primary result was pathological, an insane distortion. Not philosophy, instead—delirium!!"

Nietzsche himself characterized Rée, the author of the book *On the Origin of Moral Perceptions*, as "one of the bravest and coldest of thinkers." This occurs in the outline of *Ecce Homo*, in the section "Warum ich so gute Bücher schreibe" (Why I Write Such Good Books), by quoting Aphorism 37 (from *Human, All Too Human*). In this way, he had, he said, bathed the eminent Dr. Paul Rée in the glow of a glorious historical significance, since readers concluded "because of this one passage (that) the whole book had to be understood as a higher Réealism." (Nietzsche had already alluded to this opinion on the part of his friends in his personal dedication to Rée in his copy of *Human, All Too Human*, Vol. 1, jokingly congratulating him on becoming a "father" with the slogan "Long Live Réealism!") Lou A.-S. characterized Rée's pathological self-hate as a Jew in a letter to her friend, Ferdinand Tönnies, dated December 7, 1904:

"I have often observed half-Jewish people who suffered from their mixed nature. In itself, this split could hardly be called pathological, for it is just as normal as a limp in a person with one short leg and one long. But to see someone limp along on his two healthy legs as Rée did—! To be totally a Jew yet nonetheless to identify solely with something within himself which opposes this self in such a despicable and contemptuous manner—I never saw this in others to the degree that I saw it in him. (A simple, innocent remark about this [when Rée became aware that she had not noticed his Jewishness] caused him to faint away before my eyes. A few incidents in which Jews, not instantly recognized as such by him, had contact with us, defied, in their ludicrousness and abomination, all description) but something of this strangeness was evident in more than one Jew I knew.

"This violent self-rejection was a powerful agent, if not indeed the principal cause of Rée the thinker's disregard for the emotional and for the individual personality. He was, therefore, not as narrow-minded as he seemed; it was simply a fact that the door which led out was closed tightly enough that it almost became a wall. This door functioned nonetheless as a means of communication, if only in the most intimately personal realm—via, so to speak, the keyhole. And high above the walls, an almost ethereal goodness grew from his incredibly sorrowful self-hate. No one knew that better than I, for I rested in this goodness as a young bird sits in its mother's nest."

In 1885 Paul Rée had begun to study medicine in Berlin ("to get closer to people," Lou A.-S.) after the failure of his plans to qualify as a university instructor. After he and Lou von S. parted ways, he continued this course of study in Berlin, until the end of the semester in the summer of 1887. (Lou A.-S. regularly received news about him, without his knowledge, from a mutual acquaintance.) He finished his studies in Munich. He moved to Stibbe in 1890, setting up practice in a small building next door to the manor house. He never had any contact with the neighbors and did not take his meals in the main house. He was "the doctor who worked without pay for the whole population there" and he often financed patients who needed to go to clinics in Berlin or Breslau. He was frequently seen "bringing large donations of food and wine beneath his coat into the homes of workers who were poor or ill." He is remembered "even today (1927) as a saint there." (This memory of him was still vivid a decade later.) When not practicing, he often went hiking for miles in the surrounding woods or sat at work at his desk. After completing his book, he didn't want to continue his philosophical endeavors, "but I don't know what will happen. I'm compelled to think philosophically. If I no longer have something to philosophize about, then I might as well die."

When he heard (1900) that the family estate was to be sold (his brother later tried in vain to reverse the sale), he left his home in the middle of the night and went to Celerina in Upper Engadine, where he lived in the same hotel in which he had once stayed with Lou von S. He continued to tend to the poor. He was often thought to be a clergyman because of his "large, clean-shaven, serious face," his clothes, and his gait. On a hike through a mountain range, crossing over a smooth ridge whose rockface drops steeply down to the Inn River, he fell to his death on October 28, 1901. A worker who saw it happen (!) found him in the water. A large portion of the population attended the burial at the cemetery in Celerina. (Most of this information is taken from Kurt Kolle's *Notizen über Paul Rée* [Notes About Paul Rée], in *Zeitschrift für Menschenkunde* [Journal of Anthropology], September 1927).

As an answer to Lou A.-S.'s letter (quoted above), Ferdinand Tönnies, in his essay "Paul Rée" in the periodical *Das freie Wort* (The Independent Word), gives his own personal impression: "I knew Rée and valued him as an unusually well educated and ingenious person. He had an imposing air about him, inspired by both the quiet self-confidence of his appearance and the calm, indeed, gentle manner of speech. Among closer acquaintances, he was also thoroughly good-natured and amiable. . . . Rée loved conversations, even though he became easily puzzled and would then let his deep-set, lively eyes wander back and forth in doubt until he helped himself out of his embarrassment with a jocular phrase. . . . He aimed his gentle, ironic humor as much against himself as against others. He knew how to cloak small malices in a civil, friendly fashion. He was basically modest. Yet he placed great trust in the correctness of his thinking, because he thought of himself as one of the few totally unbiased thinkers, and he concentrated upon certain fundamental problems untiringly—for months, indeed, for years." Tönnies makes the following comments (among others) concerning Rée's letter about Nietzsche in the appendix to his *Philosophy*: "When I was frequently with Rée—this was shortly after his break with Nietzsche in 1883—he told me that Nietzsche's letters were more important than his books and that his conversations were even more striking than his letters. This judgment certainly does not stem from their conflict; instead, it is, characteristic of their inner relationship. Nietzsche was, for Rée, an interesting phenomenon—the way an artist always is for the academic. . . . Rée had no use for intuitions and tended to deny their validity in moral and anthropological matters just as he did in physics." Lou A.-S. said that Paul Rée often did not understand what she and Nietzsche were discussing and would good-naturedly ridicule the topic. When, in Leipzig, Nietzsche told them about a dream he'd had (which he later incorporated into *Zarathustra*), Rée replied: "Well, what do you expect? You had pea soup again last night." The crystal clarity of Rée's thought was splendid but "his writings lack validity."

45. *read your letter at least five times*: Lou von S.'s letter to Gillot, dated March 26 (the second date is based on the Russian, Julian, calendar), was written after she'd known Rée for about ten days and a good three and a half weeks before Nietzsche's arrival in Rome.

47. *arrival of Friedrich Nietzsche*: As though his predecessor and "role model" had begun his tour of discovery from his home port of Genoa, Nietzsche, another Columbus, boarded a freighter under sail in Genoa on March 29, 1882, bound for Sicily (toward his "edge of the world"). The only passenger, he arrived in Messina on April 1 and stayed there until approximately April 20. While still in Genoa, he wrote the following in a letter to Rée about Lou, dated March 21: "Convey my greetings to this Russian woman, if it makes any sense: I long for this type of soul. Yes, before long, I'll be on the prowl for that type. Considering what I want to do in the next ten years, I need it. Marriage is a whole other story—I could handle, at the most, a two-year marriage and this only because of what I have to do in the next ten years." The poem: "Freundin—sprach Kolumbus—traue/Keinem Genueser mehr!" (My dear—spoke Columbus—trust/No more Genoese!) reveals, in its various versions (published in *Nietzsche-Dokumenten*), that the "Russian woman" was included in

his vision of the discovery of the world. Whether it was written when the ship set sail or later is inconsequential. Nietzsche did not give it to her until the beginning of November 1882 in Leipzig, perhaps in parting: "To my dear Lou." It is also significant to note that the letters Nietzsche wrote in Messina to his sister and his friends are similar in tone to those written shortly before his collapse. Perhaps the core of Nietzsche's "Lou-Experience" must be sought in this unity of the Columbus-Vision and the image of Lou.

47. *Nietzsche made himself a third member of our alliance*: his letter (partially quoted above) is an answer to a (no longer extant) letter from Paul Rée, sent to Genoa. Malwida von Meysenbug also mentioned Lou von S. to Nietzsche in her letter of March 27, 1882 (see *Documents*, p. 103ff). Nietzsche refers to this in July 1882: "If you [Malwida von M.] find anyone for me with *this* [heroic] mode of thinking, like that young Russian woman, please let me know." Rée then writes in another letter: "By undertaking this [trip to Messina], you have caused this young Russian woman, more than anyone else, surprise and concern. She has grown so eager to see you that she wanted to travel back via Genoa in order to do so. And she was very angry to see you so lost in thought. . . . She said she wanted so much to have a nice year and that's supposed to start next winter. To do so, she is counting on you, me and some older lady, such as Fräulein von Meysenbug (did you receive that letter?) who, however, is not interested. . . . Rome is not for you but you must definitely get to know the Russian woman." Lou A.-S. could therefore write that Nietzsche arrived "unexpectedly," but Nietzsche would have been well aware of his acceptance as a third person in an alliance. Perhaps the contradiction may be resolved thus: that Lou von S. had first (e.g., at the time of Rée's letter) established the winter plan, which was akin to a renewed Sorrento plan—and then afterward established her life plan with Rée ("as soon as he learned about the plan Paul Rée and I had"), in which, of course, a third person could not be included. What resulted from the amalgamation of these two incompatible plans is the "Trinity." —*the location of our future triune existence . . . Paris . . . Vienna*: Presumably Eugène von Salomé wanted to "continue his studies" and had thought briefly of Munich, because Lou von S., who was still dependent on her family's approval of her plans, writes to Nietzsche on August 2: "I think we will have to abandon Vienna in favor of Munich." The Paris plan had probably existed since Tautenburg.

47. *with Ivan Turgenev*: In Paris in 1875, Paul Rée visited Turgenev (1818–1883) who, exiled to his estate following his eulogy for Gogol, had left Russia. He returned to his homeland in 1880, where he was welcomed publicly at the unveiling of a monument to Pushkin. (It was then, at the very latest, that Lou von S. met him personally.) He died in Paris on September 3, 1883.

47. *foster daughter Olga Monod and Natalie Herzen*: Olga Herzen, the adopted

daughter of Malwida von Meysenbug, married the French historian Gabriel Monod in Paris in 1873.

47. *Nietzsche . . . normally somewhat reserved, almost solemn demeanor*: In her book *Friedrich Nietzsche in seinen Werken* (Friedrich Nietzsche in His Writings), Lou Andreas-Salomé enlarges upon this impression:

"I would say that this reserve, this inkling of concealed loneliness, is the first strong impression which makes Nietzsche's appearance so striking. The hasty observer notices nothing remarkable; this man of average height in his simple yet very meticulous clothing, with his calm features and plainly combed-back brown hair, could easily be overlooked. His thin, highly expressive mouth was almost completely covered by a large mustache, brushed forward. He had a quiet laugh, a noiseless manner of speaking and a careful, thoughtful gait, stooped slightly. . . . Nietzsche's hands were beautifully and nobly formed. He himself thought that they disclosed his intellect. . . . His eyes truly betrayed him. Although half-blind, they showed no trace of the peering and blinking and involuntary intrusiveness of many shortsighted people. They looked much more like guardians of treasures and unspoken secrets which no trespassers should glimpse. This defective vision lent his features a special kind of magic in that instead of reflecting ever-changing, external impressions, they revealed only what he had internalized. . . . I remember that, during the first few minutes of my initial conversation with Nietzsche—it was on a spring day in St. Peter's Church in Rome—his self-conscious style and manner astonished and disappointed me."

47. *we left Rome*: The date of Nietzsche's and Rée's departure, after that of Lou von S. and her mother, has not been determined.

47. *we seem to have been fascinated by nearby Sacro Monte*: The "seem to have been" should not be understood as an uncertain memory, but rather as tactful expression. In her journal for Paul Rée, Lou von S. writes from Tautenburg on August 14: "We often recall our time together in Italy, and when we climbed the [gap in the text] narrow path, he said quietly, 'Sacro Monte—I thank you for the most exquisite dream of my life!' " Talking about that time, Lou A.-S. once said with a slight, almost embarrassed smile: "I no longer recall whether I kissed Nietzsche on Sacro Monte or not." They visited Sacro Monte on May 5, 1882.

48. *Nietzsche . . . to Basel to visit the Overbecks*: Nietzsche writes to Paul Rée in Locarno on May 8: "Am going directly to Basel, where I will be living incognito with the Overbecks until your telegram calls me to Lucerne. . . . For me, the future is closed but not yet 'dark.' I must indeed speak again with Frl. L., perhaps in the Löwengarten [Lion Park]?" On May 13, Lou von S. and Paul Rée met Nietzsche at the train station and the conversation took place the next day. Nietzsche and Lou von S. left Lucerne to visit Wagner's former estate, Tribschen. Franz Overbeck, 1837–

1905, was a professor of ecclesiastical history in Basel. After Nietzsche was appointed there in 1869, Overbeck lived with him in the same house for years. Despite the increasing difference in their directions of thought (Overbeck's always stayed the same), their friendship lasted until Nietzsche's collapse. Overbeck picked Nietzsche up in Turin in January 1889 and delivered him to the psychiatric clinic in Basel. Elizabeth Nietzsche erroneously includes a visit Lou von S. paid to the Overbecks after the Italian trip in their relationship.

48. *photograph of the three of us*: The picture depicts Nietzsche and Rée standing by the shaft of a small, two-wheeled cart. Nietzsche, gripping the handle, is looking off into the distance while Rée, lightly touching the shaft and without being involved in the action, is turned toward the observer. Lou von S., also turned toward the observer, is half-crouching in the cart. In her gloved left hand, she holds the reins, which are attached to the outer arms of both men. In her ungloved right hand, she holds the short, makeshift whip with its artificial cluster of lilacs at the tip. The backdrop is composed of a scene with a tree, a bush, and the Jungfrau mountain. The expression on Nietzsche's face could be read as visionary; Lou and Rée scarcely betray amusement. The whole picture, with the artificiality of the studio, the coexistence of indifference (Rée), stiltedness (Lou), and posed devotion to an inner image (Nietzsche), seems more grotesque and uncanny than it does amusing. (First reproduced by Erich F. Podach, *Friedrich Nietzsche und Lou Salomé, Ihre Begegnung 1882* [Their Meeting, 1882], Zurich and Leipzig, 1937. The journal written by Lou von S. to Paul Rée in Tautenburg is printed there, provided by the editor.)

48. *mother and I stayed on awhile in Zurich at the charming country place of the friends*: The Brandt family, who had once lived in St. Petersburg and been close friends of General von Salomé's family, moved to Brunnenhof in Riesbach near Zurich, where they had taken in young Lou. Lou von S. and her mother were spending the second half of May there. At the end of that month, Lou visited the Overbecks in Basel. A kind of family get-together for the Wilms took place in Hamburg.

The Brunnenhof with the Villa Brandt, its farmlands, gardens, and various workshops, was close to the sanatorium Burghölzli. The Brandts were well known in Zurich society for their charity, their willingness to help, and also for the cultivation of music in their home. A monument, "Rebekkabrunnen" (Rebecca's Fountain), was erected by a member of their family on the square in front of their house and has been situated at the beginning of Bahnhofstrasse in Zurich since ca. 1906. The Brandts had no children. They adopted a nephew who brought them much misfortune. After the death of his adopted parents, he sold all the real estate and went to Russia with his wife and children. The grounds of the Brunnenhof now belong to the Burghölzli.

48. *opening of the Bayreuth festival*: Lou von S. remained in Stibbe from June 1882 until a few days before the festival performances, which began July 26 with the first

production of *Parsifal* (this production dedicated the new stage). Nietzsche left Naumburg on June 25 for Tautenburg, skipping the festival. Only his sister came to Bayreuth from Leipzig; Lou von Salomé and Elizabeth Nietzsche met each other there for the first time.

49. *the Russian painter Joukowsky*: Paul von Joukowsky (Zhukóvsky), 1845–1912, was the son of the poet Vasíly Andréyevich Zhukóvsky, who had been Alexander II's teacher and a grandchild of the Baltic painter Gerhard von Reutern. He was a friend of Wagner's and created the scenic design for the first productions of *Parsifal*. Lou A.-S. referred to him both in the manuscript and in conversation as "Graf [Count] Joukowsky."

49. *tone-deaf*: Helene Klingenberg remarked in this context that Lou A.-S. was often unable to listen to music because it "stirred her so deeply," almost like "a blow to the head."

49. *Nietzsche and I planned . . . several weeks together . . . Tautenburg*: From August 7 until August 26, 1882. Elisabeth Nietzsche met up with Lou von S. in Jena in order to accompany her to Tautenburg. Lou von S., like Elizabeth N., lived in Pastor Stölten's home, while Nietzsche had private accommodations elsewhere. Nietzsche often visited both Elizabeth and her in Tautenburg: "She didn't bother us" (Lou A.-S.).

49. *Biedermann*: Alois Emmanuel Biedermann, 1819–1885, was one of the most important Independent Protestant theologians of the 19th century and was greatly influenced by Kant, Schleiermacher, and especially Hegel. His main work is *Christliche Dogmatik* (Christian Dogmatic Theology), 1869. The copy given to Lou von S. "as a souvenir and bond in heartfelt sincerity" contains the handwritten verse: "Der Geist erforschet alle Dinge, auch die Tiefen der Gottheit" (for the Spirit searcheth all things, yea, the deep things of God) Cor. I.2,10. Biedermann took a strong interest in her studies and general well-being. Lou A.-S. remembered that he gave her a kind of mock qualifying examination at the beginning of her studies. She had studied dogma, general ecclesiastical history on a philosophical basis, logic, and metaphysics with him. She also studied art history. Besides Biedermann (no one else was particularly important), Lou von S. also studied art history with Gottfried Kinkel (1815–1882), who evaluated her poems and, more importantly, established, via a letter of recommendation, the contact with Malwida von Meysenbug, who had once been a friend of his. At this time Lou was staying in Rome. On July 7, 1883, A. E. Biedermann wrote to Frau von Salomé, whom he had met during her visit to Zurich before the Italian trip. The letter summarizes his impressions of her daughter:

"I have had a heartfelt interest in the spiritual and intellectual life of this unusual girl since the very beginnings of our acquaintance. She approached me with such trust, a trust I fully appreciate and value. It is a trust that I try to earn and reciprocate in that, to the best of my ability, I tried to exert a healthy, sobering influence on the direction of the development of her mind and spirit. Afterward, in Italy, and even more so after her return to Germany, she lived solely in the environment of men whom I do not personally know and whose spiritual and intellectual direction is so foreign that I could not be anything but disquieted by their influence over her— especially given the fact that she has shut me completely out of this aspect of her life.

"If I had the right to be regarded by her as a fatherly friend, then I felt I also had the duty to talk to her as such. So I wrote a letter to her at the end of the year [1882] in which I openly discussed these people and my worry about their unconscious influence on her. I also reminded her of one of her comments to me that she did not wish to overstep the bounds of the naturally female in the course of her studies but wanted to orient herself independently concerning the religious and philosophical questions with which today's thought occupies itself.

"I did not receive a direct answer from her, although probably an indirect one from Frau Brandt . . . the comment that she was feeling well, that she owed me an answer which needed to be conveyed orally rather than in writing. And, indeed, she appeared—totally unexpectedly—fourteen days ago. She made the same familiar heartwarming impression on my family and me—namely, that of a pure and genuine being who had concentrated unusual energy solely on an interest in spiritual and intellectual education. She seems to be untouched and therefore untroubled by all the other natural elements of life which can be of influence and can wield power in human feeling and will. Recognizing all her intellectual aspirations, her unusual talent for and expenditure of energy in this regard, I nonetheless stated that . . . I could hardly consider a career in writing as a livelihood capable of offering and accomplishing this [providing the solid framework for internal as well as external happiness] for anyone, but least of all for a woman.

"Were I to summarize our short reunion, it would be so: your daughter is an unusual woman possessing both childlike purity and integrity of mind as well as an unchildlike, almost unfeminine direction of spirit and independence of will. In both, she is a *jewel*. I hesitate to use this word because it sounds like a compliment. And I never compliment anyone I respect—and certainly not a girl in whose entire well-being I have a deep and sincere interest and against whom I fear I would be sinning in making compliments. And I definitely do not want to pay compliments to the mother about the daughter regarding a subject which I certainly feel and know will impose on the mother painful privations of the *happiness* which she is most commonly and obviously justified in expecting from a daughter.

"Still, I judge Fräulein Louise, on the basis of her innermost essence, to be a *jewel*."

49. *that Nietzsche and I argued a bit at first*: The "seems" should be interpreted here too as an expression of tact. The phrases "argued" and "all sorts of nonsense" refer to a comment from August 14 in the Tautenburg journal: "I *knew* that when we began to

converse, which we avoided at the beginning, caught up, as we were, in the storm of feelings [from having 'argued'], that, having disposed of small talk, we would soon find our way back to each other through our intrinsically related natures." And, in an answer from Paul Rée to a lost part of the journal: "Nietzsche, oddly enough, seems to have regarded you as his bride as soon as you agreed to travel to Tautenburg? And, in his function as bridegroom, reproached you for tales of what happened in Bayreuth?" Nietzsche's source was his sister. Lou A.-S. cited in this regard the example that Elisabeth N. had supposedly reported her "flirtation" with Joukowsky in Bayreuth: "I, the innocent lamb!" She once complained to Joukowsky that she "had nothing to wear" to the parties given every other day between the *Parsifal* productions; he is then said to have hemmed a simple dress for her while she was wearing it. Perhaps such harmlessly amusing occurrences gave Elisabeth N. reason to gossip. As luck would have it, Lou left Bayreuth in the same train compartment as Bernhard Förster; her jokes with him (not knowing that he was Elisabeth's fiancé) may have also fueled the fire. Elisabeth Nietzsche had also reported to her brother (and this was another reason for the "arguments" in Tautenburg) the comments Lou von S. is supposed to have made to her in a dispute about him. This heated discussion occurred in Jena prior to the joint trip to Tautenburg, where Nietzsche was awaiting her. It was also resumed there upon their arrival while Nietzsche was seeing about accommodations. This dispute was the basis of Elisabeth Förster-N.'s lifelong hostility toward Lou A.-S. Since it is referred to frequently in the following pages, some recollections from Lou A.-S. are noted here. After the (first) rejection of his marriage proposal, Nietzsche is said to have asked Rée (who had informed him of the rejection): "Then wouldn't it be better to *live together without marriage?*" Rée, "who did not like to say more than was necessary," told her this before the trip to Bayreuth-Tautenburg so that she would know where she stood with regard to Nietzsche's "change in physical conduct." When Elisabeth referred to her brother as an "ascetic and saint" in a conversation about him in the Jena home of friends of the Nietzsches', Lou laughed and innocently told her Rée's remark. Not only did Elisabeth voice the most virulent counterstatements, but she also became physically ill (compresses were necessary). Lou's replies increased in intensity and passion: she spoke of Nietzsche's "total claim" (which she had found in his letters since Lucerne), of "egoism" (see the Tautenburg letter diary, August 21: "the egoist in grand style"), and so on. Elisabeth N. wrote to Paul Rée's mother later regarding the reference to "living together" (see the note to p. 50), but the mother could only report that her son had told her this as well. A long letter, written by Elisabeth N. to the family friend in Jena in whose house the dispute occurred, is preserved. Lou A.-S. included herself when referring to this as an amusing "little girls' affair."

49. *our subsequent experience was a rich one*: This experience together remained, in a special way, completely fresh in Lou A.-S.'s mind. It wasn't so much a matter of discussing certain themes, delving deeply into subjects together and talking them through: what was magical was the way in which the most varied topics needed only

to the "touched upon" for a common understanding to emerge, together with an awareness of this understanding: she never experienced this in such a fashion again.

Another time, talking of her relationship to Nietzsche, she emphasized that she never gave him a reason to "speak of him and me instead of speaking of the three of us." She added that she had at the time a "burning interest" to discover "what was going on inside him, what he looked like inside," specifically with regard to her earliest experiences, which still reverberated within her; she was trying to get things clear in her mind.

The Tautenburg journal provides some of the results of this "burning interest." Here are a few examples taken near the end of the extant text: "At the same time, his [Nietzsche's] goal [of knowledge] attained, by virtue of his very nature, what I would call a Christian character, in that he seized upon it to rescue himself from a painful condition, which, as it were, required salvation. The identical goal of knowledge in my case resulted in a completely happy condition. This is the most striking difference between us, which can be traced throughout our struggles for development. Nietzsche, for example, threw religion overboard when his heart no longer felt anything for it, and when, in his emptiness and weariness, he longed for a new goal which would satisfy him. My lack of faith tore like a lightning bolt through my heart, or, rather, my mind, which then forced my heart to give up this belief, to which it had clung with childlike fervor." (This also with reference to the passage: *"that I would be fascinated by something in Nietzsche's words and nature. . . ."*)

49. *preference for an aphoristic style . . . forced . . . by his illness*: On p. 129 of the Nietzsche book, Lou A.-S. adds: "It corresponded increasingly to the singularity of his mind and spirit" to listen to his own thoughts as to a "constantly interrupted dialogue."

50. *one of my letters*: The letter continues: "Are we *very close* to each other? No, in spite of everything, no. There is a shadow over my feelings although, just a few short weeks ago, I was very happy with N. But this shadow separates us, pushes itself between us. And at some hidden depth of our being, we are worlds apart from each other."

50. *together with Nietzsche again . . . October in Leipzig*: Toward the end of their communal stay, on October 24, Lou von S. invites Heinrich von Stein (whom Rée knew from Halle) to a visit in Leipzig, "in the name of our Trinity, that is, Nietzsche, Rée, and me." Stein came but Nietzsche was visiting his family in Naumburg that day. She also uses the term "our Trinity" in a note concerning their attendance at a performance of Lessing's *Nathan der Weise*. However, the following (undated) entry made in Leipzig implies what "affected [her] inner feelings": "Just as Christian mysticism (like all mysticisms) can reach, precisely in its highest ecstasy, a coarsely religious sensuality, so too can the most ideal love become sensual again, precisely because, in its purely ideal state, all the great emotions are unleashed. A disagreeable

point, this revenge of the human element—I do not love the feelings when they return in this way because that is the point of *false pathos*, where they lose their truth and candor. Is it this which estranges me from N.?"

Occasionally Lou A.-S. remarked that the "Trinity" was not actually dissolved, not even in Leipzig: "but it simply wouldn't work, if he [Nietzsche] secretly wanted something else." She offered more detailed information regarding the passage "*to make me think less of Paul Rée*": Nietzsche was said to to have described Rée (who always carried a vial of poison with him) as an "incomparable coward." Several days before the departure from Leipzig, Peter Gast (Heinrich Köselitz) saw Lou von S. there "once and had an almost hour's long discussion with her in her room." His report at that time to his friend Cäcilie Gussenbauer is reproduced here for its vividness: "She is definitely a genius of heroic character. A bit taller than I, she is well-proportioned and a blonde, with an ancient Roman look. Her ideas show that she has dared to travel to the farthest horizon of the thinkable world as well as to those of the moral and intellectual worlds—as I said, a genius in spirit and disposition" (E. F. Podach, *Gestalten um Nietzsche* [Figures Around Nietzsche], Weimar, 1932, p. 82.) Peter Gast's remark fifteen years later in a letter to Josef Hofmiller is better suited to a history of the Nietzsche archives and as a revelation of Köselitz's own character: "For her to have lived around Nietzsche for a time, and instead of having been inflamed and stirred, to have been only an observer and a cold recording machine—that's something too." Lou A.-S. has commented on other remarks made by Gast (she knew nothing of those above) that he spoke "gushingly" of her and that later, when he worked in the Nietzsche archives, he "let his salaried position determine what he said," as he himself admitted. (See the chapter "Peter Gast" in the above-mentioned book.)

50. *I know only from one subsequent letter*: Lou A.-S. recalled how, in Stibbe, she and Paul Rée often puzzled over letters from Nietzsche and conferred on how to answer them: "How can one keep from offending him?" She cited the example of when, in the quiet afternoon hours in Stibbe, she encountered the following phrases in a letter from Nietzsche at the end of November: "Clear the skies." "The cloud on our horizon covered me!" She asked Rée, who sat across from her: "What can he mean by that?" and he answered "God only knows. . . ." The letter from mid-December which begins "You both should not get too upset about the outbursts of my 'megalomania' or my 'injured vanity' " probably refers to his sister's disclosure of that dispute which became important again at the end of the Tautenburg stay: "I've talked only briefly with my sister but enough to send the newly appeared ghost back into the Nothingness from which it sprang."

Nietzsche then withdrew from his family (especially as a result of one of his mother's comments). Elisabeth Nietzsche, as soon as she heard "that it's over with Frl. Salomé," tried to reestablish the relationship with her brother through letters. In May 1883 the reconciliation between brother and sister occurred in Rome, on the condition that there be silence about the "whole matter." A letter Nietzsche wrote to

Frau Overbeck at the end of July 1883 reveals that Nietzsche had received a final disclosure from his sister three weeks before: "a letter from my sister to Frau Rée, a copy of which she sent me (by the way, a feminine masterpiece of a letter!), shed light—and what light! Suddenly Dr. Rée is in the foreground. . . ." In this second phase of his terrible attempt to save himself or to give himself up, Nietzsche turns mainly against Rée (whose "mouthpiece" Lou von S. was said to have been) just as he had turned against Lou in the first phase. Finally Nietzsche breaks from his sister, having been "made sick by this indescribably disgusting provocation" (letter to Malwida von M. from May 1884).

The course of events, particularly considering Nietzsche's psychological behavior, can be sketched here only in a simplistic form. The pool of tangible documents can provide little enlightenment since almost all the letters written by Lou von Salomé and Paul Rée to Nietzsche have been destroyed; only limited information can be gleaned from documents. The entry made in her journal by Lou von S. on New Year's Night 1883 does not reveal any conflicts with Nietzsche:

"It was in the first days of January as, tired and sick, I came to Italy to absorb enough sunshine and life for the whole year and take them back with me. How this sun brightened our Roman strolls and chats, illuminated the idyllic Orta with its boat trips and the Sacro Monte with its nightingales, how it shone on our Swiss trip through the Gotthard as well as on the days in Lucerne! And then, as I left Mama and wanted to shape my reclaimed life, we entered into that strange friendship-relationship on which our whole lives have depended ever since, even today. A relationship which may never exist again in such intimacy and reticence. Perhaps rarely, perhaps never, have two people entered into an alliance so recklessly and, at the same time, with so much presence of mind. We certainly did not know at the time what would happen when I left Stibbe that evening and crossed over, alone and anonymous, into the Unknown which, through you, has become home to me. But then came the day when we left Stibbe together and, hand in hand, entered into the 'big world' like two true comrades, knowing we could not be misunderstood. And there, in this big world, we built ourselves a nest. Despite all appearances and difficulties, our relationship proved itself *to us* and *among people* as viable. An occasional disapproving or fearful judgment sounded in the distance or from friends, but we met only with understanding, heartiness, and warmth among those people who were *close* to us and in whose eyes we lived. It turned out that no greater degree of respect and love can be gained by avoiding false appearances, by retaining the whole bundle of prejudices and deferences into which one crams a thousand of life's loveliest instincts, than can be gained by completely living out one's own personality, which is its own self-identity and legitimation. And we ourselves, in the midst of this rich, strange, and stimulating life, we became dearer and dearer to each other. Our friendship, like a carefully tended and nobly guarded plant, paid honor to our horticultural talents, bearing today a thousand blossoms and a thousand buds."

Lou Andreas-Salomé's reaction toward the various claims made by Elisabeth Förster-Nietzsche (for example, that Lou A.-S. was a Finn, a Jew; that her Nietzsche book was a "vengeful act of injured female vanity toward a poor sick person," a fraudulent misrepresentation of Nietzsche's nature, character, and teachings, and many others) is clarified in a letter she wrote to her friend Frieda von Bülow. This letter, probably written in February 1905, was a reaction to a letter from Maximilian Harden, who had published an essay entitled *Nietzsche-Legenden* written by Elisabeth F.-N. in his journal *Die Zukunft* (The Future) on January 28, 1905. The letter from Lou A.-S. and the quotations she includes from a letter by Malwida von M. clarify to a certain degree the passage about Nietzsche's unfounded "suspicions." Here too, Elisabeth N. "sets an example" for her brother, as in the assertion that Lou and Rée "lived together" in Leipzig. Lou A.-S. must have had solid grounds for her accusation against Nietzsche, since she repeated it often.

"In Harden's letter there is a word which interests me because it shows what Förster is capable of achieving. It is only because of her allegation that my N. book is the vengeful act of a scorned woman (which I had assumed *every* reader of the book would find beyond belief) that Harden claimed my book is indeed 'not nice,' in other words, an unfair treatment. In truth, it glorifies N. as much as I could honestly do; and I wrote it only because it seemed to me *then* to be a necessary kind of duty to N. since the young literati were so stupidly transgressing on the subject. As a result, Nordau attacked me as a blind disciple! How can anyone who has read it judge it as Harden does? Naturally, Förster is only of this opinion because she probably wishes it had glorified him *more*. But her hatred toward me (which I had long since forgotten) is older and its actual source unknown to me. In any case, it is of a completely personal nature (jealousy). Even before I knew her, I had been warned about her.

"As far as a reply is concerned, I could, of course, provide one, be it either angry or objective. I could have done that long ago if I wanted to put up with this person's diminishing my small portion of happiness, peace, and professional satisfaction. But my relationship to N. includes the most personal elements, such as a marriage proposal and its rejection, and the *very* unpleasant reaction of his jealous anger toward Rée which sullied us all as much as it possibly could have. M[alwida] v. M[eysenbug] wrote me at the time: 'N. just gave vent to his jealousy,' and she was simultaneously infuriated that we 'left' the unh[appy] N. because of our own affection for each other.' In the new N. volume [of the biography], Förster certainly wrote considerably more irritating things than H[arden]. For example, I supposedly chased after Rée in vain as well with matrimony in mind. Should one have to 'refute' such things?! And were *you*, as my friend, to write about this, then you would have to include all the relevant, objective proof. Otherwise, the justifiable conclusion would be that the matter can't be definitively refuted. So, either stir up the whole hornets' nest or don't react at all—that is, as far as I'm concerned, as a friend authorized by me. On the other hand, any other method of reacting—even directed at Förster herself—would be worthless, as attractive as the idea sounds to me, because I'm human after all, and would be happy to see her annoyed till she bursts. What hits me the hardest though, is that things, such as my book, *can* be so wrongly understood. But I believe that no one who knew me in the N. years can misunderstand me as Förster does. All her invective misses the mark entirely: my sins were always precisely of the opposite kind.

"Adieu! Harden will finally come to the conclusion that we don't dare contradict her."

See the information from Karl Schlechta in Vol. III of his Nietzsche edition *Werke in drei Bänden* (Works in Three Volumes), Munich, 1956, p. 1371f. about Nietzsche's "Lou-Experience."

51. *Heinrich von Stein . . . in Sils Maria*: Heinrich von Stein, 1857–1887, philosopher, aesthetician, and poet, had known Paul Rée since his student days in 1874/75 in Halle. It was through Rée that Stein was staying with Malwida von Meysenbug in the winter of 1877/78. Nietzsche probably heard of him first in a letter from Rée in October 1877, shortly before the appearance of *Die Ideale des Materialismus* (The Ideals of Materialism), which established Stein as a philosopher. Nietzsche visited Sils Maria from August 26 to 28, 1884. Nietzsche, in a letter to Overbeck dated September 14, 1884 calls Stein "a splendid example of a real person and a man; I find him to be lucid and agreeable through and through because of his basically *heroic* attitude." At the end of November he sent him the poem "O Lebens Mittag! Feierliche Zeit!" (O Life's Noon Hour! A Solemn Time!) which, at the time, was titled "Einsiedlers Sehnsucht" (A Hermit's Longing). Their relationship, which included a personal encounter on the road between Naumburg and Kösen in the autumn of 1885, was limited from that point on.

An addition to Nietzsche's cited letter after Heinrich von Stein's visit reads: " 'Struggling for God', novel by H(enri) Lou (Stuttgart, Auerbach)—*Stein* spoke of it." In this book, Nietzsche had found "a hundred echoes of our Tautenburg conversations" (to Overbeck, October 17, 1885). Previously, he had referred to the soon-to-be-published essay by Lou von Salomé "Vom religiösen Affekt" (Concerning Religious Emotions): "the same theme which I revealed to her extraordinary talent and experience in Tautenburg. I'm glad my efforts back then weren't totally in vain" (to Malwida von M., May 1884). This essay by Lou A.-S. appeared on April 23, 1898 in *Die Zukunft* (The Future).

51. *kept away from it all, refusing to read any more about it*: To the extent that Lou A.-S. did not, for example, cut open the pages of Elisabeth Förster-N.'s Nietzsche biography (1895ff), which described Nietzsche's meeting her. And even in writing the first draft of this particular chapter, she chose to ignore the later publication by Nietzsche's sister of certain drafts of his letters. Occasionally Lou A.-S. remarked that one couldn't really "trust" Nietzsche; that his "eightfold motivations" had undermined such trust. He also had, she said, something of his sister's "scheming" nature.

51. *book Friedrich Nietzsche in His Works*: It appeared in Vienna, Carl Konegan

Publishers, in 1894, and is "dedicated in faithful memory" to "An Unnamed Person" (Paul Rée). In the book (which couldn't take into account his literary estate), Lou A.-S. distinguishes three periods of Nietzsche's spiritual development. She first undertook these distinctions in a periodical in January 1891 and in other early studies as well. Already, in October 1882 in Leipzig, she had "read aloud to him and discussed with him" "A Sketch Toward Characterizing Nietzsche," which concerned his "nature" and his "transformations" (see p. 4 of her book). The three periods are: (1.) Nietzsche at the level where the "object of his religiously oriented turn of mind was not yet himself" (a Wagner disciple in terms of Schopenhauer's philosophy), (2.) N. as "the emotionless pure thinker" in a positivistic sense (from *Human, All Too Human* on), (3.) N. as "the mystical philosopher of the will." (Nietzsche had confided his doctrine of the Eternal Return to Lou von S.—"he spoke about it only in hushed tones and with signs of deepest terror," Nietzsche book, p. 222.)

51. *recall one summer in Celerina in Upper Engadine*: probably in 1885. In the previous summer, Rée and Gillot had gotten to know each other during a stay at St. Quirini-Tegernsee: "We spent many a pleasant hour there while the restless waves tumbled onto the shore and the song of the boatmen could be heard from the water. Rée and I have often rowed over to the Gillots' ourselves, where we spend the evening until the moon climbs high in the sky and calls us home. It's a unique pleasure for me to see the two men together. The past and the present interweave themselves oddly in my imagination and I feel very happy. They converse sincerely with each other and it is a pleasant sight when Gillot, in his warm manner, throws his arm around Rée's shoulders, and his face with its energy and his bright, sarcastic mouth, across from Rée's angular, guileless, dark features. . . ." (fragment of a letter). On the same piece of paper, Lou von S. deals with the mystery that Gillot remained for her: "But in order to do that, I must *be able to get to know* Gillot, as I do others, and this I can do as little today as in days gone by. He remains for me that which my feelings make of him—just think, I placed a small notebook with the title 'Who Are You?' in my most well-concealed desk drawer. It was to contain studies of Gillot. The many mute, white notebook pages provide me with an answer by virtue of their very blankness. But strangely enough, the answer is less than logical—almost as though given by a small child. The answer is not: 'You are this or that' but 'You are dear to me and I value you.' And instead of a portrait, it consists of an eternal veil."

At the time when Lou von S. was writing her first book, around the beginning of 1884, near Meran, Gillot was recuperating from a serious illness. "I think often of him and am in the habit of dreaming about him all night long. I am surprised to find myself thinking about him. Recently I was so lost in thought that, when Rée happened to open the door and come toward me, in a kind of madness, I confused him with Gillot and, trembling all over, came close to fainting." In the summer of 1884, she had her first reunion with Gillot.

52. *tried spending part of winter in Vienna once, where my brother . . . with Nothnagel:*

winter 1884/85. After completing his medical studies, Eugène von Salomé worked for a time at the First Viennese medical clinic, which had been founded and directed by Hermann Nothnagel, the internal medicine specialist, 1841–1905. Salomé left the clinic in 1886 and established himself in St. Petersburg as a pediatrician.

52. *my first book*: After Heinrich von Stein had told him of the book during his visit to Sils Maria, Nietzsche read *Struggling for God* the year it appeared:

"Yesterday I saw Rée's book about the conscience:—how empty, how boring, how wrong! One should speak only of those matters with which one has had experience.

"I had a totally different impression of the half-novel written by his soeur insépar-able Salomé. Rather ironically, it came to my attention at the same time as his did. All formal elements are girl-like, effeminate and, considering the pretext that an old man is supposed to be the narrator, nearly comic. But the *thing* itself has its serious side and higher level. Even though it definitely is not the Eternal-Feminine which elevates this girl to *new heights*; it is perhaps the Eternal-Masculine.

"I forgot to say how much I prize the simple, clear, and almost antique form of Rée's book. *This* is the 'philosophical habitus.'—Such a shame that more 'content' is not found in such dress! Among Germans, it cannot be honored highly enough if someone, in the style that R. has always used, forswears the true German Devil, the genius or the demon of unclarity." (October 15, 1885) Paul Rée's book (*The Origin of the Conscience*), like *Struggling for God*, appeared in 1885. For *Julius and Heinrich Hart*, see note to p. 58.

52. *originally formed around Ludwig Haller*: Ludwig Haller, in later years a senior governmental executive officer, was the author of *Alles in Allen. Metalogik. Meta-physik. Metapsychik* (All in All: Metalogic, Metaphysics, Metapsychics). Its epi-graph was: "Auf daβ Gott sei Alles in Allen" (but it is the same God which worketh all in all: I Cor. 12.6), Berlin 1888. He died during the printing of the two-volume set, of which only the first volume (the one he had prepared) was actually published. In the beginning the meetings generally took place in Haller's apartment. In a letter to Lou von S. (probably in 1885), he writes: "I do not need to reiterate to you what an important moment in *my* life it is to have our small circle assemble. Without these meetings, I would not have succeeded in achieving the goal toward which I have striven for years." Lou A.-S. wrote an essay (which has not been found) about Haller, after his death.

54. *lowered the curtain before himself*: compare the portrayal (also the image of the curtain) in the Nietzsche book, pp. 147–149. Regarding Nietzsche's self-deification, see the Nietzsche book, p. 213ff.

54. *among the others*: Lou A.-S. had listed most of the names of the following with a cross, insofar as she had learned of their deaths. *Georg Brandes* (Cohen), (1842–1927), Danish literary historian, lived from 1877–1883 in Berlin. F. C. Andreas

NOTES · 179

knew him during his studies of the Iranian manuscripts in Copenhagen (1868–1870). His work *Hauptströmungen der Litteratur des 19. Jahrhunderts* (Main Trends of Nineteenth-Century Literature), Berlin, 1872–1891, using a positivistic-Darwinian approach, was widely known. Brandes championed Naturalism in literature. *Hans Delbrück* (1848–1929), historian, was a private university instructor in Berlin. In 1882 he dedicated his work *Das Leben des Feldmarschalls Grafen Neithardt von Gneisenau* (The Life of Field Marshal Count Neithardt von Gneisenau), written the same year, to Lou von S. with the words: "if not to read—then indeed to remember."

Paul Deußen (1845–1919), publisher and disciple of Schopenhauer, translator and, in the spirit of Schopenhauer, interpreter of ancient Indian holy writings. He had been Nietzsche's friend since school days and was, at this time, a private university instructor at the University of Berlin (and later a professor at Kiel University). He had just (1883) finished his *System des Vedânta* (System of Vedanta). Deussen tells in his posthumously published autobiography, *Mein Leben* (My Life), 1922, that "one day, perhaps 1883 [actually 1882], Dr. Paul Rée and Louise v. Salomé . . . who had distinguished herself with her sharp and clear mind" appeared at his home. "A philosophical circle was set up, including (besides Lou, Rée, and me) Dr. Romundt and later Heinrich v. Stein, private university instructor. In the meantime, Lou wrote her book *Struggling for God*, which appeared in December 1884. I was one of the first to whom she gave a copy. . . . I must admit that, while reading it, my love for Lou caught fire and burned brightly. . . . My friend Ebbinghaus maintained that they were 'a nun's daydreams' but I found much of her spirit in the book and I fell in love with her mind. The fire soon dampened when I noticed that within our philosophical group, Lou preferred the somewhat murky views of Heinrich v. Stein to mine. The friendship remained, but only as a friendship." He knew Paul Rée from a trip taken long ago in the area of the Lake of Lucerne when, having arrived late, he had had to share accommodations with a stranger. "Right! In the other corner someone already lay in bed. 'Good Evening!' I said. 'Good Evening' echoes a soft, pleasant-sounding voice. 'Allow me to introduce myself: Dr. Deußen from Marburg.' 'Pleased to meet you! I am Paul Rée, doctor of philosophy.' I considered some of the various subjects . . . covered by the title Doctor of Philosophy and consequently asked . . . carefully: 'Philosophy in the wider or the narrower sense?' 'Philosophy in the narrowest sense,' replied the stranger. Again a small pause, and then I said: 'Have you associated yourself more closely with any particular philosopher?' To this question, the stranger uttered but one word and it was this single word which drove me in one step to his bedside where I took his hand in mine. A total stranger became a friend, a brother. This one word was the name Schopenhauer."

J. Gildemeister is the brother of the well-known translator Otto Gildemeister. *Hugo Göring* was a physician. *Paul Güßfeldt* (1840–1920) was a scientist who traveled to, among other places, the Andes in 1882–1883. *Wilhelm Grube* (1855–1908), sinologist, was at that time assistant director of the Museum of Ethnology in

Berlin and a university lecturer. W. *Halbfaβ* was a high-school teacher and a classical philologist. *Max Heinemann* was a public prosecutor who had set some of Lou v. S.'s poems to music: "They should appear in print this winter" (1885). He became estranged from her when he mentioned that he had attended an execution. *Ferdinand Laban,* born 1856, was a librarian for the Royal Museums in Berlin. He had published *Die Schopenhauer-Litteratur* in 1880 and was close to Heinrich von Stein. *Rudolf Lehmann* (1855–1927), later well known as a teacher, was at this time a university lecturer. *Heinrich Romundt* (1845–1919), follower of Kant, had been Nietzsche's friend since their university days together in Leipzig. As a private university instructor in Basel, as already mentioned, he established the Nietzsche–Paul Rée connection. Later he was a high-school teacher. *Georg Runze* (1852–1919) was a Protestant theologian and later taught at Berlin University. *Heinrich von Stein* (see the note to p. 51). His participation in the meetings is shown conclusively by two short messages to Paul Rée (January 8, 1885) and Lou von S. (December 12, 1885): "I'm looking forward to the continuation of the Bruno readings." In an earlier letter to Paul Rée (October 28, 1881), he expresses the "difference" of his "notion of the world" from that of his friend (as he calls Rée) and also writes about his perception of Nietzsche after the break with Wagner. Most of the letter is printed here in light of these important connections, as well as the fact that it represents the intellectual divergence of two members of the philosophical circle:

"There certainly is a difference between your explanation of feelings and mine based on the same world view. I fail to see why nature, on its course to let certain relationships of affinity consciously appear as the feeling of love, should have taken the detour of placing it only in the instinct of the nursing mother and would then reproduce it as a delusion in other cases. . . . Why should nature not adhere to the same process directly, without detours, in all interhuman relationships in order to imbue the instinct of completely healthy association with the majestically understandable feeling of sympathy?

"With these questions I have moved into your territory and have tried to move around on it. My actual standpoint is much different because only this ideal significance of feelings stimulates me to contemplation and inspires me to speak out. Everything external is an insignificant game in comparison. . . . How vain does the course of world destiny appear, with its continual repetition of the victory of the depths. . . .: All heroes everywhere only tragic passersby, but nonetheless magnificent beyond all bounds to watch. Only on the basis of feelings can history be understood: the soul contains the true sense of the times—even of those times where history had nothing to say. You agreed with me that your great and richly talented friend Friedrich Nietzsche was supposedly moved by a similar enthusiasm of the soul to production of a precisely historical scope. And this, I believe, touched me so deeply in his works, bound me so inextricably to his main work: *Über die Geburt der Tragödie"* (The Birth of Tragedy). He is an artist but with an intellectually productive virtuosity, and that is why he was created as the intellectual herald of the most all-encompassing conception of art [namely, Wagner]. The impression of true art is what directs us in our yearning sighs for a new world, a new culture. And therefore we want to make true art the focus of all related efforts; we want to make it the true point of view for a radically different Weltanschauung.

"Even if he has gone in a direction of a complete, almost skeptical intellectualism, I still do not believe that this is the last and decisive turn in his spiritual life. Yes, I do not regard this by any means as the 'wrong track'—and here I exclude the unfortunate fact that certain personal relationships have been broken off as a result of these publications [since *Human, All Too Human*, Vol. 1]. His virtuosity is indeed intellectual, even if I grant the fact that the prevailing tone of his temperament is artistic; the development and training of such a virtuosity can in no way avoid the sharpest skepticism. A . . . heroic need—is, granted, the foundation for all of this. Nietzsche possessed that and still does: he who has been in favor cannot fall out of favor; he *believes*, even if only in the most far-removed depths of a quiet, yearning wistfulness. It all depends on this credo, however, and out of the *credo quia absurdum*, we are able to form the *credo nesque enim est absurdum* [I believe, because it is not absurd]."

The philosophical circle of friends around Paul Rée and Lou von Salomé was apparently formed of Rée's old friends and acquaintances (Heinrich von Stein, Romundt, Tönnies, Deußen) who, in turn, brought in their friends. The philosopher Friedrich Paulsen, a close acquaintance of Ebbinghaus and then also of Rée, seems to have had loose ties with the group. The first consolidation occurred at the end of 1882. Besides Haller, Deußen, Ebbinghaus, Delbrück, Stein, and Brandes, letters from 1883 also mention Tönnies, Halbfaß, Runze, and Lehmann, who formed "a small colony" with Rée and Lou in Churwalden during the summer vacation. Ferdinand Laban was a member of the group in the winter of 1883/84. In the first months of 1884, Lou von S., who had suffered for years from a weak constitution, "fully recovered and grew ever stronger—actually leaving with an entirely changed body." That summer, on the way to the Tegernsee, where Gillot was staying, she met Heinrich von Stein in Munich. Heinemann also took part in the summer visit to Upper Engadine in 1885 (about which Lou writes above). He had contacted her after having read *Struggling for God*. Baron Carl von Schultz, Gildemeister, and Göring are mentioned outside the context of the group in 1886. Thinking back to the friends of those years, Lou Andreas-Salomé once remarked: "They were real people—pure and simple."

54. *Ferdinand Tönnies/Hermann Ebbinghaus*: Ferdinand Tönnies, (1855–1936), one of the founders of modern German sociology, was at this time a university lecturer in Kiel. He became known particularly for his classic treatise *Gemeinschaft und Gesellschaft* (Community and Society) in 1887. Lou A.-S. called him the most brilliant conversational partner, aside from Nietzsche, she had ever met. In his work *Der Nietzsche-Kultus: Eine Kritik* (The Nietzsche Cult: A Critique), 1897, he argued for "an appeal to caution, to prudence, to sobriety." He maintained that the Nietzsche book written by Lou A.-S. had the "honor of having opened up a deep,

personal, and objective insight into this unusual phenomenon." Hermann Ebbinghaus (1850–1909), at the time a private university instructor in Berlin, was an experimental psychologist who later taught in Breslau and Halle. Both men belonged to the relatively numerous circle of friends around Lou von S. and Paul Rée. And they all passionately courted Lou. A letter written by Ferdinand Tönnies on July 11, 1883 from Flims to Friedrich Paulsen gives an idea of the communal vacations in the Rée period: "We live here in a highly charming trio. . . . Fräulein Salomé manages this household with superior confidence and an exquisiteness of tact which is totally admirable. Truly, she is a totally extraordinary being. So much knowledge in the head of a twenty-one-year-old girl would almost evoke horror if not for the genuine tenderness of her soul and her consummate modesty. . . . Rée is very industrious. . . . His evenly keeled, humorous, and witty nature always completely delights me." See Nietzsche Documents p. 321f and 288ff.

55. *I had seen him fall prey again to his addiction to gambling*: On September 12, 1882, Paul Rée wrote as follows to Lou von S., who was living at his parents' home in Stibbe:

"You were right in what you said last night, absolutely right. Not as though I was born with weakness of character; it was not in my nature from the very beginning, and I've had no trace of it for the better part of my life. But I'm inferior in the battle with a stronger enemy. Not because I was weak but because the opponent was superhumanly strong. Oddly enough, I too have ruined myself mostly by staying up through the night. For months, I intentionally stayed awake all night, albeit in a different way (mostly wandering the streets of Berlin) and for a different purpose than you. I don't think that I have fought any less energetically than you, but my opponent was, incredible as it seems, even more terrible than your opponents. It conquered me completely. Exhausted, I finally gave up the battle. I still remember that, at the time, I compared myself to a monk about whom Seume writes in his autobiography, *Mein Leben* (My Life), 1813. He had done everything thinkable to free himself from the coercive recruiters who sold soldiers to America back then. When, however, everything proved fruitless and he had to board ship, then he lay down in his hammock and remained there, without washing, without combing his hair, and so he rotted away in his vermin and his filth.

"I'm afraid that we must part company; because, although I offer you protection and stability in the world, you are too honest to want this if the most profound, deepest, congenial fondness between us is shaken only in the slightest. Yet that is the case. Because, on the one hand, weakness of character is now a part of my being; indeed, it is almost the key to my being—that is to say, to that being which I have more and more become in the last four, five, six years. I was actually already dead; you had awakened me to a mock life, but such feigned semblance in a dead person is revolting. On the other hand, I could not get rid of a feeling of anxiety, based on the existence of a characteristic which I feel strongly in myself and which I know you dislike. The sense of uncertainty I mean has to do with being disliked by you, doing things which are disagreeable in your eyes.

"Therefore—let us go our separate ways to our graves."

Under this, in the margin, the answer from Lou von S.:

"No, absolutely not! Let us live and strive together, until you have *retracted* this! L."

55. *fundamental misunderstanding persisted*: See the note to the phrase "without being able to tell the full truth about this step to my friend" in the chapter "What's Missing From the Sketch"; actually, see the entire beginning of the chapter. Lou von S. could only reassure Paul Rée that nothing could change her feelings toward him. In the winter semester of 1885/86, Rée began to study medicine after the "tenured philosophy faculty" in Strasbourg had "waved him off with both their hands and feet" (so Rée wrote to Paulsen about his attempt to qualify as a university lecturer). Lou von S. continued to live alone in the pension and one day opened her door to a stranger: Andreas, who gave German lessons to Turkish officers there. His feeling toward her was immediate, and never wavered. In her case, however, it was some time before she felt equally certain about things. She, who had refused all offers up to this point without hesitation, wrote Rée of Andreas' courtship and her intention to "have relations" with him. In her letter she added typically: "if you have no objections." Rée answered, equally typically, with "whatever you do is fine," until he thought he was being confronted with a decision made against him. The engagement took place on November 1, 1886, the wedding on June 20, 1887. Paul Rée probably left in the early spring of 1887.

56. *accidently fell to his death*: In a letter to Frieda von Bülow, written after Rée died, Lou A.-S. says: "The primary experience for me late this autumn was one with which I was unable to cope for many weeks, for rather terrible reasons that can only be explained in person. It was Rée's death. You probably read that he fell to his death in Celerina (Upper Engadine), where we spent the summers and where he had been living, totally alone, for years. For a while I lived only in old letters and much became clear to me. The past came eerily alive. My main impression was: Too much! I've had too much! Too much of what is good and rich for one person's lifetime! It makes one feel humble."

Rée's memoir mentioned above, written on March 17, 1888 (about a year after Paul Rée's departure) reads: "Today, 6 years ago, I met you. I was much younger then, more than 6 years younger. A child, full of its first pain, who then healed. And I had the first inkling of the rich life in front of me. How often I think of all this and with what limitless clarity of thoughts. But I don't write it down as I used to do, not so long ago, always putting down on paper everything that I did. I believe that everything in me now shies away from words. I often dream of you—nothing in particular—it's always the same, simple thing: I see you again and then I cry in my dream. Sometimes I find myself talking or gesturing just like you—totally involuntarily and accidentally—and then I always feel how dear you are to me. I remember an argument we had where, in the thick of the quarrel, you said (with your mixture of goodness and irony): 'If we argued until we separated and, years later, happened to see each other again somewhere, how terribly pleased we would both be!' And your eyes suddenly filled with tears. I replay that scene so often now and think: *yes, yes.*"

Lou A.-S. also felt this way. She thought that she would never break off with Rée and she termed their parting "irreparable." She thought of it with pain, not nostalgia.

58. *those we got to know* (*the Berlin circle, since* 1887): *Gerhart Hauptmann* (1862–1946) wrote the story *Bahnwärter Thiel* (Signalman Thiel) in Erkner, among other works. "*Signalman Thiel*, Wilhelm Bölsche's *Mittagsgöttin* (Midday Goddess), and Bruno Wille's *Wacholderbaum* (Juniper Tree) were conceived in the dreamy stillness of the forest of the Brandenburg March" (Nadler). Hauptmann's social drama *Vor Sonnenaufgang* (Before Sunrise) had been heralded by Theodor Fontane even before its premiere at the Lessing Theater of Berlin's Independent Theater. It was this play which gave literary Naturalism its breakthrough in Germany. A message: "My dear and cherished woman, I must be granted a visit! Gerhart" indicates the (completely platonic) friendship between Hauptmann and Lou A.-S. Later, when the longing for glory overtook him, Lou A.-S. kept her distance. She was quite taken with his first wife, Marie Hauptmann. *Arne Garborg* (1851–1924) is considered one of the most important figures, both on an intellectual and a human level, in Norwegian literature of his time. He and others tried to utilize in literature the Landsmål, the purely Norwegian language free of Danish elements. He came to Germany in 1890. After his first literary efforts, which were influenced by Naturalism and Decadence, he reintroduced religion to literature in *Müde Seelen* (Tired Souls). *Hulda Garborg* translated Lou A.-S.'s book *Ibsens Frauengestalten* (Ibsen's Female Figures) into Danish, added a preface written by her husband, and published it in Copenhagen in 1893. *Bruno Wille and Wilhelm Bölsche*, "friends in a rare kinship of opposites" (Nadler), founded their Friedrichshagen community in 1890, turning away from a narrow urbanism. In the same year, Bruno Wille (1860–1928) opened his Independent People's Theater with a production of Ibsen's *Pillars of Society*. After he rejected party-line socialism in 1894, he renamed his theater the New Independent People's Theater, with the goal of bringing workers into contact with art. Bölsche and the actor Turk aided him in this undertaking. Wille's Friedrichshagen struggles as a freethinking teacher, his own "experiences with philistinism," form the basis of *Das Gefängnis zum preußischen Adler* (The Prussian Eagle's Jail), 1914. Wille was best known for his pantheistic-romantic novel, *Roman eines Allsehers: Offenbarungen des Wacholderbaumes* (Novel of One Who Sees All: Revelations of the Juniper Tree), 1895. A caricature of unknown origin found in Lou A.-S.'s papers depicts him in the year 2000, dressed in his nightshirt, with a dog on a leash, and carrying under his arm a manuscript "Philosophie des

reinen Mittels" (Philosophy of Pure Means). This title is an allusion to his text of the same name which appeared in the periodical *Freie Bühne* (Independent Theater). He changed the title in 1896 to *Philosophie der Befreiung durch das reine Mittel* (The Philosophy of Deliverance by Pure Means). His friend Wilhelm Bölsche (1861–1939) arrived in Berlin in 1887 and published *Die naturwissenschaftlichen Grundlagen der Poesie* (The Scientific Foundations of Poetry) that same year. Following Brahm and preceding Julius Hart, he was the editor of the periodical *Independent Theater* ("For the Struggles of Our Time") from 1890 to 1893. His antispiritualistic novel, *The Midday Goddess*, infused with elements of nature poetry, appeared in 1891. In 1898 Lou A.-S. discussed critically in *Die Zukunft* (The Future) the first volume of his well-known three-volume work *Das Liebesleben in der Natur* (Lovelife in Nature), which had just been published. According to the few extant letters, meetings of the "whole colony" took place mostly at Bölsche's from 1890 to 1893. *The Hart brothers:* Heinrich Hart (1853–1906) and his brother Julius (1859–1930) were critics as well as poets and from 1882–1884 tried to clarify and evaluate the literary trends of their time in the periodical *Kritische Waffengänge* (Critical Engagements). Along with Fontane (*Vossische Zeitung* [Vossische Newspaper]), they were probably the most important critics in print in the eighties and beyond (in the *Tägliche Rundschau* [Daily Review]). Lou A.-S. probably met the Harts before they joined the Friedrichshagen group around Bruno Wille and Wilhelm Bölsche. Later, in 1900, they founded the religious brotherhood Neue Gemeinschaft (New Community) in Schlachtensee. The Swedish writer *Ola Hansson-Marholm* (1860–1925), who lived in Friedrichshagen from 1889 to 1900, supported Danish writers, particularly Jacobsen, and turned against the Naturalists Ibsen and Brandes. Strindberg encouraged him to write his essay on Nietzsche in 1890. At the time he was writing in German. Using the pseudonym *Laura Marholm*, his wife wrote dramas and novellas. *August Strindberg* (1849–1912) had just arrived from Switzerland when Lou A.-S. met him in Friedrichshagen in 1892. He had a second, short marriage in 1893 in Berlin and left a year later for Paris. *Max Halbe* (1865–1941) had not yet had his great theatrical success with the 1893 romantic drama *Jugend* (Youth), set in his homeland of Vistula. *Arno Holz* (1863–1929) provided a model for Naturalism in 1890 with his drama *Die Familie Selicke* (The Selicke Family). In his work *Die Kunst, ihr Wesen und ihre Gesetze* (Art, Its Nature and Its Rules), he declared that "Art must, once again, become Nature." His 1896 comedy, *Sozialaristokraten* (Socialist Aristocrats), is a satire of the Friedrichshagen circle of aristocratic socialists, complete with "portraits" of Wille, Mackay, and even young Holz himself. *Walter Leistikow* (1865–1908) painted the Brandenburg March countryside, especially the Grunewald. *John Henry Mackay* (1864–1933), of Scottish descent, had been in Berlin since 1898 and was a follower and editor of Stirner. In his novel, *Die Anarchisten* (The Anarchists), he breathed life into the theory of "individual anarchism," which opposes all use of force in society. Set in London, it was published in 1891. *Richard Dehmel* (1863–1920) who, besides Leistikow, was the only other person from the Brandenburg March in the group, produced his first volumes of poetry in those years: *Erlösungen* (Salvations), 1891, and *Aber die Liebe* (But Love), 1893. *Fritz Mauthner* (1849–1923), of Bohemian-Jewish extraction, was a cofounder of the periodical *Freie Bühne* (Independent Theater). In the novel *Der letzte Deutsche von Blatna* (The Last German of Blatna), 1890, he portrays the situation of the Germans in his homeland. Mauthner was also known as a parodist (*Nach berühmten Mustern* [After Well-known Models]) and a satirist. In 1901/02, he published *Beiträge zu einer Kritik der Sprache* (Contributions to a Critique of Language) and professed his belief in a "godless mysticism." *Otto Brahm* (1856–1912) began as a critic and a literary historian. With the founding in 1869 of the Independent Theater Association, he became its director and publisher of the periodical of the same name. His first production was Ibsen's *Ghosts* and his second was Hauptmann's *Before Sunrise*. In 1894 he took over the Deutsches Theater. The other "Independent Theater" refers, therefore, to Wille's Independent People's Theater, which was later called the Berliner Volkstheater (Berlin People's Theater). *Maximilian Harden* (Witkowski) (1861–1927) began as an actor and then, in 1892, founded the weekly periodical *Die Zukunft* (The Future), which was a forum for a wide variety of opinions. His literary attacks on the Kaiser and aristocratic society had political repercussions. *Carl Hauptmann* (1858–1921) received his doctoral degree in 1893 in Zurich. His dissertation, written with the positivist (critical empiricist) Richard Avenarius, was entitled *Die Metaphysik in der modernen Physiologie: Erster Teil* (Metaphysics in Modern Physiology: First Part). His early literary works were closely associated with Naturalism: *Marianne*, 1894, and, particularly, *Ephraims Breite* (Ephraim's Size), 1899. Rilke met him in Worpswede. *Otto Erich Hartleben* (1864–1905), a dramatist, was the author, among other works, of the comedy *Hanna Jagert*, 1893, and the well-known officer's tragedy *Rosenmontag* (Shrove Monday), 1900. "Moppchen" was the nickname of Hartleben's later wife. *Eugen Kühnemann* (1868–1941), later a literary historian in Breslau, wrote his book *Herders Leben* (Herder's Life) in 1895. He says in his preface that he would "most like" to see his book "in the hands of young artists." In a letter to Lou A.-S., after completing the volume, he called it "your book."

59. *Georg Ledebour . . . let these lines serve as a greeting*: Georg Ledebour, born in 1850, was a socialist politician who, at this time, was editor of a Social-Democratic newspaper. He was one of the founders of the Independent Social-Democratic Party (formed by breaking away from the SPD during World War I). He later rejected the idea of amalgamation with the Communist Party. In 1924 he founded the pacifistic Sozialistischer Bund (Socialist Federation) and, in 1933, emigrated to Switzerland. He died in Bern in 1947. See the explanation of "let these lines serve as a greeting to him" in the chapter "What's Missing From the Sketch," p. 130 above, with commentary.

59. (*Parisian milieu, 1894*): *Antoine's "Théâtre libre"*: In 1887 the actor Antoine

André founded the Théâtre Libre in Paris, open only to season ticket holders. This theater, the model for the Independent Theater Association (where Antoine gave a guest performance with his troupe in Berlin in 1887) performed plays by Ibsen, Strindberg, and Gerhart Hauptmann, among others. The actor and theater director Aurélien-Marie *Lugné-Poe* founded his Maison de l'oeuvre in 1893 and performed Ibsen and Maeterlinck, among others. *Paul Schlenther* was, along with Otto Brahm, a cofounder of the Freie Bühne (Independent Theatre). Lou A.-S. reported that it was she who put *Knut Hamsun* in touch with his later publisher Albert Langen. Hamsun (1859–1952) had published his first successful novels, *Hunger, Mysterien,* and *Neue Erde* (New Earth) elsewhere. *Therese Krüger,* a translator into and from Danish, translated part of Lou A.-S.'s Nietzsche book for a Danish periodical. She was also Herman Bang's translator. *Herman Bang* (1857–1912) began as a director and journalist (theoretician of Naturalism) in his Danish homeland. One of his first prose works was the novel *Hopeless Sexes,* written in Danish in 1880. In a 1903 essay about both the Danish novels *The White House,* 1898, and *The Gray House,* 1901, Rilke wrote that Bang "wanted to seize his childhood again." The president of the French republic of Sadi, *Carnot,* was assassinated by an Italian terrorist on June 24, 1894. Alexandre *Millerand,* later the head of state, was a socialist, as was the peace advocate Jean *Jaurès,* who was murdered immediately preceding the First World War. A professor of philosophy, he was a splendid orator.

60. *Wedekind*: made famous by his first drama, *Frühlings Erwachen,* (Spring's Awakening), written in Munich in 1891. "Then I went . . . back to Paris and became a secretary to . . . a Danish painter and art dealer named Willy Grétor. . . ." The novella by Lou A.-S. in which the "Wedekind misunderstanding" was incorporated as "padding," is the story *Fénitschka,* 1898. The delicate situation in which Lou A.-S. involved herself by her innocence regarding signs of male interest is recognizable in this story—as are the words (even if not actually spoken) Lou used in order to extricate herself and Wedekind: "The blame is mine, Mr. W., for I have never yet met a dishonorable man." The next day—it may be noted here—Wedekind appeared in formal attire to beg her pardon, and a friendship was quickly formed. The *Galgenlieder* (Gallows Songs) mentioned here are the well-known ones by Christian Morgenstern. In her short journal entries while in Paris, Lou A.-S. notes on July 28: "Wedekind came to see me, discussed doing a drama together in the Palais Royal." The plan to collaborate on a drama was mentioned again on August 4: "In the evening, Wedekind here for the drama." Then, however, Lou A.-S. speaks only of her own work on this drama. During her stay in the Swiss mountains (mentioned on p. 62.) with the Russian doctor Savély (whom she describes in a note as a "fine companion"), she not only finishes the drama (August 26 "Drama done") but also produces a clean copy and revises it: "In the morning, finished the revisions of the drama." She reads it aloud to Russian acquaintances in Paris. Nevertheless, she continues to work on this play in three acts (we do know that

much at any rate) in Berlin (October 7). It is not mentioned again after this date. Nothing more is known about the work (nor about the original collaboration with Wedekind). The play has not survived.

61. *widow of Georg Herwegh*: widow of the well-known political writer Georg Herwegh (1817–1875), who had enjoyed his greatest success in the years before 1848. She had saved her husband from being taken prisoner during the collapse of the uprising in Baden, in which he had taken a less than glorious part.

61. *Zwilling . . . selling flowers*: After her return to Germany, Lou A.-S. wrote a short story in October 1894 in order to provide them with financial support: "If you want to do me a great, great favor, please pass the collection plate using the enclosed story. Every word is true and I'm raising money for these two poor individuals whom I like very much" (letter to a friend).

62. *something arose in me like a primal vision*: At first the passage read thus: "something arose in me like a vision of *an altered world totality*—I don't know how to express the emotional nuance of the unexpected surprise any more clearly. The idylls of paradise disappeared in the fading light of the magical landscape, and, unavoidably" [the text breaks off, and was to be continued approximately]: "the feet tread on a irrevocable stoniness." The "remembered moment" was that of "the loss of God."

63. *Frieda von Bülow*: Baroness Frieda von Bülow (1857–1909) was the daughter of a Prussian legation councilor. In 1887 she followed her brother Albrecht to the colony in East Africa (attained for Germany by Carl Peters) where she founded the first patient-care stations in Zanzibar and Dar es Salaam. In the following year, her own illness forced her to return. She met Lou A.-S. in Tempelhof at the beginning of 1892. After May of that year, her brother fell in battle in Africa and in June 1893, she traveled back for the second time, staying about a year, in order to wind up his work on the plantation. Lou A.-S. and Rilke stayed with her at Bibersberg near Meiningen in the summer of 1899 when they were preparing for their long Russian trip. Due to their portrayal of the colonial conditions at the time, Frieda von B.'s novels have a certain importance, based upon her African impressions and a personal encounter with Carl Peters (in *Im Lande der Verheißung* [In the Promised Land]).

The letters which Lou Andreas-Salomé wrote to Frieda von Bülow toward the end of the latter's fatal illness (from November 1908 until almost the final day, March 10, 1909) not only testify to their friendship but also reveal Lou A.-S.'s view of life in middle age, as called forth by the circumstances. (Some excerpts from what Frieda von Bülow, who knew of her impending death, wrote: "One becomes deeply depressed when one experiences personally how much sorrow, pain, and helplessness can befall us unhappy human beings. . . . I have suffered more torture in the last six days than in the other 51 years of my life put together. . . . One longs for death." She speaks of "two gloomy apparitions always standing next to the bed"; one who tells her that she can "not assure a comfortable, pleasant existence" for her sister Sophie as she "so strongly" wanted to and the other who says: "The great farewell to everything will soon come." It is a sign of her character that she terms the former "even more sinister" than the latter.)

"My dear, I humbly offer you this gray bit of a note as a small greeting. . . . I do think that, when they reflect on it later, childhood is the best time for most people. It was the least happy time of my life, however, and the same could probably have been said about you, if you had not had Grete with you (Margarethe von B., see the note below). Two childhoods of the same type experienced *together* are indeed paradise. You might not have been able to say that of the next period, youth, since one never knows if your erotic years and intellectual productivity would have been compatible. So, perhaps, the recollections end with the best and sweetest in life. What came then incited you as a woman and human being to become who you intrinsically are and to do so independently, since you no longer had Grete. I always imagine that it is in these years of youth that we wrestle our inner selves free from life, to which we cling so tightly. Courage and passion are the virtues of youth; we become and later possess only what we fought for then. Later it is as though we take a step back from life, gain a bit of distance from it, we exist more for ourselves, occasionally coming up with something already digested: children, work, and so on. From that point on, we really don't need, strictly speaking, to continue living; rather, something is already living within us, into an eternity about which we know nothing—an eternity in which our internal form might possibly emerge with a new exterior which might be just right for a higher, more refined existence, figuratively speaking. These are not just dreams. In the final analysis, all our best, most instinctive ideas revolve around such presuppositions: that it is not our current physical life which is most valuable, and that we distrust those who think it is; that all the most wonderful and moving experiences in our souls are not externally visible; that everything of true value is oblivious to itself and invisible to others—all true nobility and refinement is based on such ideas. I think that everything, at some point in time, will be externalized physically, on a much more refined plane; we only know of such a small number of possibilities for existence.

"Such thoughts occur because all the natural sciences have, in the last few years, turned in this direction, just as (and because) all of the even halfway intelligent scientists are now interested in metaphysical questions. It was not different *in earlier days*, but, half a century ago, when we were young, the wasteland of scientific dogma wore blinders and didn't even see what was in front of its nose.

"More days and days, and nights and nights, my dear—how difficult each individual hour must have become for you! Each like a terrible weight, pressing you down until there is nothing which can be put on the other scale. Indeed, one forgets that there even is another *side to the scale* and that it is mysteriously counterbalanced with weights, which, because of their special nature, cannot be felt in certain situations. And *that* is so terrible. There is no other comfort possible than to know:

the counterbalance *will* occur, even if you have been pressed to the floor with terrible lead weights! They are only cardboard weights, believe me, when you look back upon them, after they are gone. And the dread of them is also gone, just as mothers giving birth lose all sense of pain after a while. Hold on to that *mechanically*, so that it happens, *order* yourself to do it with all your might! Don't be afraid. Pull yourself together in the victorious belief that such diseases are *births*. They are the *most difficult experience* that one can undergo (unless it is accompanied by a fever, so that one experiences it only half-consciously). Because what is and remains most difficult is the alienation from one's own body. All other suffering is external and that we can fight. But this, this is apparently ourselves, and we are therefore captured by it. Precisely because we 'are' not bodies but only 'have' bodies, does it seem so monstrous—when the body silences, so to speak, everything in us and seems to assume our place. Our instinct for self-preservation is so at one with the body that it can only tear itself away forcibly. But in reality, it is not at this moment that our Self is no longer identical with the processes of the body; this has already long since been the case. It is so shaped *within itself* and so concentrated in form that, free of the body, it would exist in and of itself as in a much more individual, elegant 'corporeality.' Spirit, mind, and body—these are only our words: in a sense, we call everything physical, which, with our crude means, we can dissect and see. Whatever is beyond that, we call spiritual. One step up on the ladder from this— and not such a huge one—would be what we now call the spirit of a physical sort, of the mind, and this in turn would be the mirror, the receptacle for influences and effects that lie even higher up the ladder—and we call these 'spiritual.'

"Throughout life, all serious people show an instinct for self-preservation which goes far beyond the physical, in all their significant endeavors, their beautiful experiences, their voluntary sacrifices—and how many hundreds of sacrifices of comfort, happiness, and even life, for some idea, or some love. None of these instances fall outside the circle of self-preservation—nothing which is alive can do that; it would be perverse and common, not noble. No, it is only that the Self, for them, was already focused elsewhere long ago, where it is protected, secure, and obeys *its* own laws for growth. Even those who are *healthy* withdraw their selves so completely in their advanced years that the Self hardly seems apparent on the exterior. The body only holds it, paralyzes it, imprisons and obstructs it. This 'prison term' is what you now feel so dreadfully because of the disease, and everything must constrict so tightly around you often—so tightly and so often—that I sometimes break out in a sweat from empathy with both the fear and the pain. I want to hold you! We can do as we like but it *must* be endured! What is *above you*, my most treasured one, demands it. Your own Self will emerge from this. They are labor pains—not something terrible or ignoble, like your dreams used to suggest. Life, eternal life, wants it this way. 'Die in order to live' the life in which we are all one. A person striving upward! I can't write anymore, I am so totally, completely, with you. . . .

"My dear, I scold myself for writing so many things you may not even wish to read. But the good thing is that you don't *have* to read it; it is not like a bothersome conversation, for it doesn't have to be discussed—it depends on you. It is also prompted by the fact that I have had so many thoughts in these years regarding physics, chemistry, and the like. And I would have liked to have talked with you about them when they were simmering. In particular the strange certainty that the process we call life is actually a process of death and *vice versa*—both are the same in their nature. It has been known for a long time that, wherever there is 'life,' something inherent to the organism decays, dies; the renewal that then occurs is in no way a proof of 'life'—it can be found, for example, in sleep, in the fatigue from digestion, etc. For life to be 'free,' a great deal must be mortal. Thus, life is a continual 'flight and escape from the corporeal.' When we say: the body *is necessary*, we only mean: it is necessary for us in order to have a *reflected, visible image* of life. But life 'lives' only in opposition to the body, because it appears only when and to the extent that something physical 'dies.' What is organic, or even spiritual, and conscious, is differentiated most clearly from the inorganic by the extent and degree of its *mortality*, that is, of the loose structure of the material elements which it constantly dissolves in order to be free—in other words, to appear as 'life.' One can almost define everything organic and spiritual by the phrase: 'by way of death to life.' In the final stages of this freeing process, in sickness or old age, and most completely in death, life, because of this dissolved physical state, becomes almost unnoticeable, imperceptible to whatever is still bound by the body (less forcefully expressed: 'whatever is still dying'). At that point, one can only see the negative: that which no longer manifests itself in matter—that which is escaping. But that is the point at which life is ready to attain its Self most positively—the center of its Self, which we can only sense by intuition, since it lacks the residue and material by which we recognized it. As truly as God lives, it is so!"

63. *Margarethe von Bülow, already a known writer at that time*: died in January 1884 at the age of twenty-four during a rescue mission. Margarethe von B. was much more talented and original than her sister as a writer. Her most mature work is the novel *Jonas Briccius*, 1886.

64. (*Viennese circle, 1895/96*): *Arthur Schnitzler* (1862–1931) had already begun his literary career with the dramatic sketches *Anatol*, 1893, and the play *Das Märchen* (The Fairy Tale). Lou A.-S. wrote to him in April 1894 about these works.—*Richard Beer-Hofmann* (1866–1945) had only published *Novellen* (Novellas) at this time. His important novel *Der Tod Georgs* (Georg's Death), 1900, was of interest to the young Rilke. *Hugo von Hofmannsthal* (1874–1929) was already enjoying his first success with his poems and small dramas. *Felix Salten* (Salzmann) (1869–1945) was an essayist and a story writer. *Peter Altenberg* (Richard Engländer), (1859–1919) published the first collection of his sketchlike *Studien* (Studies), and *Wie ich es sehe* (As I See It) in the following year, 1896. The sketch referred to by Lou A.-S. is probably *Zwei Fremde* (Two Strangers), which was preserved in the literary estate,

but was not published in the above book. The "well-known saying" about Altenberg (by Alfred de Musset) can be found on the title page of the early printings of *As I See It* and reads" "Mon verre n'est pas grand—mais je bois dans mon verre." (My glass is not large—but I drink from my glass.)

65. *Marie von Ebner-Eschenbach* (1830–1916) wrote most of her works in the eighties, beginning with *Božena* in 1876, continuing with the short story *Glaubenslos* (Without Faith) in 1893, and followed by the collection of short stories *Aus Spätherbsttagen* (Late Autumn Days) in 1901. Lou A.-S. had already expressed her admiration and respect for Marie von Ebner in her essay *Ketzereien gegen die moderne Frau* (Heresies Against the Modern Woman) which appeared on February 11, 1899, in *Die Zukunft* (The Future): The modern woman, who is also moving onto the battlefield as a writer, "is now using such a terribly large portion of her intimate strength for the constant repetition on paper of the nature and essence of her being. When one approaches her personally, does she still convey the impression of a rosebush in bloom or . . . of someone who has given away something more dear and irreplaceable than an excess of flowers? I can remember the hour in which I confronted this question for the first time. It was in Vienna [in 1895] in a quiet, old, elegant room, and I was sitting across from an elderly female writer to whom the comment that she wrote 'in a feminine manner' was probably never uttered as a reproach. Does she write in a masculine way then? Oh no. But when one looks into her deep, intelligent eyes, and when one sees the incredibly delicate smile which plays on her kind lips, then one suddenly knows how . . . little of the great wealth within her can be found in the words of these texts; in the end, all those sheets of paper resemble the pale, delicate petals of the rose in contrast to the deeply rooted, everlasting solid tree which shed and cast them to the four winds. This poet whose hand I kissed, so full of such thoughts, was Marie von Ebner-Eschenbach."

The high regard which Marie von Ebner-Eschenbach had for Lou Andreas-Salomé on a human and literary level can be seen in brief letters she wrote from 1895 to 1913. Her letter of August 7, 1901, is particularly expressive: "Honored lady! I finally allowed myself some rest after a long and productive period of work. And I read one of the most beautiful stories there is: *Ma* by Lou Andreas-Salomé. If it is a portrait, then it is a Velasquez.

" 'Among contemporary writers, Lou Andreas is the most intellectual and psychologically profound' [presumably a sentence from a review printed with the book]— I echo that with letters as large as the Uspénsky Cathedral [in Moscow, mentioned in *Ma* as well as in the diary of the Russian trip]. All my respect, inspired lady, for your art and your wisdom. Wisdom is always a benefactress; she gave you the idea of this strange child, whose small figure appears comfortingly before us when we see the wonderful Ma returning home to her lonely apartment after her daughters' departure.

"Thank you, dear lady, for writing this book and for sending it to me. By doing so, you gave me a sign that you remember me kindly."

She had already commented on *Aus fremder Seele* (Out of Another's Soul, A Late Autumn Story), 1896: "A great literary talent has tried to solve an insoluble problem. She was not successful, but she fills us with respect" (M. von E.-E., *Aus einem zeitlosen Tagebuch* [From a Timeless Diary], 1916).

See also Lou A.-S.'s remarks about Marie von Ebner-Eschenbach upon learning of her death. These are in a letter to Freud of March 15, 1916.

66. *essays, as I had earlier on my theatrical reviews*: The first essays written by Lou A.-S. (from 1891–1893, in other words, up to the first Paris trip) dealt with topics in the psychology of religion, e.g., *Der Realismus in der Religion* (Realism in Religion) and *Gottesschöpfung* (Divine Creation), then topics from the later Nietzsche book, and finally, in 1893, *Theater Reviews*: about Duse's performance, about Wedekind's *Spring's Awakening*, Hauptmann's *Hanneles Himmelfahrt* (Hannele's Ascension), and others. They appeared mostly in the *Freie Bühne* (Independent Theater), edited first by Bölsche, then by Julius Hart, then Wille. The "daily essays" referred to here, written up until the second group of theater reviews during her acquaintance with Max Reinhardt (from 1906 on), dealt with religious and literary psychology, and concerned the question of women, Russian matters, etc. They were published in a wide range of periodicals. From ca. 1911 on (up to the essays on depth psychology), most essays on related topics were published in *Literarisches Echo*.

66. *Baroness Anna Münchhausen-Keudell*: the mother of Baron Thankmar von Münchhausen, known from Rilke's letters. The friendship with Anna von Münchhausen lasted until Lou A.-S.'s death.

66. *Helene von Klot-Heydenfeldt*: born in Livonia in 1865. Her book *Eine Frau: Studie nach dem Leben* (A Woman: A Life Study) was probably written in 1890. She married the architect Otto Klingenberg in 1897 and, commencing in 1899, they lived in Berlin, where Rilke visited them. Helene Klingenberg died in April 1946, in a small Mecklenburg village to which she had fled in 1943 during the heavy air raids on Berlin. Lou A.-S.'s words in her memory are analogous to a note of thanks from a late letter by Helene Klingenberg: "You are and always will be in my thoughts. I will never be able to express adequately my thanks to you. I can only treat my fellow man as you have me."

67. (*Munich circle, 1897*): *Graf* [*Count*] *Eduard Keyserling* (1855–1918) had up until this point only published stories in a Naturalist vein. His significant works, dramas and stories, first appeared after 1903. The visit, which was paid too late, was not during the Munich period with Rilke. *Ernst von Wolzogen* (1855–1934) had written a bohemian tragicomedy and social novels, among others. In 1900 he founded his "Überbrettl" in Berlin, which transposed the Montmartre-Cabaret onto a higher level into German. August Endell built a theater for him in Berlin. *Michael Georg Conrad* (1846–1927) was known for, among other works, a futuristic fantasy novel

In purpurner Finsternis (In Purple Darkness), 1895. His periodical, *Die Gesellschaft* (Society), founded in 1885, was one of the most important literary periodicals up until the turn of the century. It had a wealth of collaborators with the most varied opinions and was published by Wilhelm Friedrich in Leipzig, who also published *Struggling for God*. *Jakob Wassermann* (1873–1934) published a novel about his origins, *Die Juden von Zirndorf* (The Jews of Zirndorf) in 1897. He became more well known for *Die Geschichte der jungen Renate Fuchs* (The Story of Young Renate Fuchs) in 1900.

67. *August Endell*: (1871–1925) from Berlin, studied aesthetics, psychology, and philosophy in Tübingen and Munich. In 1896 he went to Italy for the first time and, after his return, published the short essay *Über die Schönheit* (On Beauty). Lou A.-S. read it and went to see him spontaneously, probably in autumn 1896. It was at this time that Endell got to know the craftsman Hermann Obrist, who convinced him to put his theoretical work into practice. Together with Obrist and others, he aroused interest in a new artistic craft and in the new architecture of *Jugendstil*. The studio Elvira in Munich is one of Endell's first buildings. Most of his works were built in Berlin, where the text for *Die Schönheit der großen Stadt* (The Beauty of the Big City), 1908, also originated. Themes like "Die Zerstörung des Lebens durch Arbeitszerlegung" (The Destruction of Life by the Division of Labor) also occupied him. In 1918 he became a professor and director of the Art Academy in Breslau. Endell died in 1924 after long years of suffering.

68. *one spring evening at the theater*: Rilke knew Lou A.-S. as a writer (*Ruth*) and author of the essay *Jesus der Jude* (Jesus the Jew), which had appeared in the April 1896 volume of the *Neue Deutsche Rundschau* (New German Review—the continuation of the *Independent Theatre*). This essay, with its "Visions of Christ," had deeply moved him. The first encounter with "the famous poet and African specialist" (Frieda von Bülow) probably occurred two days before the theater performance, on May 12, 1897: "to Wassermann, the Viennese [Rilke]." Lou A.-S., however, did not remember this "twilight hour" (Rilke in his first letter to Lou A.-S.). She does not mention Rilke's name in her diary until May 14: "Sick last night; later with Endell to the premiere of Schewitsch's *Dunkle Mächte* (Dark Powers), where we met Puck [Photo studio Elvira] and others; went with them and Rilke to Schleich's, dined very merrily until 1:30 A.M.; home with Endell and Rilke." The next day Rilke wrote his first letter to Lou A.-S. The eleven *Visions of Christ* (which remained unfinished) are now in the Rilke Archive. Of these eleven, five were to have appeared in Michael Georg Conrad's periodical (Sämtl. Werke, [Complete Works], III, p. 127ff).

68. *Wolfratshausen*: The communal stay in Wolfratshausen in the Isar Valley (an hour's walk from the Starnberger Lake) lasted from ca. mid-June to the beginning of September 1897. The picture mentioned here of the second little house in Wolfratshausen is reproduced in the Rilke memorial volume, written by Lou A.-S.

68. *the periodical* Wegwarten (Chicory Flowers) appeared in three slim issues in 1896. It was supposed to expose the "people" (Volk) to the contemporary literature of the time (mostly lyric poetry).

70. *edge of the forest in Schmargendorf:* Just after their time together in Wolfratshausen, Rilke lived in Wilmersdorf near Berlin. He didn't live in Schmargendorf (in the Hotel Waldfrieden [Woodland Peace]) until the beginning of August 1898.

70. *long trip to Russia:* According to the short daily entries by Lou A.-S. (which were not available to the editor for the first edition), the first Russian trip, taken with Professor Andreas, began on April 25, 1899. Its route was from Warsaw to Moscow (visited Leo Tolstoy on the 28th, Good Friday, in the evening; on April 30, Russian Easter: "celebrated Easter night in the Kremlin"). Directly afterward, the time in Petersburg, from May 3 to sometime after the middle of June (including another trip to Moscow near the end of May), was spent with Lou A.-S.'s family. They returned home via Danzig (Oliva).

The second, long Russian trip, taken at the beginning of May, also went via Warsaw to Moscow and from there for a (second) visit with Tolstoy in Yásnaya Polyána near Tula. "31 May, departure from Moscow around noon, bound for Tula. Leonid Pasternak [who painted Tolstoy as well as Rilke] and Boulanger [an acquaintance of Tolstoy's] in the train; telegram to ascertain Tolstoy's location. . . . 1 June, early, ca. 8 A.M. to Lazárevo, other directions received there. Took a freight train back to Yasínsky, from there via troika horses and ringing bells to the Yásnaya Polyána village and Tolstoy's estate." Boris Pasternak, who described the encounter in the train in his *Geleitbrief* (Letter of Safe Passage) had accompanied his father at the time: ". . . a man in a black Tyrolean cape . . . with him, a tall woman. She might have been his mother or his older sister. . . . The stranger spoke only German. Even though I knew this language well, I had never heard it spoken this way before." The trip then led them southwestward toward Kiev, down the Dnieper to Kremenchúg, from there via Poltáva, Khárkov, Vorónezh, Koslóv—all in all, eastward—to Sarátov on the Volga. From there by steamer upstream via Samára, Simbírsk, Kazán, Nízhny-Nóvgorod (now Gorky) to Yaroslávl, via wagon to Krestá Bogoródskoye, where they spent several days in the country, then southward to Moscow. After a week-and-a-half stay there, back to the (upper) Volga on June 18 to the Gouvernement Tver (now Kalínin), northwest of Moscow, to visit the peasant poet Drózhzhin in Nizóvka and his estate owner in Novínki, Count Nikoláy Tolstoy, relative of Leo Tolstoy. From there, on June 23, departure via Nóvgorod to St. Petersburg (July 26). The day afterward, Lou A.-S. traveled to her family in Rongas, Finland, and Rilke waited in St. Petersburg until their return together on August 22.

70. *second visit to Tolstoy:* According to Lou A.-S.'s diary, this took place on May 19 of the Russian calendar, therefore on June 1, 1900. Both visitors depicted the event: Lou A.-S. in her diary and Rilke in a letter from Tula on May 20 (Russian calendar)

as well as in the Worpswede Diary from September 15, 1900. (See also Complete Works, VI, p. 967ff.)

71. *Tretyakóvsky Picture Gallery in Moscow*: The brothers Pável Mikhaýlovich and Sergéy Mikhaýlovich Tretyakóv had begun their famous collection of mostly Russian paintings in the sixties. In 1892 they donated it to the city of Moscow.

72. *we could feel at home in the Russian Izbá (peasant's hut)*: The longest stay was for four days in the village of Krestá-Bogoródskoye near Yaroslávl and in the village of Nísovska with the peasant poet Drozhzhin in the Gouvernement Tver. See the Epilogue, appended to this chapter, which Lou A.-S. wrote later.

72. *peasant poet Drozhzhin*: Spiridón Dmítrievich Drozhzhin (Drozin) (1848–1930) came from a family of serfs. In 1860 he went to St. Petersburg, where he held low-level jobs for a long time. When Lou A.-S. and Rilke visited, he had long since returned to his native village of Nísovka in the Gouvernement Tver (on the upper Volga) where he spent the winters writing. Influenced by Pushkin, he is said to have begun writing poetry early. His songs touched on Nature, love, work, and the life of the village poor. He later received an honorary pension from the Soviet government. Sófia Nikoláyevna Schill had already sent one of Drozhzhin's volumes of poetry to Rilke in Schmargendorf in February 1900 and Rilke had translated several poems. Drozhzhin's recollections of Rilke are printed in *Inselschiff* (The Insel Ship), Vol. X, Summer 1929. Lou A.-S. and Rilke lived with him and his family for several days before they moved to the nearby estate of Tolstoy's relative. The strongest impressions of the life on this estate and of the people there were recorded in the Finnish afterword to the diary and then incorporated into *Ródinka*. A picture of Rilke and Drozhzhin can be found in Lou's memorial volume for Rilke, and in this volume as well.

72. *Russian God of Leskóv, who "lives in the left armpit"*: Lou A.-S. also referred to this picture in her memorial volume for Rilke—perhaps remembering Leskóv's story *Am Rande der Welt* (On the Edge of the World) (translated by Irene Neander): "I must confess to you that I love our Russian God more than all other images of the divine—this God of ours who creates his own residence beneath our bibs. . . . We do not find him in the incense smoke of their [the Greeks'] Byzantinism but rather He is among us and simply strolls the same way we do through the countryside. Without incense, He is in the fine, cool breaths of air wafting under the bath benches and huddles like a dove in the warm pocket of space between the breast and shirt" (Father Kiriák's words to a bishop). A "study" done by Lou A.-S. about the famous prose writer Nikoláy Semyónovich Leskóv (1831–1895) is entitled *Das russische Heiligenbild und sein Dichter* (The Russian Picture of a Saint and Its Poet). It was "based on five Russian essays about N. Leskóv by A. L. Volínsky" which were published in 1897. The study, whose only extant pages are the first ones, is perhaps a

joint effort from the Schmargendorf period (it is in Rilke's handwriting with the title by Lou A.-S.). In April 1920 Lou A.-S. published a review of the novel *Die Klerisei* (The Clericals—actually *Der Popenkreis* [The Pope's Circle]) in *Literary Echo*. In it she suggests that the stories *On the Edge of the World* (see above) and *Der versiegelte Engel* (The Sealed Angel) should be translated next.

73. *"You have fallen from the nest"*: the end of the poem "Wenn ich gewachsen wäre irgendwo . . ." (Had I grown up somewhere . . .), the twenty-first in the *Buch vom mönchischen Leben* (Book of Monastic Life).

73. *"We work at building you with trembling hands"*: the beginning of the fifteenth poem in the *Book of Monastic Life*.

74. *beginnings . . . in the early stages of the Book of Hours, on our first trip to Russia*: Lou A.-S. assumes this based on her impressions of Rilke "working" during the trip. For more information about the entire paragraph, see the note to the statement in the text "That which rose in you, almost without intention, as 'prayer,' " which is found in the Epilogue to this chapter.

74. *"See that he knows his childhood once again"*: from "Mach Einen herrlich, Herr, mach Einen groβ . . ." (Make One Splendid, Lord, Make One Great . . .), the ninth poem in the *Buch von der Armut und vom Tode* (Book of Poverty and of Death). "create his childhood again": see the Rilke memorial volume, p. 42f.

75. *"I believe in all which has remained unsaid"*: the twelfth poem in the *Book of Monastic Life*.

76. *"I was far away, where the angels are"*: approximately in the middle of the poem "Ich komme aus meinen Schwingen heim . . ." (I am coming home from my swaying). This is the eighteenth poem (from the end) in the *Book of Monastic Life*. Lou A.-S. commented that as soon as the Luciferian thought of this poem became clear to her (early on), she could then prophesy Rilke's fate.

76. *"Poverty shines in splendor from within"*: last line of the poem "Sie sind es nicht. Sie sind nur die Nicht-Reichen" (They are not it. They are only the Not-Rich) also belongs in a larger thematic context. This last line, which is set off and emphasized almost like a one-line poem, is located in the middle of the *Book of Poverty and of Death* and introduces the positive connotation of poverty.

77. *description of the poorest of the poor during his first stay in Paris*: in the letter of July 18, 1903, which Rilke, in Worpswede, wrote to Lou A.-S. several weeks after the first Paris stay. In it he combines certain related impressions from this period (which was interrupted by a stay in Viareggio). The portrayals appear (sometimes almost

verbatim) in the first part of the *Aufzeichnungen des Malte Laurids Brigge* (The Notebooks of Malte Laurids Brigge). While writing this, Malte lives in the same rue Toullier where Rilke once actually stayed. The passage Lou A.-S. cited: *"I often long to say aloud, that I'm not one of them"* reads in the letter: "I must often tell myself that. . . ." Lou A.-S. quoted mostly from memory (the poems as well); this is shown by the following: The phrase "To make things out of fear" is already in the letter with the "descriptions" in the following context: "If things had been better, quieter, more friendly, if I had kept my room and if I had remained healthy, then perhaps I would have been able to do it: to make things out of fear." And Lou A.-S. answers: ". . . there you are mistaken: that you helplessly suffered all these things, without repeating them on a higher level. . . . Now it has happened: the poet in you creates out of human fears." Rilke could have either confirmed or acknowledged the fulfillment of his words "making things out of fear." (See Rilke memorial volume, p. 32.)

77. *spiritual salvation Rodin offered*: This refers to the phase of relatively close personal contact with Rodin (beginning with Rilke's visit on September 1) and, simultaneously, to the relationship of disciple and master. This phase concluded with Rilke's "secretary" period during his second Paris visit—that is, with Rodin's temperamental outburst in May 1906. It also refers to a phase, beginning in 1908, where there was a certain re-establishment of the personal relationship. Lou A.-S. means the first phase at its height. (See the Rilke memorial volume, p. 37f.) By *modelé*, Rilke, following in Rodin's footsteps, meant "That which forms sculpture, the surface areas, . . . the type of surfaces, as contrasted to contours, . . . whether they are rough or smooth, shiny or matte," a "solid, three-dimensional basic element," which must be distinct from the "form" (letter to Clare Rilke, September 5, 1902).

78. *a late letter (1914)*: from Irschenhausen on September 9, 1914. Lou A.-S. underlined the word "purpose."

79. Book of Hours: *the continuation . . . on the Mediterranean at Viareggio*: in *Of Poverty and of Death*. The quotation from it: *But if it's you: weigh down until I break"* are the concluding lines of the introductory poem. The line *"Lord, give to each a death his own"* introduces the sixth poem of the book: "O Lord, give to each a death his own / The Dying that comes from each life / in which he had love, meaning and suffering" which is thematically related to the line *"poverty shines in splendor from within."*

79. *Rainer's feverish childhood dream*: for this, and for Malte's not-wanting-to-be-loved-again, see the entry by Lou A.-S. in her Freud diary from October 10 to 16, 1913, the "dream analysis."

80. *a letter of 1911 from Duino Castle in which he reminisces*: letter of December 28,

1911. The comparison Malte is making with the bomb precedes the metaphor of an elevated watershed.

80. *like that of the "God who did not requite love"*: Toward the end of the *Notebooks*, before the Story of the Prodigal Son, it is said of Abelone: "but could her honest heart delude itself that God is only a direction of love and not an object of love? Didn't she know that there is no requited love to fear from him?" The story of the prodigal son is told as "the legend of the one . . . who did not want to be loved." See the statements by J.R. von Salis in his book *Rilkes Schweizer Jahre* (Rilke's Swiss Years), Frauenfeld and Leipzig, 1936, p. 204, and the remarks by Lou A.-S. in her memorial volume for Rilke, p. 60f, about this thought of the "God who did not requite love."

81. (*Nun's Letters*), *etc.*: Continuation in the first draft: "To be loved—almost a hindrance to complete devotion, on which everything depends; the 'God who did not requite love'—a truly helpful God; the return of the prodigal son—a misunderstanding of a religious impulse, which looks for its own instead of looking away, looking upward. Thus the poorest become the richest, the holiest, and the most blessed, because they have 'achieved' the total poverty for which Rainer longed as for a perfect possession. Yet the images of such destinies signified to Rainer only the pressure toward creative activity itself, toward the hour of creation. When, anticipating an incomprehensible blessing, a part of the Elegies (individual stanzas, magnificent fragments) came into being, hopes blazed up in him—hopes that he would indeed be able to satisfy the stern face of the angel of God's message, regardless of how mercilessly this face gazed down on him. (—no longer the faceless God, into whose face man sinks as though into the face of all life itself)."

81. *from what would become the Sixth Elegy*: This fragment, written in either 1912 or 1914, is separated by a gap from the main body of the "Helden-Elegie" (Hero's Elegy). After Verses 32–41 were inserted in Muzot, to fill in the gap, this fragment became the conclusion of the Sixth Elegy in the following form: "Then the hero stormed through the abodes of love,/lifted up by each of them, each beat of the heart meant for him,/already turned aside so soon, he stood at the end of smiles,—changed."

81. *a conversation . . . with Rainer . . . in our garden*: during Rilke's second visit in Göttingen from July 9 to 21, 1913.

81. *"they exist—they exist!"*: from the letter written in Muzot on February 11, 1922. (As actually punctuated: "They exist. They exist.")

82. *heed our pleas*: continuation and clarification in an earlier version: "This 'inter-

nalization of the God- and angel-like' expresses only the moment of conception, only birth in and of itself. It excludes everything superfluous, everything preceding and following it in time, for these things are not only of lesser value, they are totally valueless. . . . just to act, as though it *existed*."

82. *and to his body as "the ape of his spirit"*: See the passage in the letter of July 4, 1914, written in Paris: "In my situation, in which it was of the utmost importance to maintain the spiritual in a dangerous balance, it was only natural that my body, in its lethargy, drew the worst example from this mental attitude, and made itself an ape of my spirit and, in its own state, at the slightest provocation, became productive in its own way."

82. *flirtations with the occult and mediums*: particularly during stays at Duino Castle in the circle of people around Princess Marie von Thurn and Taxis. See Rilke's correspondence with her. See also Max Mell, *Begegnung mit Rilke* (Meeting Rilke) in *Corona*, Vol. 6, No. 6, 1936.

84. *In the mystery of poetic conception there is no denial of the relationship between the dreadful and the beautiful*: As generally as this insight is expressed by Lou A.-S., it nonetheless reflects the fact that the fate of Rilke's soul was very much on her mind. Her last (extant) letter to him, from December 12, 1925, might serve to illustrate her thoughts in more detail and her attempts to comprehend Rilke's abysmal suffering— abysmal because of the interlocking of psychically determined and physically deter- mined suffering. Lou A.-S. had an overview of only the psychic components, although she considered the other a possibility ("This entire process preys upon corresponding physical weaknesses").

On October 31, 1925, a year and two months before his death, Rilke admits in his last detailed letter to Lou A.-S. that he has lived "for the last two years" (that is, since the end of October 1923), "more and more in the midst of terror," in a "terrifying circle" whose origin he recognizes as a "self-induced disaster," a "devilish obses- sion," a "nonsensical temptation." He also terms this a "game" which "these mean devils" are playing with him. The more exact description is not included in the published letter, but is not necessary because the entire answer from Lou A.-S. has been published.

(Rilke's portrayal of the terror in which he says he lives brings to mind, in both its graphic expression and nature of the symptoms, a letter from January 20, 1912, he wrote to Lou A.-S.: "how very often this disastrous circle dances around me for weeks at a time"; "a hypersensitivity of the muscles," "my physical being runs the danger of becoming a caricature of my mind," etc.)

Rilke wrote of the "circle of black magic which envelops me, as in a Breughel painting of hell" (1912: "certain bad habits which, one day, will close around me like walls"). And yet he himself was able to distinguish between this and the "phobia" (fear of cancer) which he said he had been experiencing "for a month" (since the end of September 1925), caused by "appearances inside my lip" which, however, were apparently part of the leukemia syndrome.

Here are the most significant portions from the answer written by Lou A.-S. on December 12, 1925. (Those passages which have not yet been published are set in brackets.)

"Rainer, the whole point is that it is not a devilish obsession. [It is *because* your feelings of guilt are tied to it, and have been since childhood, that it has such bad effects. . . . As children, and even later, we are plagued by a moralizing guilt which only accidently, as it were, finds expression in corporal punishment. Then, when we've outgrown that, this guilt invades the bodily processes themselves, breeding disaster: guilt engenders a hysterical tendency toward the pathological in whatever organs it chooses. This is brought about by the morbid interest and attention directed to the organs, the increased flow of blood and hypersensitivity focused on one area, similar to the erotic sensations that occur in the penis. Such hypochondria can also be understood as a kind of self-love of the organ in question, except that it is not perceived as such. Rather, it is the lack of desire, the torture, and quasi-hate toward one's own body which are felt, because the organ is not suited to such attention and has no erotic qualities—instead, it has been robbed of its natural functions, and, once disturbed, will avenge itself.] This entire process preys upon corresponding physical weaknesses, regardless of how minimal they may be: It *cannot* be otherwise: They grow out of proportion in size and terror, expressing themselves in who knows what form. . . . We wrote about this years ago and you gained valuable insights then. Please do not be annoyed by the repetition, Rainer, continue reading. . . . [When you look at yourself now and see your willingness to confirm your guilt as it is manifested on both your throat and tongue, what does that tell you?] Oh, it's all so clear, only it wasn't clear to me back then [in Wolfratshausen]: I was such a simpleton. Because of *that*, God has struck *me* with guilt: When we met each other and I could have helped you, I did not have the knowledge and experience I have now. As a result, your condition grew worse over time. [Even the fact that it is expressed higher on your body rather than lower is a worsening of the situation.] But, nevertheless, this did not subdue and destroy you, Rainer! The same great mercy reigned above you, which makes use of the primal levels of the infantile: the creative diversion into work, which, for that reason, is intertwined so closely with the physical, for from that realm it impels one erotically toward the physical as work, rather than its practical objectification, no longer having room for that excess which originally overwhelmed us and made *everything* one. . . . To fall into pain, desertion, into subjection to your own body is not just a reaction to the strain of writing. It is, rather, the experience of something belonging to that creative process, the other side of it, and the devil is only a *deus inversus*. Whoever sees the image of the divine must also see its reverse side. But he is still in the divine realm, embraced and enveloped by that which remains eternally-maternal, even though we humans of limited consciousness must pay for those transcendant ecstasies."

85. *as you wrote* Cornet: in autumn or at the beginning of winter in 1899, on a night when "clouds which were eerily fleeing past the moon served as a stimulus [to write]" (letter to Baron Thankmar von Münchhausen, March 6, 1915).

86. *you placed that one poem in my room*: in Wolfratshausen. The poem is included "in the *Book of Hours* one year later," in the section *Buch von der Pilgerschaft* (Book of the Pilgrimage), 1901, where it is the seventh poem. This veiled yet nonetheless published love poem calls to mind another love poem, also hidden, in the flow of the dramatic dialogue in *Amphitryon* (II,4) by Heinrich von Kleist (Rilke certainly did not know of it at that time):

Take from me
My eye, I'll still hear him; My ear, I'll sense him;
Rob me of touch and I'll still breathe him;
Take eye and ear, touch and smell,
Strip me of all senses and leave me my heart:
Thus granting me the bell I need,
To search a world, and I will find him still.

Lou A.-S. apparently wrote down Rilke's poem from memory ("the page of manuscript" has not been preserved). Regardless of whether the first version is the one she gives, or whether or her memory has altered it, the way she remembered it is stronger and more regular than the *Book of Hours* version "Fuβ noch" instead of "Füβe," "Reiβ mir das Herz aus" rather than "Halt mir das Herz zu," "so will ich" instead of "so werd ich," and—in regular meter—"Und wirfst du mir auch in das Hirn den Brand" rather than "Und wirfst du in mein Hirn den Brand."

Although not included here, Ernst Zinn's critical commentary (p. 837f., Vol. III of the *Complete Works*) provides more information about this poem written to Lou A.-S. by Rilke.

87. *in the evening twilight at Krestá-Bogoródskoye*: In this village on the upper Volga near Yaroslávl, Lou A.-S. and R. M. Rilke lived several days in an Izbá, an empty peasant's hut. Lou A.-S. talks about this on p. 72 above. In her diary of the Russian trip, she describes the evening before departure: "I meet up with Makaróvna [a peasant woman whom they had both befriended] on a meadow I had not yet discovered. Since it is harvest time, she is mowing behind her Izbá. This meadow with the scenery behind it is like a dream. I take flowers and listen to Makaróvna talk one more time: a rush of warm words this time, and I feel how she has captivated us. It is pouring outside. Then comes the horribly sad packing. It is as if one is leaving home."

87. *cart horse returning to his nightly herd*: This mutual recollection of the white horse is also recorded in the diary. As is well known, Rilke dedicated "its image" to Orpheus with Sonnet XX from the first part of the *Sonette* (Sonnets). How deeply the

recollection was imbedded in him as a jointly "witnessed myth" can be seen in Katharina Kippenberg's story in the fourth and final version of her "essay" (R. M. Rilke, 1948, p. 163). One evening, while riding in a train, she and Rilke caught sight of a white horse on a meadow. "Rilke and I were both engrossed in contemplation of this horse. 'Now he's going to leap up and gallop off!' I shouted. To my astonishment, I saw the blood rush to Rilke's face. It was flushed so darkly it seemed it would never fade. As though deeply moved, he sat there silently, looking downward, and gave no reply."

87. *room behind the Kremlin*: Remembering the stay in Moscow during the long Russian trip where Lou A.-S. and Rilke lived "behind the Kremlin, as though among the bells" (Lou A.-S.).

88. *we had been traveling up the Volga for several weeks*: It lasted only about a week.

88. *which rose in you, almost without intention, as "prayer"*: The "prayer" in the first part of the *Book of Hours* originated in the autumn *before* the long Russian trip. Of those in the second book which were incorporated into the book *after* this trip in the following autumn (from September 18 to 25, 1901, in Westerwede), at least the poems "Lösch mir die Augen aus" (Extinguish My Eyes) were created earlier "as the residue of the fundamentally sensual," as Lou A.-S. once expressed herself. Rilke's entry from September 1, 1900, in his *Schmargendorf Diary* in Worpswede tends to confirm this recollection of Lou A.-S.: "Because then there were only sounds in me: once in Poltáva . . . , once in Sarátov . . . , later in the midst of the Volga waters . . . , but I know no words from the fabric of these sounds; yes, I can no longer remember if they were paired with words." From memory, Rilke enters in his diary a poem from Moscow, several verses from a song "outside Kazan in the evening," the beginning of a poem that might "have been an echo from Yaroslávl-Krestá" (*Tagebücher aus der Frühzeit* [Early Diaries], 1942, p. 232f). Lou A.-S. commented on the whole paragraph: "I have recalled it from memory, exactly as it was," that is, in precise detail.

88. *impulse to give creative form . . . in conflict with total receptivity to that which was to be expressed*: Here too Rilke's diary entry can be compared: In Moscow, in "May 1900," he said to Lou A.-S.: "Yes, everything that has actually been seen, *must* become a poem!" Looking back, he remarks: "I did not make use of them [the possibilities], as with so many on this trip. There were countless poems I did not grant a hearing." Rilke and Lou A.-S. were told the anecdote about Herr and Frau B. before they began the trip to the Volga.

89. *were taking our usual noon walk*: in Kiev in the days before they embarked on the Dnieper ship, (Russian) Pentecost, 1900.

89. *periods of anxiety . . . the physical attacks*: "Throwing himself onto the ground out of fear" (such as on the lonely path through the acacia forest), "attacks of crying, about everything" (Lou A.-S.). Concerning the phrase "the most difficult aspect of the matter . . ." (p. 89), LAS remarked: "that was the first explanation that we had had."

90. *the letter arrived*: This letter has not survived. The second letter, "in a different tone," is from August 1900.

90. *enter into open spaces and freedom*: Lou A.-S. recalls that at the end of the Volga trip in Yaroslávl they both discussed the idea of Rilke's staying for a while at Worpswede. The picture Lou A.-S. paints here of her ending the first phase of the relationship is confirmed by documents from shortly after the trip's conclusion. The words "back then" ("struggling to understand it myself") refer to the time Lou A.-S. spent at her eldest brother's estate in Finland while Rilke waited in St. Petersburg for their joint trip homeward. How deeply this "true" and "never be true" was actually felt, can be judged by the reader, who must consider the correlation between the experience of love and the "God Experience."

91. *in the hour of greatest need*: In June 1903 Rilke resumes correspondence after a period of some two and a half years and refers pointedly to this agreement: "but who knows if I will be able to come at the darkest hour." This arrangement continued to be valid in that Rilke always knew that he would be allowed to come "in the hour of need"—and not only then. The equilibrium between the two, established at the onset of their relationship, ruled throughout all the years of their friendship and excluded the possibility that Lou A.-S. became only the helper and Rilke only the complainer. She often said that they had no need for a regular exchange of letters.

The following poems written by Rilke to Lou A.-S. are printed here because they have their origins in "an hour of greatest need" and therefore belong in this period. Only the first of these is known: Lou A.-S. had quoted it (as Ernst Zinn had correctly surmised, from memory) in her memorial volume for Rilke, p. 13. But both of the other poems have also survived. In the summer of 1912, Lou A.-S. had recounted the trilogy, also from memory, to young Dr. Paula Matthes (who, at that time, had been close to her): "Lou recited them to me, in a corner of her balcony, almost as if quietly singing to herself. I wrote as she spoke. I am willing to walk through fire to attest to the absolute correspondence of each word to what was said. Because the words left a deep impression on me as well" [letter].

The first poem is also printed here in Paula Matthes's recorded version; the divergences from the version in the Rilke book speak for the genuineness of this version—as does the temporal priority (1912 versus 1928): "seit sich" instead of "weil sich," "ich steh und warte" for "Ich starre drauf hin," "meines Lebens Gesetz" rather than "meines Lebens Gehalt." Only "*wirres* Gedränge" (instead of "irres") is, irrefutably, a mishearing.

I

I stand in the darkness as though blind
since my gaze no longer finds you.
The crazed throng of the day is
my curtain behind which you live.
I watch to see if it will rise,
that curtain behind which live my life
as well as my life's rule and commandment—
but also: my death.

II

Without mockery you shaped yourself to me
as the sculptor's hand caresses to mold the clay,
a hand with the power of creation
to form a figure from a dream—
yet it tired, the interest dwindled,
let loose its grip, and I fell, shattered.

III

You were the most maternal of women
and a friend just like a man.
Outwardly you appeared a woman,
and more often you were a child.
You were the tenderest of my encounters,
and the most unyielding with which I wrestled.
You were the height that blessed me—
and became the depth that swallowed me.

One assumes that the trilogy was written after the separation from Lou A.-S. ("Letzter Zuruf" [Last Cry], February 26, 1901). As a poetic statement of the romantic relationship with Lou A.-S., this trilogy is as significant as the retrospective testimony of the mature Rilke found in another trilogy from 1911: "Ich hielt mich überoffen . . ." (I remained too open . . .). At least the so-called autobiographical verses of this latter trilogy are reprinted here:

Who can express,
what happened to us? We recovered everything,
for which there was never time. I matured
in that strange stimulus of youth passed by,
and you, my love, held my heart captive
in some kind of wildest childhood.

91. *heroic impulse toward "toujours travailler"*: Rilke mentioned Rodin's rule of "toujours travailler" to Lou A.-S. for the first time in a letter of August 10, 1903: "Il faut toujours travailler—toujours—he told me once when I spoke of the alarming chasms which opened up between my good days. He was scarcely able to understand it. . . ." The letter from Lou A.-S., which she herself refers to here as having been returned to her from Rilke's literary estate, is also dated August 10, 1903.

92. *Your letter still spoke of misery. In spite of everything . . . ready . . . to return home*: verbatim: "als derselbe Verstrickte in meinen Thurm zurückzukehren" (as the same entangled person to return to my tower), letter of October 31, 1925.

92. *"fête d'un fruit perdu"*: The poem is inscribed in the book *Vergers* for the French poet Jules Superville and reads:

Nos pertes, n'est-ce sur vous
que nos rêves s'érigent?
Seulement nos rêves? Que dis-je?
Pertes, vous portez tous

nos plus tendres élans!
Vous êtes ces caves anciennes
oú les vins de nos vignes deviennent
grands invisiblement.

C'est sur vos voûtes qu'on pose
tous ces étages émus.
Qu'est-ce en somme, la rose
que la fête d'un fruit perdu?
(R. M. Rilke, Poèmes français, Paris, 1935)

92. *shortest poem in the* Book of Hours: Now the last, fourth stanza of the seventeenth poem (from the end) in the *Book of Monastic Life*: "Du wirst nur mit der Tat erfaßt . . ." (You are seized only with the deed . . .). According to the "monks'" notation in the Göttingen manuscript of the *Book of Hours*, this "Nachtgebet am 1. Okt. [1899] (spät)" (Late Evening Prayer on Oct. 1 [1899]) was written in Schmargendorf. The verse is here considered a part of the "residue of the fundamentally sensual."

94. *receptive to Freud's depth psychology*: Lou A.-S. probably got her first detailed impression of it from her friend Dr. Poul Bjerre, a Swedish doctor, while she was visiting Ellen Key in Sweden in August and September 1911. She traveled with him from there to a convention in Weimar. Sigmund Freud (1856–1939), together with Dr. Josef Breuer, a Viennese doctor, published the fundamental work *Studien über Hysterie* (Studies in Hysteria) in 1895. The particular psychotherapeutic method of "psychoanalysis" was born when Freud substituted free association for the hypnosis

which he and Breuer had been using. Since ca. 1902, Freud gathered young doctors around him to instruct them. The conference in Weimar in September 1911, where Lou A.-S. met Freud face to face, was preceded by similar ones in Salzburg (1908) and Nürnberg (1910). The reader is referred here to the correspondence between Freud and Lou A.-S. for more information about their first meeting, as well as for a general elucidation of this entire chapter.

The relationship between Lou A.-S. and Freud remained clearly defined, as may be seen in an exclamation of Freud's in conversation: "But you haven't changed at all [as a student of psychoanalysis]. You are still the same old you," to which Lou A.-S. replied: "And so are you."

It should be noted about the chapter that it was read aloud to Lou A.-S. four days before her death. She made remarks such as "It's good up to there, no overemphasis" (p. 119); "That makes everything seem so innocent" (p. 121); "Strange how almost no one looks at these things clearly" (p. 122); "knowledge doesn't help there" (p. 125). Her comment about p. 125 "that's almost pure philosophy . . ." "analysis and symbolization are not *infinitely* different—Klages was wrong there" points to the core of Lou A.-S.'s philosophical view of things.

95. *very first grandiose spadework of Freud*: Whichever "spadework" (since the discovery of the "Oedipus complex" in individual analysis) one sees as the "very first," they are all "grandiose" in their consequences as revelation of important unconscious processes: "early childhood sexuality," "repression," "resistance," "transference," and many others.

95. *motives of our rational mind . . . Mephisto*: in the "Prologue to Heaven," he says of man, the "small god of the world": "A little bit better would he live/If heaven's light you weren't so wont to give/He calls it reason and uses it to be/more animal-like than any other animal we see."

96. *might turn discoverers into inventors*: "out of the *discoverer* of truth, which previously was synonymous with the philosopher, he has become, to a certain extent, the *inventor* of truth . . . ," Nietzsche book, p. 168.

103. *wanted to work with Alfred Adler*: Alfred Adler (1870–1937), Viennese doctor, worked jointly with Sigmund Freud at first, then slowly drew away from him (beginning in 1907 with a publication concerning organ inferiority) and founded what was known as "individual psychology." Freud's letter from November 4, 1912, in which he answers Lou A.-S.'s request, characterizes the situation at the time and is typical.

The reasons Lou A.-S. chose Freud over Adler are clearly expressed in her letter to Alfred Adler of August 12, 1913. This letter also serves as a preliminary introduction to her observations on Freud.

"I have wanted to write you for a while in order to formulate or at least to touch on certain things which I now see differently than last summer when I wrote you for the first time. Do you remember what I mentioned then: that I could go along with much of what Freud said despite some theoretical differences (which I found then more significant than they actually were), and that I was not bothered by this? It now seems to me that this is typical for the whole state of affairs, for I now think that the whole theoretical debate over Freud is in many instances a misunderstanding which can never be resolved by a simple delineation and comparison of theories. I can't deny the fact that my interests have always been focused in this direction, and that these things became important only in questioning their integration in the overall philosophy. But that is almost the best lesson I've learned from Freud: the continually renewed and intensified joy in the facts of his discoveries themselves—a joy which is always there, even at a new beginning. Because, in his case, it is not a matter of collecting and identifying the "material" details, which can be granted their dignity only by a purely philosophical discussion. He does not excavate old stones or utensils but the fact that we ourselves are in all of these things and, because of this, the insights which are so clearly evident to us are not any less serious than are the experiences of a child which teach him to say 'I' for the first time. If one were to reduce the results of Freud's research to a general phrase or to summarize them in a somewhat differently focused abstract synthesis than before, they would be neither substantially furthered nor altered in nature. It would be roughly equivalent to the following. If, in investigating altruism, there were justifiable agreement that altruism is only egoism—we would reply: certainly, but in order to research this, one would immediately have to form subcategories, make distinctions and classifications so that, despite this standardization, which would inevitably be too loosely woven, the net from this fishing expedition into the human soul would allow precisely what we are trying to discover to slip through. I know that, for you, the inclusion of everything in a single phrase [drive for power, 'male protest'] is not of the greatest significance. Rather, your primary focus is on proving them to be based on a feeling of inferiority and its reliance on the organic. . . . Psychoanalytically speaking, I do not agree that the feeling of inferiority, stemming from the organic, is a basic feeling in the psyche, and I have a philosophical justification for my objection. The organic as such neither explains nor determines the psychical for us; instead, the former portrays, so to speak, the latter (and vice versa). For this reason, even if the portrayal seemed to be a complete and valid one, I could explain or derive nothing from what was happening in the psychic state, and the same also applies if the circumstances are reversed. Psychology, having its own methods and means, has the right to allow this puzzle, this darkness, this X, to remain unsolved. Regardless of what can be said about this epistemologically, psychology follows its own course, just as the natural sciences do, unimpeded. If neither psychic nor somatic evidence of precedence can be produced, then I don't see why the psychical should be understood negatively—unless flaws are generated and kept alive by lies and tricks. Admittedly, one can seek power for reasons of powerlessness, but only because we understand the drive for power (or whatever we want to call it for the moment) as a synonym for life itself, which prevails everywhere, directly and indirectly, as the eternally-same. It does not make any sense to me that this is indulged, not only in ceaselessly changing images of itself, in fictions, and in symbols, but that it is also supposed to be an empty mirage above a void, a negation of a negation. Even during the first evening with you over tea, I raised this objection when I teasingly requested that you 'please define the "female" more positively' [in contrast to the phrase 'male protest']. The 'female means' remain for me today, in spite of your counterarguments then, that which in the 'secondary protective mechanism' shows its claws (not only the fictitious velvet ones—but instead, masked as such) as our instinctive, fundamental basis. And with that, I find myself back at the beginning, with Freud's 'Ubw' [Unbewusste: Unconscious] and all the reasons why his 'digging' underneath—namely under all these images which I feel are positive—is more conclusive to me than all the brooding over it."

105. *his long years of suffering*: The "years of suffering" began in 1923 with the diagnosis of cancer of the jaw and ended, after many operations and much pain, with his death in 1939. See the correspondence between Lou A.-S. and Sigmund Freud and particularly Ernst Jones's Freud biography, Vol. III.

106. *my husband had been named to a professorship in Persian*: See the commentary to the detailed discussion on p. 118 in the chapter "F. C. Andreas."

107. *Heinrich Vogeler's etching "Love"*: an etching by Heinrich Vogeler, who was once quite well known. Born in 1872, he had been a member of the Worpswede artists' colony since 1895. In this etching, two lovers, dressed in idealized costumes from the Middle Ages, sit leaning against each other. They look out onto an equally fairytale-like medieval landscape. Behind them and in front of the viewer is the spirit of love, playing a harp. The whole picture is characteristic of the Jugendstil. Vogeler became a communist and died in Russia in 1942.

108. *a story* Das Haus: with the subtitle "Familiengeschichte vom Ende des vorigen Jahrhunderts" (The Story of a Family From the End of the Previous Century), Berlin, 1919, Ullstein Publishers; 2nd edition, Berlin, 1927, Deutsche-Buch-Gemeinschaft Publishers. The sister of the young Balduin (René Rilke) has characteristics of Lou A.-S. herself; the "letter he had written to me" is Rilke's letter from January 15, 1904, in a shortened form. Having assumed that a book's publication year (in this case, 1919) is close to the date of its composition (here, 1904)—the time span between creation (1901–1904) and publication (1923) of *Ródinka* was even longer—people have talked about the "psychoanalytic" character of Lou A.-S.'s narrative work. But, with the exception of *The Hour Without God*, all these books were written well before she encountered psychoanalysis. (Also the dream play *Der Teufel und seine Großmutter* [The Devil and His Grandmother], drafted in 1914, does not contain anything *specifically* psychoanalytical.) Within the theoretical writings, such a thread does run through *Drei Briefe an einen Knaben* (Three Letters to a Boy) but it is difficult to recognize had it not been for her specific reference in the book. The search for an explanation of the

particular character of Lou A.-S.'s prose writings probably stems from the comment Lou A.-S. herself made that she did not want to create "works of art": she claimed her texts had "sacrificed [some of their] lifelike character to a greater attention to form." Therefore, more life results in less of the "art." In contrast to her own statement that, when writing, she felt engaged in a masculine task, one would think that this creating in a manner true to life (internally true, not necessarily in terms of an external portrayal) is indeed feminine in nature. Yet this opinion loses all validity when one realizes that the very essence of her writing is an adherence to life (from the perspective of art) and not a replacement of life. Its nature lies not in opposition or confrontation but in a "giving-back" *because* it is not written for a "reader" but remains a secretive storytelling for God, after everything has already "rested in his gentle hands." To express it nonmetaphorically, it is a completion and celebration of unity.

108. Ródinka: subtitled "A Russian Recollection," Jena, Eugen Diederichs, 1923. *Ródinka* encompasses *both* Lou A.-S.'s truly Russian periods ("Russian recollections"): her memories from childhood and her impressions of the long Russian trip with Rilke. The childhood memories in *Ródinka* are so similar to those in the short story *Im Zwischenland* (In-Betweenland) that even the names of the children, Musya and Boris, are the same. She does not use her most personal impressions from the long Russian trip (mentioned in the Rilke chapter and its epilogue) but rather the "Russian" ones—e.g., the visit to the Höhlenkloster in Kiev, particularly in the "Sommer auf Ródinka" (Summer in Ródinka), the stay at Novinki, Count Nikolay Tolstoy's estate. These memories, from such very different times, are united primarily by the figure of Vitály, who is modeled after a Petersburg boy seen once by Lou von S., who had moved her with his strength and personality. She places him in his native home of Ródinka ("small homeland") and has him grow up, so to speak, in her imagination. She brings him together with the figures from the estate and others still vivid in her mind. She herself is not represented in the book except in the beginning as the young Musya.

108. *Max Reinhardt . . . the Kammerspiele . . . he was founding*: Max Reinhardt (1873–1943) succeeded Otto Brahm as the director of the Deutsches Theater, which evolved from the Independent Theater. In 1906 he founded the "Kammerspiele" (Chamber Theatre), which was linked to the Deutsches Theater and performed plays on a more intimate scale. Gerhart Hauptmann had probably put Lou A.-S. in contact with Reinhardt. At the beginning of December 1905, he had read aloud to her and several others *Und Pippa tanzt* (And Pippa Dances); by January 1906 it had gone through rehearsal and its premiere. The Berlin theater visits with their concomitant wealth of contact with actors, critics, new and old acquaintances, transpired (except for January 1906) from mid-February to mid-April (in March with Rilke) and again in November and December of that year. In 1907 they took place from mid-January to the middle of April and on several days in December. Friedrich Kayβler, Alexander Moissi, Gertrud Eysoldt, and Else Heims were those in Reinhardt's circle who were particularly close to Lou A.-S.

109. *Stanislavsky's troupe passed through*: the troupe of actors from the Moscow Artistic Theater, which was founded in 1898 by its director Konstantín Sergéyevich Alexeyév, known in his capacities as actor and theater director as Stanislavsky. On tour in Europe, the troupe gave performances in Berlin of *Czar Fyodor* by Aleksey Tolstoy, *The Lower Depths* by Gorky, *Uncle Vanya* by Anton Chekhov, and *An Enemy of the People* by Henrik Ibsen, in February and March of 1906. Russian dramaturgy gained worldwide fame through Stanislavsky and his troupe. Stanislavsky required the actor to stay in character, even in everyday life as far as humanly possible. He rejected value judgments based on roles: "There are no small roles, only small actors."

110. *both known Ellen Key for about the same length of time*: In 1898 Lou A.-S. reviewed the book *The Abused Power of Women* by the Swedish writer Ellen Key (1849–1926), who thereupon visited her in Berlin. In 1900 her book *The Century of the Child* appeared in German. Well-known at the time, at least by name, the book wished to give the new century this designation. Rilke reviewed the book in 1902 and a lively correspondence arose between Rilke and Key; it was she who arranged Rilke's stay in Sweden from the end of June to the beginning of December 1904. Lou A.-S.'s visit with Ellen Key in Alvastra, Sweden, from mid-August to mid-September 1911, has already been mentioned.

110. *Sistiano at the conclusion of a southern trip*: November 1910. Sistiano is not far from Duino, where Rilke had stayed for a few days in April of that year (first visit). *In Munich*, where Lou A.-S. and Rilke spent time together from March 19 to May 27, 1915, and from March 26 to June 1, 1919 (their last meeting). *In the Basque district in France* where Lou A.-S. stayed late in the summer of 1905. Rilke was in Spain from November 1912 to February 1913. The *longest trip south* (the Balkans) occurred in the summer and fall of 1908.

112. *One year later I was in Vienna*: This period of study lasted from the end of October 1912 until April 1913. Immediately following the Freud seminars and discussions, she recorded her impressions and thoughts from this time in the diary *In der Schule bei Freud* (In Freud's School).

113. *Professor Freud . . . wrote . . . : "now what do you have to say about brothers?!"*: When the war broke out, he wrote: "Do you still believe that all the big brothers are so good? Expecting a comforting word from you. . . ." When Lou A.-S. responded with a profound lament of despair, he replied with the letter from November 25, 1914.

116. *His grandfather . . . a highly gifted North German physician*: The maternal grandfather of Friedrich Carl Andreas, the (tropical) doctor Dr. Waitz, who was a friend of Hufeland's, wrote a book about the care of sick children in the tropics. The name Bagratuni is written in the Russian form (Prince) Bagratión. Andreas was the Christian name of the head of the family. F. C. Andreas was born in Batavia on April

14, 1846. On the engagement announcement he still used the name Fred Charles: he later went by the name of Carl. He died in Göttingen on October 3, 1930.

118. *Andreas received the chair in Göttingen for Persian and West Asiatic Languages*: The Iranist and Indo-Germanist at the University of Frankfurt, Herman Lommel, writes in a still unpublished note about his teacher F. C. Andreas: "After he had read an outstanding article by Andreas in Pauly-Wissowa [an encyclopedia], Eduard Schwartz sought out this great historian, who was not known to him. With Wackernagel's help, Schwartz secured a position at Göttingen for the unemployed scholar as a professor of Near Eastern languages. This title was chosen because the fact that he was the greatest Iranist of his time was not enough for the minister; one had to emphasize that he knew Semitic languages (especially Aramaic and Syrian) and that he was fluent in Old and New Armenian." The statement *one of his favorite students told me* refers to oral as well as written messages from Herman Lommel to Lou A.-S.; the quotations in the text are taken from Professor Lommel's notes (she naturally assumed he would agree to their incorporation because of their shared interest). Afterward she sent him a copy of the chapter for his approval. The editor would like to thank him for permission to use his notes. For information on Andreas, see: Götz von Selle, "F.C.A.," *Indo-germanisches Jahrbuch* (Indogermanic Yearbook), Vol. XV.

121. *his close friend Franz Stolze*: He was the photographer on the astronomical expedition in which Andreas took part as an assistant for epigraphy and archeology. He was the only person Andreas met in Persia. The Stolze family lived in Berlin and his relationship with them continued long after the Tempelhof-Schmargendorf period.

122. *the quatrains of Omar Khayam in Rosen's translation*: Friedrich Rosen (1856–1932), friend of F. C. Andreas from his Berlin years, was an Orientalist and a diplomat (in 1921 he was the secretary of state for the German Empire). In 1909 he published his translation of (selected) quatrains under the title *Die Sinnsprüche Omars des Zeltmachers* (The Aphorisms of Omar the Tentmaker). A Persian poet, Omar Khayam lived ca. 1100.

122. *Nature . . . "Both at the same time"*: An accurate rendering of the sense of Goethe's confessional verses: "Nature has neither core/Nor shell,/She is simply all in all" from the poem: "Ins Innre der Natur—/O du Philister!/Dringt kein erschaffner Geist" (Into Nature's interior—/Oh you philistine/No spirit yet created enters).

124. *elemental and intimate do not declare themselves openly*: In this last "Sketch," where human language almost fails her, Lou A.-S. once more describes the mystery of her marriage to Friedrich Carl Andreas. It may help to understand this enigma if the reader looks at it the way she herself did, years earlier, when it still seemed clear to her. On October 31, 1888, she offered the following comparison of her former friendship with Paul Rée to what she specifically called her "love" for her husband:
"One usually says that friendship allows for criticism, but that love is beyond all

criticism. And it is also said that friendship occasionally demands an awareness of its reasons for existence; love, on the other hand, loves totally and blindly. And some impose the restriction: totally and blindly except in the case of serious moral defects. I believe that these two analyses should be reversed. In the first place, I am more critical of my husband than I was of my friend Paul Rée and, secondly, my feelings for Rée had far less to do with my judgment of him than does my opinion of my husband.

"I tried to understand Rée, calmly and objectively, during our long and close life together as friends. I got to know some very dear and a few completely disagreeable characteristics of his. But the very fact that they were his almost balanced them out. I was wholeheartedly fond of him and, even if he had been different, it wouldn't have mattered.

"My love for my husband began—I can't express it any other way—with an inner demand. This produced an attitude which was critical of him to the point of pain. The pain was in my interest in the results of the criticism—with Rée, the results didn't really matter. This seemed quite natural to me. There is a difference between looking for some friendly attachment and searching for a *wedded union*. In the latter case, not only is a distinctly higher profound fondness included, but also the desire and ability to relinquish one's individual being. And I think the less one is tied to bargaining for or demanding greater or lesser advantages, the more natural it seems to give oneself and bind oneself. It isn't a question of a committing but of being committed—is there something in us which already unites and weds us, something which lies beyond all friendly interests, something much deeper and higher, a joint aspiration which we Both share? It is a matter of realizing whether we already belong in each other (not only to each other), and this in an almost religious, or at least in a purely ideal, sense of the word. Love itself is, however, not purely ideal, but I swear I've never understood why people whose love consists primarily in sensual attraction *get married*.

"For this reason, friendship is often more indulgent than love, and it's true that love and contempt are mutually exclusive. But I just want to add that what is so often called moral respect is not involved; love can even tolerate crime, but we must not violate the domain of a person's most deeply individual morality, where adoration and devotion are rooted. Because it is precisely at this point that two people must intersect, that their highest, most intrinsic ideals must mesh, and should this prove not to be the case, no crime is necessary to kill love.

"The man I loved but did not criticize was Gillot, although I loved him truly—ideally, as I define it. The difference between this and the way I feel now is based on age: in the later stages of youth whatever one strives for ideally incorporates itself directly in a person, and for this reason one loves that person. Later, when people and ideas are more clearly differentiated, one no longer searches for a divine mortal; instead, there is unity in a mutual, internal devotion to that which both revere and hold dear. No longer does one person kneel before another, but Two kneel together. The perfect example of the first type is a personality which wants to rule and affect others with his energy—like Gillot. The perfect example of the second type, well, that's Fred[eric] as he lives and breathes, in his total devotion to what he feels is valuable or worthwhile, in his disposition, soul, and character, in his deep hatred of dishonesty, false appearances, misrepresentation, and in his desire for knowledge.

"Were I to have loved another man as I did Gillot, I would have run from him, because I would have believed in the possibility of passion but not in the possibility of marriage and A Life. I was very conscious of the fact that the alliance with my husband nonetheless took me back to my early youth, and in particular to the time of my relationship with Gillot—but only as far as the threshold of the small Santpoort church in which Gillot himself became a priest, changed from a *God* into His priest, became He who confirmed me in my quest for all things great and beautiful. My confirmation took place at that moment in which the identification I mentioned earlier was transformed into pure childlike enthusiasm and, simultaneously, at the moment of *farewell*, when I recognized that I would live *alone, without him* in that quest, although I could have stayed with him."

This significant diary entry, written by Lou A.-S. after she had been married a year and a half to F. C. Andreas and giving no indication of an internal threat to that alliance, leads to two related observations.

The first is that Lou A.-S., when writing about the mystery of her marriage in *What's Missing From the Sketch*, apparently did not remember this diary entry, which is based upon direct, firsthand experience. *Why* she abandons this interpretation is not a question we can discuss here. What can be asked however, is whether her marriage remained a mystery to her because of its origin—and for that reason could never be dissolved.

The second observation arises when one reads the description of the "forms of love" (in the chapter "The Experience of Love") as she saw them: male-female love, maternal love, and finally, only hinted at, that love which is "the rarest and most glorious human relationship created by Eros"—and then reads the diary of 1888. It is then clear that, not only as Lou A.-S. says, "the basic nature of the first great love in [her] early youth [Gillot] was no doubt related to what [she had] just been describing" but it is indeed part and parcel of her relationship with her husband as well. Regardless of the number of statements compared, the characteristics of the "most glorious human relationship created by Eros" also apply to what she calls "wedded union" in the diary entry quoted above. But even as the connection between "wedded union" and love for Gillot is characterized precisely here, so too is it superseded: "No longer does one person kneel before another, but Two kneel together." It is only at this point in a relationship that such a "creation of Eros" can completely emerge.

The devastation Lou A.-S. experienced when she became consciously aware of her love (the male-female variety) for Georg Ledebour may be understandable when one recalls what she says in her diary about marriage as a "wedded union." Lou A.-S. is right, in *Lebensrückblick*, apart from her love for Rilke, to speak only of her affection for Ledebour. Gillot, Andreas, Ledebour, Rilke: no other name lasted. Paul Rée stands alone.

124. *being able to tell the full truth about this step to my friend*: To have told the whole

truth about this "wedded union," which excluded sexual relations, would have belittled Andreas in Rée's eyes.

125. *comparisons are instinctively drawn from the realm of creatures*: The realm of creatures to be understood here, as elsewhere, as the nonhuman realm of universal creation, that which is *merely* creation. Or, expressed positively, that which is still *fully* creation, not simply a less human, auxiliary creation. That Lou A.-S. "instinctively draws these comparisons from the realm of creatures" not only indicates the "limited nature of all human measure" but also says something about her. It illustrates that, for her, the most forceful and direct language stems from the "realm of creatures" and not of man. There is no infidelity in that realm. The phrase "love of animals" means nothing—"love for creatures" says everything. The equation of creature with the nonhuman realm of universal creation may be indebted to the phrasing of Romans 8, 19.

128. *Solf, who was devoted to him throughout his life*: Wilhelm Solf, 1862–1936, was later the secretary of state in the German Colonial Office. Probably the closest person to F. C. Andreas, he went to the German colonies in 1898 as part of his duties in the Colonial Division of the Office of Foreign Affairs.

130. *a man both of us found striking and likable*: Georg Ledebour. A note from those days discloses that their meeting of the minds, following earlier acquaintance, took place in Friedrichshagen in the spring of 1892 (the last Templehof year), and, that in June, she decided not to see Ledebour for a year—a renunciation made possible by the solidity of their inner relationship. One reads further that, exhausted by the struggle, she broke with him a year later. The note however, also indicates that, despite the permanence and mystery of her "wedded union," she would henceforth be confronted with the enigma of the "compulsion" of the connection with her husband.

Lou A.-S. placed a poem from the time before she knew Georg Ledebour in the manuscript of her remarks about this important encounter. It was still in the original envelope.

March Happiness

On bare and windblown limbs
hangs March's last snow, damp and soft,
I walk as in a fairy land
Entering the silence of evening's darkness.

Brightly echoing, deep in the forest's heart,
The twitter of a titmouse, the only sound,
like a promise of Nature:
a call, a greeting, the tidings of Spring.

As though she'd sent a harbinger
To make us all forget the snow and frost
Until a Spring which is not yet there
Is spied by eyes, bewitched and dreamy.

Now! He may never again beguile me—
Let this March happiness still be mine:
To stand at peace in Winter's landscape
And listen to the call of Spring.
                        1890, Tempelhof

132. *love then came to me quite quietly and naturally*: Lou A.-S. is referring to her love for Rainer Maria Rilke. From the days of the "quiet and natural [love]" in Munich-Wolfratshausen in May 1897, only Rilke's letters (in prose and verse form) are extant; nonetheless they reflect the reciprocity of Lou's feeling. The problematical nature of their relationship stemmed not only from the difference in their ages but also, as was clearly manifested during the long Russian trip, in the personal problems each was working out. Whereas "all [Rilke's] hopes came to a head," Lou A.-S. regained her independence through the innermost personal experiences that this trip provided. She was now capable of facing "the unavoidable circumstances which reigned" in her life, "joyfully."

Now, however, approximately half a year after the Russian trip, she puts not only the acceptance of her fate into question, but places her romantic relationship with Rilke (which had occurred four years earlier) in a surprisingly new perspective. In her "Letzter Zuruf" (Last Cry) to Rilke, on February 26, 1901, which implored him to be wary of the dangers of another bond with a woman, she finds her justification for this warning in "the cherished memory we share of Wolfratshausen, when I was like a mother to you." The explanation for this change in outlook is provided by the "Last Cry" itself: a new love-experience with its sensuous glow (which, completely fulfilling her, leaves her partner that much more in the background), so outshines the occurrence of the "quiet and natural [love]" that she believes she is following the "great plan of life" which is said to hold for her "a gift beyond all comprehension and anticipation."

What she had envisioned gradually proved to be a self-deception. He who observes the course of her life understands that what happened to her was an inevitable experience, but nothing more. To what extent it affected her intrinsic experience of Eros is difficult to say. The "unavoidable circumstances which reigned in her life" proved to be permanent. Once her view cleared, the truth of her first love emerged— an encounter which embraced the partner and held him as never before or again with any other. Thus, the words which open "April was *our* month, Rainer . . ." are both a memory and the confirmation of a discovery.

APPENDIX: ORIGINAL TEXTS

LAS (p. 7):

Du heller Himmel über mir,
Dir will ich mich vertrauen:
Laβ nicht von Lust und Leiden hier
Den Aufblick mir verbauen!

Du, der sich über alles dehnt,
Durch Weiten und durch Winde,
zeig mir den weg, so heiβ ersehnt,
Wo ich Dich wiederfinde.

Von Lust will ich ein Endchen kaum
Und will kein Leiden fliehen;
Ich will nur eins: nur Raum—nur Raum,
Um unter Dir zu knieen.

LAS (p. 15):

Lieg ich einst auf der Totenbahr
—ein Funke, der verbrannt—,
Streich mir noch einmal übers Haar
Mit der geliebten hand.

Eh' man der Erde wiedergibt,
Was erde werden muβ,
Auf meinen Mund, den Du geliebt,
Gib mir noch Deinen Kuβ.

Doch denke auch: im fremden Sarg
Steck ich ja nur zum Schein,
Weil sich in Dir mein Leben barg!
Und ganz bin ich nun Dein.

LAS (p. 20):

Gewiß, so liebt ein Freund den Freund,
Wie ich Dich liebe, Rätselleben—
Ob ich in Dir gejauchzt, geweint,
Ob Du mir Glück, ob Schmerz gegeben.

Ich *liebe* Dich samt Deinem Harme;
Und wenn Du mich vernichten mußt,
Entreiße ich mich Deinem arme,
Wie Freund sich reißt von Freundesbrust.

Mit ganzer Kraft umfaß ich Dich!
Laß Deine Flammen mich entzünden,
Laß noch in Glut des Kampfes mich
Dein Rätsel tiefer nur ergründen.

Jahrtausende zu sein! zu denken!
Schließ mich in beide Arme ein:
Hast Du kein Glück mehr mir zu schenken—
Wohlan—noch hast Du Deine Pein.

LAS (p. 42):

Altrußland

Du scheinst in Mutterhut zu ruhn,
Dein Elend kaum noch zu begreifen,
So kindhaft scheint noch all Dein Tun,
Wo andre reifen.

Wie stehn Dir noch die Häuser bunt,
Als spieltest Du sogar im Darben:
Rot, grün, blau, weiß auf goldnem Grund
Sind Deine Farben.

Und doch: wer lang darauf geschaut,
Enthält ehrfürchtig sich des Spottes:
Ein Kind hat Rußland hingebaut
Zu Füßen Gottes.

LAS (p. 43):

Wolga

Bist Du auch fern: ich schaue Dich doch an,
Bist Du auch fern: mir bleibst Du doch gegeben —
Wie eine Gegenwart, die nicht verblassen kann.
Wie meine Landschaft liegst Du um mein Leben.

Hätt ich an Deinen Ufern nie geruht:
Mir ist, als wüßt ich doch um Deine Weiten,
Als landete mich jede Traumesflut
An Deinen ungeheuren Einsamkeiten.

Rilke (p. 73):

—Du bist aus dem Nest gefallen,
bist ein junger Vogel mit gelben Krallen
und großen Augen und tust mir leid.
(Meine Hand ist Dir viel zu breit.)
Und ich heb mit dem finger vom Quell einen Tropfen
und lausche, ob Du ihn lechzend langst,
und ich fühle Dein Herz und meines klopfen
und beide aus Angst.

Rilke (p. 73):

Wir bauen an Dir mit zitternden Händen
und wir türmen Atom auf Atom
Aber wer kann Dich vollenden,
Du Dom.

Rilke (p. 74):

Mach, daß er seine Kindheit wieder weiß;
das Unbewußte und das Wunderbare
und seiner ahnungsvollen anfangsjahre
unendlich dunkelreichen Sagenkreis.

Rilke (p. 75):

Ich glaube an alles noch nie Gesagte.
Ich will meine frömmsten Gefühle befrein.

Was noch keiner zu wollen wagte,
wird mir einmal unwillkürlich sein.
Ist das vermessen, mein Gott, vergib.

—

Und ist das Hoffart, so laß mich hoffärtig sein
für mein Gebet—

Rilke (p. 76):

Weit war ich, wo die Engel sind,
hoch, wo das Licht in Nichts zerrinnt—
Gott aber dunkelt tief.

Die Engel sind das letzte Wehn
an seines Wipfels Saum;
daß sie aus seinen Ästen gehn,
ist ihnen wie ein Traum.
Sie glauben dort dem lichte mehr
als Gottes schwarzer Kraft,
es flüchtete sich Luzifer
in ihre Nachbarschaft.

Er ist der Fürst im Land des Lichts,
und seine Stirne steht
so steil am großen Glanz des Nichts,
daß er, versengten Angesichts,
nach Finsternissen fleht.

Rilke (p. 76):

Armut ist ein großer Glanz aus Innen.

Rilke (p. 79):

Bist *du* es aber: mach dich schwer, brich ein:
daß deine ganze Hand an mir geschehe
und ich an dir mit meinem ganzen Schrein.

Rilke (p. 79):

O Herr, gib jedem seinen eignen Tod.

Rilke (p. 81):

Wie hinstürmte der Held durch Aufenthalte der Liebe,
jeder hob ihn hinaus, jeder ihn meinende Herzschlag,—
abgewendet, schon schon, stand er am Ende der Lächeln:
anders.

Rilke (p. 84):

Laß dir Alles geschehn: Schönheit und Schrecken.

Rilke (p. 86):

Lösch mir die Augen aus: ich kann Dich sehn
Wirf mir die Ohren zu: ich kann Dich hören
Und ohne Fuß noch kann ich zu Dir gehn
Und ohne Mund noch kann ich Dich beschwören.
Brich mir die Arme ab: ich fasse Dich
Mit meinem Herzen wie mit einer Hand
Reiß mir das Herz aus: und mein Hirn wird schlagen
und wirfst Du mir auch in das Hirn den Brand
So will ich Dich auf meinem Blute tragen

Rilke (p. 87):

Dann brachte mir Dein Brief den sanften Segen,
ich wußte, daß es keine Ferne gibt:
Aus allem Schönen gehst Du mir entgegen,
mein Frühlingswind Du, Du mein Sommerregen,
Du meine Juninacht mit tausend Wegen,
auf denen kein Geweihter schritt vor mir:
ich bin in Dir!

Rilke (p. 93):

Ich geh doch immer auf Dich zu
    mit meinem ganzen Gehn
denn wer bin ich und wer bist Du
    wenn wir uns nicht verstehn—

Matthias Claudius (p. 123):

Siehst du den Mond dort stehen?
Er ist nur halb zu sehen
Und ist doch rund und schön—

Heinrich von Kleist (p. 202):

Nimm mir
das Aug, so hör ich ihn; das Ohr, ich fühl ihn;
Mir das Gefühl hinweg, ich atm ihn noch;
Nimm Aug und Ohr, Gefühl mir und Geruch,
Mir alle Sinn und gönne mir das Herz:
So läßt du mir die Glocke, die ich brauche,
Aus einer Welt noch find ich ihn heraus.

Rilke (p. 205):

I

Ich steh im Finstern und wie erblindet,
seit sich zu dir mein Blick nicht mehr findet.
Des Tages [w]irres Gedränge ist
ein Vorhang mir nur, dahinter du bist.
Ich steh und warte, ob er sich nicht hebt,
der Vorhang, dahinter mein Leben lebt,
meines Lebens Gesetz, meines Lebens Gebot—
und doch: mein Tod.

II

Du schmiegtest dich an mich, doch nicht zum Hohn,
nur so, wie die formende Hand sich schmiegt an den Ton,
die Hand mit des Schöpfers Gewalt.
Ihr träumte eine Gestalt—
da ward sie müde, da ließ sie nach,
da ließ sie mich fallen, und ich zerbrach.

III

Warst mir die mütterlichste der Frauen,
ein Freund warst du wie Männer sind,
ein Weib so warst du anzuschauen,

und öfter noch warst du ein Kind.
Du warst das Zarteste, das mir begegnet,
das Härteste warst du, damit ich rang.
Du warst das Hohe, das mich gesegnet—
und wurdest der Abgrund, der mich verschlang.

Rilke (p. 205):

Wer spricht es aus,
was uns geschah? Wir holten jedes nach,
wozu die Zeit nie war. Ich reifte seltsam
in jedem Antrieb übersprungner Jugend,
und du, Geliebte, hattest irgendeine
wildeste Kindheit über meinem Herzen.

LAS (p. 215):

Märzglück

An kahlen, windverwehten Zweigen
Hängt letzter Märzschnee feucht und weich,
Ich schreite wie durch Märchenreich
Hinein in abenddunkles Schweigen.

Hell tönt aus tiefen Waldesgründen
Das Zwitschern einer Meise nur,
Wie Selbstverheiβung der Natur:
Ein Ruf, ein Gruβ, ein Frühlingskünden.

Als müβt sie einen Boten schicken
Um den man Frost und Schnee vergiβt,
Bis einen Frühling der nicht ist,
Die Augen traumbethört erblicken.
Nun! Darf er nie mehr mich bethören—
Dies Märzglück doch soll mir geschehn:
In winterlandschaft stillzustehn
Um einen Lenzruf anzuhören.

INDEX